Reviews of *Tl*
by]

"*The Complete Energy Body* is a foundational work detailing and explaining what the entire human energy body is and how it works. Comparing and contrasting modern science with ancient shamanism, Smith delivers a compelling view of consciousness and reality."

—Editor, *New Dawn*

"*The Complete Energy Body* is brilliantly and exquisitely written, and relevant to our present world. What you have done is extremely valuable."

—James L. Oschman, PhD
 Author, *Energy Medicine: The Scientific Basis*

"Kenneth Smith does a commendable job leading us from point to point, example by example, revealing that as science progresses we learn what the shamans have known and practiced all along."

—*Townsend Letter*, Review by John McMichael, PhD, CEO
 The Institute for Therapeutic Discovery

"Kenneth Smith emphasizes a correspondence [of science] with the teachings of mystics and shamans through the ages and the need to re-evaluate such 'transphysical' phenomena as out-of-body experience and ESP. *The Complete Energy Body* is an excellent guide to this often surreal and increasingly important discourse."

—Editor, *Fortean Times*

"Kenneth Smith does a remarkable job comparing shamanism and wavefield physics. I found his writing to be very clear and easy to understand. This book is brilliant. It blew my mind."

—Leslie, Amazon reader

Copyright © 2024 by Kenneth Smith
Published by EB Dynamics, LLC. All rights reserved.

Cover art by Vizerskaya
Cover and interior design by Smythtype Design
Images of the energy body by Jennifer Geib

Portions of this book have previously been published in books by Ken Eagle Feather and Kenneth Smith.

ISBN 9798878465625

Library of Congress Cataloguing
out-of-body experience, shamanism, mysticism, consciousness

Power Up
Your Energy Body

Out-of-Body Experience & Expanding Consciousness

KENNETH SMITH

EB Dynamics, LLC
Wilmington, NC

*To the electric bass guitar, an ever-evolving foundation
for the band and the rhythm of life.*

Special thanks to Patrick H, Eliot H, and Leslie T.

Contents

1. Entering the Luminous World 7
2. Creating the Energy Body 28
3. Energy Body Dynamics 53
4. Our Multi-Dimensional World 79
5. Managing Your Energy Body 100
6. A Foundation for Out-of-Body Experience 124
7. Out-of-Body Aerobics 144
8. In-the-Body Experience 168
9. Life with an Energy Body 191

References 226
Illustrations 235
Index 236
About the Author 241

1 ⟩ Entering the Luminous World

This book is a recapitulation of a long and sometimes arduous path. It is a means of integrating experience, deeply learning from it, and moving forward. It represents a trajectory from feeling lifeless and vacant to wanting to learn, to savor, and to be able to acknowledge what that means. I'll start at the beginning.

There I was many years ago, smoking weed in the hospital's hepatitis bathroom with a fellow patient. He had Hepatitis B, the kind that is only transmitted through blood and bodily fluids, so I wasn't worried about contracting it from him or bothered that anyone would enter the bathroom. It was a restricted area. Besides, my attending physician, evidently ahead of his time, thought that a little marijuana would help restore my mental and physical health.

My thinking was fuzzy back then, but I felt driven by an unseen and unknown force. My fellow patient and I talked philosophy. He was into Zen Buddhism, and our discussions led me to an active interest in Taoism, another dominant Eastern mystical philosophy. For maybe the first time in my life, I was interested. Yet, all the while, I wondered how the heck I got here and was equally confused about how to get out. I was lost, estranged from myself and life, and in a constant state of mental and emotional rebellion. My stomach and intestines were torn up due to the self-inflicted torture of being on an unsustainable path. I had to find my own life. Our conversations started giving me answers.

Drugs like marijuana, psilocybin mushrooms, and peyote allow perception to loosen up so that new insights can occur, and sometimes they are life changing. I'm not advocating their use. To the contrary, the perspectives and exercises in this book can perform the same function of shifting consciousness without taking the physical toll that drugs produce. Plus, non-drug insights are often firmer, clearer, and more lasting. These kinds of drugs, however, have value in the same way prescription drugs have value.

Each time I smoked, I would realize something. I soon came to each session—as I thought of them—deliberately looking for answers. The smoke taught me well, eventually teaching me how to leave it far behind. Drugs like these contain power. They shift perception and expand awareness, accessing deep parts of ourselves and revealing natural conditions of life.

An increasing number of medical evaluations and clinical trials demonstrate the unquestionable value of this general class of mind-altering drugs for therapeutic application. Psilocybin, mescaline, and marijuana, for example, have been used to treat a range of disorders that include PTSD, alcoholism, depression, epilepsy, and glaucoma. Often, when consciousness expands to normalize and incorporate those potentials, patients no longer need drugs. They have awoken healing within. They no longer need to get somewhere; they are there.

Outside of professional guidance, people who experience lack of meaning, disillusionment, and estrangement with life are often drawn to psychedelic drugs and decidedly addictive drugs like alcohol and cocaine. They allow people to feel something, anything. Sometimes they awaken something that has been hidden. However, it is easy to rely on them instead of doing the personal work of expanding consciousness, and it can be easy to get hooked on them. As a result, something more powerful than drugs is needed to replace them. In my case, shamanism provided that reference.

Shamanism is a mystical path that centers on perception, and variations of it are found in all parts of the world. I also discovered that shamanic teachings emphasize drugs are used only when a person is too slow to catch onto the processes the teachings themselves produce.

These drugs are sometimes referred to as "power plants" since they energize the person, transporting perception into other dimensions or ways of looking at life. They have an effect of significantly altering consciousness. On the other hand, since this is a forced shift, it takes a toll on the body. As I would learn, a mystical path helps build an inner strength for personal growth that transcends the need for drugs.

If properly developed and managed, a shamanic avenue to exploring perception produces the necessary energy to change one's life for the better. One such avenue is out-of-body experience (OBE). This ability is available to everyone; it is natural to humans. It also turns out that the process of becoming aware of the capacity, learning to manage it, and exploring other dimensions enhances awareness of our daily world and of life on Earth.

Shortly after being discharged from the hospital, I was introduced to Carlos Castaneda's third book, *Journey to Ixtlan*.[1] Not only was it interesting, but it also made sense. It fed me. It took me a year to read it, then I re-read it in a matter of days. As I would later discover, his books are not about shamanism as traditionally defined, but rather offer lessons on becoming aware of and managing the human energy body, a blending of energies that surrounds and saturates the physical body and gives rise to abilities such as OBE. Only his first two books, *The Teachings of Don Juan* and *A Separate Reality*, portrayed the use of perception-altering drugs. These books propelled Castaneda into notoriety, probably due to them being released in the 1960s during the heyday of psychedelics.[2,3] He went on to publish several more best-sellers. By placing these practices in the bright light of day, Castaneda's books changed the trajectory of shamanism, and time will reveal its evolution.

While he was an anthropology student at UCLA, now-deceased Castaneda began publishing his experiences with don Juan Matus ("don" is an appellative conveying respect), a Native American shaman-seer who considered himself a warrior, a hunter of knowledge. Don Juan charged Castaneda with writing directly about his teachings, not how Castaneda interpreted them. As a result, his books are presented as dialogue and stories, not as traditional academic portrayals.

As he explained, they are an emic approach to anthropology based on participation rather than academic research.

Don Juan taught Castaneda that we live in a world of luminous energy, and that the make-up of our energy bodies determines perception and behavior. Along the way, he outlined the history and trajectory of a little-known lineage of shamans. Some people think Castaneda is a brilliant anthropologist, others think he's a fraud. Stemming from my experiences, I'm in the former camp.

Relating to *Journey* as a textbook, I began my shamanic adventure. Implementing the exercises presented in it, I learned the gait of power, a technique for running at night even over rough terrain. I also used four techniques that enable someone to find a teacher, a result of having stored sufficient energy from their use. The techniques consisted of disrupting routines, erasing personal history, using death as an advisor, and assuming responsibility.

I would eventually learn that dreaming is a core feature of shamanism in general. Some relate to this as journeying or using altered states to explore this and other dimensions. Used here, dreaming has a more technical definition than usual as it includes OBE as one of many skills. Balanced by personal development in the daily world, OBE provides an avenue to awaken the entire energy body, to power it up for a better life.

Since Castaneda and I were bound by the same teachings, I experienced similar occurrences to those he wrote about. The steps were basically the same, but due to our different personalities, the order and content of lessons varied. Once, while reading an anthropology textbook in my studio apartment, I absent-mindedly entered a state of suspended animation. I lost track of reading. I mindlessly gazed at the wall. Suddenly, the room disappeared, and in its place was a brilliant, soft light of different hues. The room became rich with vibrant lines and bundles of light. I had spontaneously experienced what don Juan called *seeing*. I had glimpsed the luminous world of shamans.

All in all, Castaneda's books are a reference to an ancient tradition of explorers that is making headway in modern times, including in the world of science. For those familiar with Castaneda's story, the focus shouldn't be the drama swirling around him and his crew but rather his excellent rendition of shamanic teachings and what they offer all of us. But this book is not about Castaneda. Don Juan tasked him to bring a tradition of investigating and utilizing the energy body to the light of day, and this effort continues that focus.

Rocky Mountain Butt Kick

Because the energy body and its resources are not part of the current, mainstream worldview, its expression is often disconcerting. This is part of learning, just as a child needs guidance and supervision when learning to cross a street. The following story is an account of the sometimes-unsettling nature of learning.

While living in Florida, and being marginally conversant with some basic shamanic exercises, I felt a deep desire to move to Colorado. Packing my car to the roof, I headed off as though singing John Denver's hit song, "Rocky Mountain High." Once in Colorado, I toured the state, not knowing exactly why I was there nor what my next step would or should be.

Then one day, after hiking through woods near a tiny town deep within the mountains, I sat on a log in a small clearing that offered a good view of the surrounding area. While gazing at the towering pine trees and the sparkling, blue sky, I found it difficult to place my attention on anything. Amidst the magnificence of creation, I lapsed into a mild euphoria. My mood abruptly changed when I felt the distinct and overwhelming sensation that, if I did not leave the mountains immediately, I would die. Accenting this message, an eagle flew directly overhead.

Looking back, I regard this feeling as having resulted from my childish affectation with the surroundings. I had abandoned my emotional control to the splendor of the area, and as a result, the power of the mountains would devour me—or so I felt. At any rate, I didn't wait to see if trolls would emerge from the forest with dinner on their minds and me as their prey. Making a hasty retreat, I swiftly packed my car and drove away.

After traveling north to retrieve other possessions I had stored, I took I-25 south out of Denver. That evening I checked into a motel in

Pueblo, Colorado. Now out of the deep mountains, I felt complacent and in no hurry. To wind down from the drive, I sat on the motel room bed, reading a magazine. Glancing up, I noticed a circular apparition hovering in the far corner of the room. It appeared without a sound. It was translucent with a soft glow. It was well contained, although it had no definitive boundary. There was movement of light resembling swirling oil on water within the circumference of the two-foot-wide specter. It was like a small energy body.

At first, I had no reaction other than curiosity. Then, with lightning speed, it lurched toward me. Recovering my presence of mind, which seemed to have been blown to bits, I found myself crouching on the floor some six feet from the bed, cowering in a corner like a rodent awaiting execution. I felt demolished and alone. At a loss as to what had happened, I immediately checked out of the motel. I drove back to Florida in two days, stopping only for food and fuel.

Several months later, I experienced this same energy. While driving through rural Maine en route to Canada, I stopped at a motel for the night. After showering, I sat in a chair and began meditating. The same twofoot-wide energy appeared without a sound. Without really knowing why, I was able to watch it with nonattached interest. It slowly moved toward me. Then I knew it for what it was, a manifestation of my self-doubts about anything and everything. It inched toward me, then vanished. Although doubt has remained an adversary in many situations, I've never again encountered the specter. For me, overcoming doubt was my path to learning. For others, it could be things like stubbornness, arrogance, or timidity.

Meeting don Juan

As with the feeling prior to my Colorado journey, in the late summer of 1975, I felt a strong urge to move to Arizona. This time my intention was clearer. My priority was to meet a shaman teacher, preferably someone as knowledgeable as don Juan. I also decided to enroll in the University of Arizona.

Shortly after arriving in Tucson, while walking down one of the main streets, I saw an old Indian walking toward me. He projected a youthful but mature grace. He was of medium height and in good physical condition; his hair seemed the color of liquid mercury and was combed straight back. Dressed in a blue shirt and khaki pants, he appeared quite ordinary. Yet he seemed different from the other Indians I had seen since arriving in Arizona. His easy stride and peaceful yet purposeful posture drew my attention to him.

I had dropped off my car for repairs and was late for class. In a hurry, aside from awkwardly staring at him since he looked somehow familiar, I paid no great attention to him. He looked at me as though I were a dolt. Not until I reached my classroom did I realize that the Indian was the same person I saw in an earlier vision while living in Florida. A mild, euphoric panic filled me. I somehow knew it was don Juan. I resolved, should I ever see him again, to meet him.

Two days later, I noticed him near a neighborhood market on the edge of town. This time he looked like a derelict. His shirt hung over his pants belt. His hair looked unkempt, and clumps of beard had sprouted. He stumbled and weaved as though drunk. Upon scrutiny, I saw that his walk was deliberate. He intended to walk in such a manner.

By doing so, he caused me to wonder if indeed I had recognized him as the person in the vision. His aim was impeccable. He had zeroed in on my doubt, and this required that I quickly evaluate the situation. Upon recognizing his walk as an act, with supreme effort I approached him. My confidence had overcome my doubts, but only slightly. Mumbling, I said hello. He looked at me as though I were missing the entire point. For a few seconds, I could not break his stare. My body told me I knew exactly what was happening. My reasoning left me cold, searching for something to say or do. I turned and walked away.

I felt embarrassed that I didn't address him directly, that I didn't use my total knowledge of the situation. As I walked away, I heard his silent voice scream inside my head, "Lose your self-importance!" I felt crushed, but immediately understood. Even more than doubt, the thing that stood in my way of fully addressing him had been my reluctance to appear foolish. By trying to avoid this, I had ended up playing the fool. Still, I walked away with a nagging certainty that he had been and would continue teaching me.

The next time I saw don Juan proved equally aggravating. I was walking around the city, just to be active and outside during a warm and pleasant afternoon. As I rounded a street corner, I saw him walking on the far side of the street. When he knew I had recognized him, he started ducking and weaving his head and upper body as though he were a boxer. Utterly taken by surprise, doubt surged through me. I could only think that I had become involved with a crackpot who liked to shadow-box in broad daylight, rather than with the famed don Juan. Flabbergasted, I didn't say anything and continued walking. At the same time, he struck something indefinable within me. The immediacy, drama, and control of his actions left a profound mark.

Most times when I saw him, I would be out for a casual walk. Once, when I felt I had to verify that he was the don Juan of Castaneda's books, I ran into him in the suburbs. He, too, was walking. When he saw me, he stopped and offered a faint, mischievous smile. Stopping at his side, I asked him his name. He looked slightly startled; perhaps he had not expected that question. He wasn't one to lose stride, though. I watched him bring his energy directly back in line.

He replied, "Juan."[4] Then, when he wanted to know what I was up to, I noticed a very curious thing. His mouth did not move in unison with his words. I heard English, but his mouth moved as though he spoke another language. His emotional intent seemed to carry the words I heard. When I asked him if he had taught Castaneda, he nodded his head yes and made a remark about being saddled with another white man. His eyes twinkled with amusement.

We met another time as I was walking home after visiting a friend. I noticed him on the far side of the street in the front yard of a small house. He was carrying a large piece of wood. A Mexican woman accompanied him. I called his name. He abruptly turned away from me and headed toward the backyard of the house. I shouted at him. The woman looked quizzically at me. I pointed at don Juan. She shrugged and turned away.

Then I saw don Juan's head turn a very bright crimson. I could distinguish the normal physical features of his body but not his head.

He looked like a human candle. Ignoring me, he disappeared behind the house. I felt I had breached some rule by yelling at him before taking the time to assess the situation. He evidently wanted some other behavior from me. Awed and dismayed, I continued walking home.

Yet another time I *saw* him as a complete energy body. There were no physical features. In place of that was a full energy body brimming with lines of light. The surrounding environment was also filled with light. I had the sense that he had provided me with the energy to shift to another frame of reference, viewing him as being of light rather than as being physical. He used his power to boost mine.

To finally accept him without doubt as don Juan required years of sifting through my concerns. The effects of my experiences lined up with his instruction. It was obvious I was gaining shamanic knowledge. But only through a careful assessment of feelings, of omens or signs indicating specific circumstances, by asking him if he had taught Castaneda, and by receiving an affirmative reply for each method of inquiry, did I come to the certainty that, yes, it was my fortune to apprentice under don Juan, a figure for whom I had immense respect because of Castaneda's books. Using references in the shamanic worldview, I had stored sufficient personal power to realize my goal of finding my teacher. While I didn't expect to find don Juan, his presence maximized the continuity between Castaneda's books and my hands-on training.

By the time I met don Juan, he had developed the amazing ability to physically exit and return to the ordinary world. I view him as a person who has stepped beyond the common definition of what it means to be alive. To me, he resides in another dimension while retaining the capacity to manifest his body on Earth. He always appeared suddenly, seemingly out of nowhere.

Upon reflection, I always had two memories of his appearances. The first is that of him walking toward me out of the vanishing point. That is, I remember him walking toward me from a distant place on the physical horizon, a point where, if he were one step further away, my perception of him would vanish. The second memory is that of *seeing* him flow out of a field of light as though he were descending an imaginary staircase. In this memory, his body glows with luminosity. When the two perceptions intersected, I would see him instantly appear in physical reality.

Don Juan's stature always captured my imagination. His build exuded natural power and strength. Deep wrinkles in don Juan's forehead accented an otherwise smooth face. Except for one occasion, I always saw him dressed in khaki or dark-green cotton work pants. He always wore a cotton shirt. He once wore a sweater, looking like a middle-class gentleman. More than anything, his relation to the world set him apart. His walk was more of a glide, as though he were carried along by a force outside of himself. He balanced and blended his energy with his environment, even when he was up to trickery.

On the one occasion that he did not wear his usual clothes, he dressed as an old woman. I was returning to my apartment after an afternoon in an area of downtown Tucson with fountains and trees, where musicians sometimes play. Walking home, I noticed an old woman walking toward me. She wore a plain, off-yellow dress that had frills around the collar and sleeves. What made her stand out from the crowd was that she didn't walk as much as she pushed and rolled her weight from side to side. She looked gruff in an odd, yet feminine, way. When we passed, her eyes lit up with a strange hope.

Don Juan's impression was so good that I didn't see him. As usual, I was so caught up in my thoughts, I had no attention for anything beyond myself. Only later did I laugh upon recognizing his antics. His impersonation was superb. And the hope in his eyes was that I would recognize his disguise.

After a few years, he instructed me to write books about Castaneda's books. He wanted me to "shed light" on them. At that point, I had no background, no training, and certainly no proficiency as a writer, but I took his assignment to heart. Years of academic and on-the-job training turned me into a professional writer. It was during my travels before and after my apprenticeship that I studied education, journalism, and religion at various colleges and universities. In the process, I learned several styles of writing and was earning a livelihood stemming from don Juan's assignment.

The last time I physically connected with don Juan, I was driving on the outskirts of Tucson. He was walking toward downtown on the far sidewalk. There was little traffic, so I stopped my pickup truck in the middle of the road and called out, asking him if he wanted a ride. He shook his head no and gestured ahead, suggesting he only had a short distance to go. I yelled that I would see him later. He smiled and waved. This was the first time I didn't feel tremendous apprehension upon encountering him. Gone, too, was the stern feeling he always used with me. A few weeks later, due to an illness in my family, I moved back to Florida, and a new awareness gradually took hold.

After leaving Arizona, don Juan entered my dream world to provide instruction. In one dream, he appeared suddenly, changing the content of my dream. He rode a bicycle in front of a supermarket. Upon recognizing him, I had the sensation that he pulled me up out of my physical body and into the dream itself. The scene then shifted to that of a forest with a winding river. I attempted to fight this sensation, but when I noticed don Juan again, I relaxed. A multicolored phrase "The Second Ring of Power" then flashed into the dream emblazoned over the river. Here, he had attached the river's symbolic significance to the capacity for dreaming known to shamans as the second ring of power, or the use of the second attention—a term I've recast as the second energy field.

Using the second energy field as a vehicle for perception and varied experience was underscored when Castaneda himself entered my dreams. Although there has never been any evidence that he intended these meetings, they did provide a useful lesson. In one dream, he formally presented himself to me. He wore a white shirt, tie, and a conservative, three-piece suit. In doing so, he demonstrated his impeccability in the first energy field, a concept associated with daily life. He had shown me that he was well-ordered and at ease. I never met Castaneda in the physical world.

For Castaneda aficionados, why I met don Juan remains a puzzle. Why was I "chosen" for this path (using don Juan's reference about an act of cosmological power or universal design, if you will)? I speculate about this on occasion. I think because I immersed myself to such a great degree in Castaneda's books, I simultaneously established a connection with don Juan. I had used don Juan's instructions to Castaneda as though they were directed at me. I had wrapped myself in don Juan's teachings and in his energy. I had developed unbending intent. As a result, he responded from his invisible residence to my quest to find a teacher by returning his awareness to the physical world. But this was only the dynamics of it. It doesn't address the actual why. Don Juan's take on this is to not seek that answer, as it is beyond human reckoning, and to simply accept the path as a challenge.

A lasting impression of don Juan is that he reminded me of a U.S. Navy SEAL who was an influential neighbor during my high school days. Very engaging, he saw the best in people and did what he could to bring that out. This association was also meaningful in that the lineage of shamans referenced herein historically also operated in small, highly skilled teams: different types of warriors with vastly different missions, yet both extending the boundaries of what is known and considered possible.

On My Own

Compelled by similar feelings as before, over time I moved about and worked for organizations with which I felt kinship. For instance, I worked on staff at Edgar Cayce's Association for Research and Enlightenment (A.R.E.), headquartered in Virginia Beach, Virginia. Over 14,000 documented "Readings" from Cayce provided a wealth of information spanning health, reincarnation, personal development, and even business. Starting on the loading dock, I later was part of conferences and marketing. Years earlier, I used their library to research the lost continent of Atlantis for a high school geography paper.

I then worked for The Monroe Institute (TMI), located in the Blue Ridge Mountains near Faber, Virginia. TMI was founded by sound and consciousness pioneer Robert Monroe, famous for his book, *Journeys Out of the Body*.[5] TMI specializes in offering in-residence courses where participants explore awareness via the Hemi-Sync™ technology Monroe developed. Basically, slightly different audio signals are placed in each ear to promote the synchronization of the brain's hemispheres. This allows examination of different states of awareness. Beginning as a receptionist, I branched out to managing their home study courses—all the while attending their in-residence programs. Leaving TMI, I began my first book, *Traveling with Power*, which presents some of my experiences during these programs.[6]

Due to a personal connection I made at TMI, I later became employed by The Institute for Therapeutic Discovery. The Institute focused on leading-edge medical research that included the placebo response, using sound for healing, and other energy medicine modalities. I was also employed by the Institute's sister company, Beech Tree Labs, Inc. Beech Tree typically uses naturally occurring molecules to address several unmet medical needs. It is a small company with a large patent portfolio for therapies, including those for viruses like Covid-19, Ebola, and herpes. It was during this time that I discovered common denominators between ancient shamanism and leading-edge quantum wavefield research. That story formed the basis for my previous book, *The Complete Energy Body*.[7]

I should mention here that I am in no way advocating that anyone follow in my footsteps. It was by effort, luck, and circumstance that I had managed to find my way into the world of don Juan and Carlos Castaneda. Especially since this path is outside the normal references of reality, such an adventure can be perilous at times. But it leads to a better understanding of life. It is from traveling this off-road path that my books arise, not from an idealized representation of shamanism or a desire for followers.

The Energy Body

The energy body is your birthright. It involves your complete anatomy. Elementary and primary school courses include where the physical body comes from, its basic anatomy, and skills in using it. In this book, we examine fundamental elements of the energy body, including where it comes from and what it is.

Many books have been published about parts of the energy body, chakras and meridians being examples. Ancient teachings from different parts of the world portray a more comprehensive anatomy of the energy body. For example, eastern teachings have provided a detailed map of a nadi-chakra network within the energy body and in so doing have expanded knowledge of the basic seven chakras. In the west, practitioners of a branch of shamanism originating in Central Mexico have been examining the full energy body for centuries. Like the whole of science, the entirety of knowledge within this tradition is immense, covering most aspects of existence. Some of these findings are presented in this book.

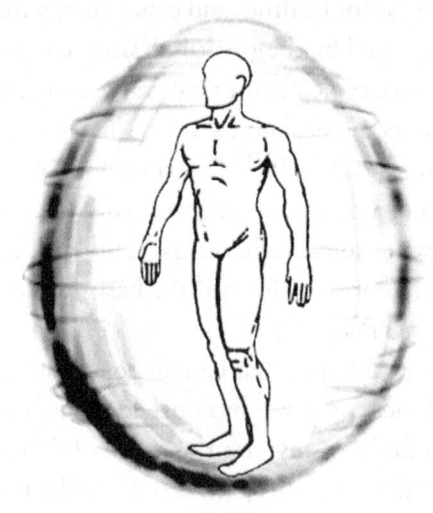

Figure 1.1
The Energy Body
Well-contained and coherent energy surrounds and permeates the physical body.

Over centuries of investigation, shamans have dedicated their efforts to exploring and mapping the energy body. They live in a universe of energy and are the scouts of human potential. But you don't need to be a shaman or mystic to develop your energy body. Shamans provide a reference that can be applied by anyone, simply because we all have an energy body. While some practices pertain to shamans, their essential findings apply to one and all—and that's what this book is about.

Energy body capacities are active to some degree in all of us. Examining energy body dynamics reveals these processes and their effects. For instance, we dream but they're usually vague. Some people have lucid dreams, meaning they are aware of dreaming while dreaming. Shamans have defined steps to take dreaming to higher levels, including OBE, for the purpose and effect of awakening the entire energy body.

For most people, the functions of the energy body are latent. In most social circles, it is not even recognized as existing, let alone used. The instruction that is provided is usually limited, focusing only on pieces of it (like auras, chakras, or acupuncture meridians). Activating the energy body means bringing it to life, being able to use it just as you use your physical body, and thereby accelerating personal growth.

The more you power up your energy body, the more abilities you have. The greater your abilities, the more you can power up. As a result, the entire world comes more to life. A basic question arises: If you have an energy body, why not know about it? Once you grasp its nature, you will have discovered that life has been as though you've been trying to walk without legs.

A central premise of shamans is that conditions within the energy body determine perception and behavior. The study of the energy body therefore concerns consciousness: its source, its dynamics, and the means for using it. The shamanic blueprint of an energetic world provides a unique reference to understanding the human condition. It is not meant to confine anyone to its boundaries. Quite the opposite.

This Book

After publishing several books relating to the energy body and shamanism, some published under the name Ken Eagle Feather, I sought to distill and consolidate my work and provide foundational perspectives, like presenting building blocks of atoms without going into all of the physics. This book is therefore a summary of decades of investigating the worldview and practices of shamans. It provides key perspectives of how the energy body works. While my books are complementary, you don't need to have read one to understand the others. They're independent of each other.

In addition, you don't have to be a shaman, or even interested in shamanism, to derive value from this book. And while familiarity with Castaneda's books adds flavor, you don't need to have read them. While my books might act as commentaries on don Juan's teachings, you don't need the backdrop of Castaneda's rendering to understand don Juan's points that I reference to bolster my presentation. That said, Castaneda delivered accounts of some very remarkable first-hand experiences with don Juan. His books stand tall and shine brightly.

The singular effort here is to deliver a concise view of the energy body with specific goals relating to OBE and the expansion of consciousness, both having general application. They are separate but related skills that work exceedingly well in tandem, illustrating applications such as learning and health. Laced with tried-and-true exercises, this book provides guidance on how to use the energy body. If you want to explore in detail the concepts in this book, *The Complete Energy Body* provides that resource. *On the Toltec Path*, penned as Ken Eagle Feather, offers more information on this lineage of shamanism.[8]

To set the stage for the work at hand, key findings shared by shamans and scientists are presented, particularly those of new quantum wavefield researchers. We begin with a short explanation of where the energy body comes from, of the energetic environment that produces and maintains life. This is supported by an overview of shamanism and science.

It is the way in which shamans make their discoveries, such as the sophisticated use of dreaming and directly *seeing* energy, that defines them as shamans. Likewise, the practices of scientists define them as such. This rendition of the energy body, however, has universal application. It deals with common denominators applicable to all humans, regardless of vocation or profession.

After looking at how the energy body is created, we examine the make-up of the energy body and how it works. We apply this to connecting personal growth and out-of-body experience—two principal sides of the energy body—and how they interact. This includes your relation to your daily world and to other dimensions, as both rely on the same energy body processes. They balance and elevate each other.

Combined, and with the right map, you have an avenue leading to the natural self, a state of having awakened the energy body.

Toward this goal, this book provides practical perspectives that, along with how-to exercises, help you gain understanding and experience in order to use your energy body. Personal development is measured by expanding awareness, achieving more balance with and in life, gaining more appreciation of the intricacies of worldviews, and having greater ability to use innate resources. This profile applies to your daily world and to OBE. An out-of-body experience indicates you have sufficiently learned to control your dreams and have gained the ability to consciously travel to and within other dimensions. Connecting OBE with your daily world is accomplished by exercising dreaming skills, relating to life as multi-dimensional, redefining reality, stepping deeper into the world of energy, and developing precision intent.

Again, you don't need to follow shamanism to derive benefit from knowing about it. The energy body itself is universal. As part of human anatomy, its mechanisms don't belong to any discipline. Shamanism does, however, provide an approach to understanding it. Even using the skeleton of these perspectives, the basics, is sufficient to turn your life around or enhance it.

Terminology

Our lives are filled with technical jargon that crystallizes our views of the world. Terminology is a kaleidoscope of interrelated terms that bestow meaning. Experiences are colored by their descriptions as they're filtered through a lens of interpretation which is based on terms. This is valuable, if not necessary, to live. But it also shows why it is important to understand the underlying dynamics of explanations and interpretations to avoid being stuck in a prison of our own making.

Terms build descriptions, and descriptions provide for navigation. These can be a manual on how to use a computer or a breath-taking constellation on the high seas. Don Juan says there is no world at large, only a description which we learn to visualize, and then the description becomes equated with reality.[9] No matter their origin, descriptions of reality act like spells, shaping the perceptions and behaviors of those under their influence.

During childhood, awareness gradually builds based on a stream of information, culminating in a view of the world that can be expansive or limiting. We're bound to a description of the world if we want to make sense of our lives. Science is built on terms relating to a material world. Shamanism is built on a world of energy. Both are descriptions. Both are valid from within their own points of view. However, the quality of a worldview hinges on how expansive and dynamic it is, what it allows us to bring into consciousness and therefore to exist.

For a new class of quantum wavefield researchers and for shamans, any point of view, any description, is an interpretation. A description is a rendering in time, an ordering of perception based on current knowledge, and a reflection of something that is vastly larger than and beyond human comprehension.

Different terms can also have equivalent meaning. For instance, information can be words on paper or a type of energy—which is the capacity for doing work, to be able to change something. What shamans have referred to as *emanations* carries much of the same meaning that some quantum scientists place on the *wavefield*. When I use the term "physical" in this book, it indicates a common reference to our daily world, knowing full well that it is not material but another form of energy.

Adding to these complexities, the conversations between don Juan and Castaneda were in Spanish. His written words may not specifically correspond to their dialogue. Over the course of his writing, Castaneda changed some terms. Consistent with terms often having multiple meanings, the initial term brujo, for instance, became categorized differently as Castaneda learned.[10] Likewise, he used several terms in referring to the overall teachings.[11] For example, Toltec, seer, sorcerer, shaman, and warrior were used at different times, in different situations, to provide nuance to and greater comprehension of the path.

Don Juan told Castaneda he initially used the word "sorcerer" to get his attention. After all, examining that world would be an anthropologist's dream. But later don Juan told Castaneda that following a path of sorcery was like following a dead-end road. It didn't lead anywhere.[12] Reflecting Castaneda's increased learning, the use of the term "seer" eventually gained preference to describe both ancient and modern practitioners. Castaneda also used the term "shaman" in his later works.

Don Juan also used different terms when explaining the same topic, such as referring to the known world as the first attention and the unknown as the second attention. This gave more insight to his teaching and expanded the vocabulary. For anyone, changes like this help prevent becoming hooked on the definition of a certain word. This also produces less reliance on a description and more confidence in one's own felt sense of the world.

Within the prerogative given to me by don Juan, I changed first and second attentions to first and second energy fields because I think this is more descriptive and consistent with portraying a world of energy. OBE, for instance, requires placing your attention on the second field. However, the wider scope, to my reckoning, is that you're involving yourself with a field of energy distinct from the first energy field of the daily world. Where you place your attention within the first or second fields then determines what is perceived. This will be explained in later chapters.

Further complicating terminology, different views of the same thing may clarify or distort understanding. Scientists label OBE as a transphysical or extreme phenomenon, while others relate it to advanced human potential. OBE also relates to other extreme events such as near-death experience and survival, or reincarnational considerations. Yet some researchers entirely discount the legitimacy of OBE, while others attribute it to an illusory effect of a brain disorder. Shamans, however, regard OBE as one element of dreaming and consider it to be a natural human capacity. Broadly speaking, these are behaviors and abilities that challenge the existing framework of reality. Like a painting, this frame focuses perception on some images while eliminating others.

In the early 1970s, with the publication of Monroe's book *Journeys*, the notable psychologist Charles Tart and Monroe popularized the term out-of-body experience. Working together to figure out Monroe's out-of-body travels, they began using this since the prevailing term at that time, *astral projection*, carried certain connotations about the experience, a description they wanted to sidestep for better clinical objectivity.

Don Juan himself sometimes sought to change terms to make the meaning more relevant. He said he didn't like "dreaming," for instance, as it didn't quite fit with his sensibilities, but his changes didn't stick.[13] His guidance for changing a term was that it had to be verified by *seeing*, by directly perceiving the world of pure energy.

As don Juan said, there is no official version of shamanic knowledge. The passage of time requires new ways of interpreting and explaining it.[14] With that in mind, I've modified a few of Castaneda's terms for consistency between worldview and practice. And for simplicity, I explain and use a more uniform terminology than found in Castaneda's work.

Summary

In a traditional sense, philosophy is an organized way to learn. Both shamanism and science have their own ways of learning that shape what is being learned, the boundaries of what can be learned, and the results of their investigations. Whether coming from the worlds of hard science or of philosophy, it takes many years for new ideas to gain widespread acceptance. Findings on the energy body are no different. While it has been studied for centuries, it'll be a long time before it is included in mainstream reality. But the process is ongoing.

To better make your own assessments, I think it is fair that you know some of my background as well as gain some perspective of the shamanic and scientific worldviews. All this feeds into and forms the content of this work. Old perspectives evolve into new vistas. Humans have traveled from a flat-Earth reality to beyond a geocentric depiction, to the determination that Earth revolves around the Sun, rather than vice versa. We are now part of an emerging epoch, a space age where circumstances and knowledge, and our view of the world, are quickly changing. In keeping with shamanic teachings, it is your responsibility regarding how you apply this unfolding information.

Our quality of life, if not our survival, hangs in the balance due to many forms of environmental pressure. We need new perspectives and answers. Don Juan thinks that for humans to survive, our worldview must change. A material world must be displaced in favor of a world of energy.[15] This shift would naturally include defining humans as being energy bodies. All of this is taken into consideration to hopefully provide you with something of value. In the next chapter, we look at how worldviews form, the intricacies of perception, and some of the shared perspectives among shamans and scientists regarding how the energy body comes into existence.

2 ⟩ Creating the Energy Body

To examine out-of-body experience (OBE) and its relation to personal growth and consciousness, it is helpful to know a few basics about how perception works. After all, OBE is a unique form of awareness, and it isn't something taught in public school. Let's start with broad strokes.

TO HAVE A WORLD TO VIEW

Reality is a human-made endeavor, a description of the world, a wide-angled explanation about what we think exists. It is a way to bring the world into view, to give life meaning, and to survive—but it is not the world itself. It is a representation of the world. A scientific worldview, for example, typically drills down on what makes up a material world, taking awareness into more expansive and detailed explanations of this reality. A shamanic worldview, in turn, describes a reality made only of energy and how the energy body determines perception and behavior. A common denominator is that the collective findings of scientists and those of shamans organize into their respective schematics which present well-defined pictures of life. However, neither is absolute.

A worldview, be it based on personal perspective or on an all-encompassing reality, frames perception and provides options for behavior. If OBE is not part of accepted reality, it will be discounted and perhaps ridiculed. This version of reality can even prevent it from occurring since reality is a force shaping consciousness. A worldview incorporating OBE allows freedom for it to occur, sets the stage for giving an experience meaning, and might even offer skills for how to make it happen.

As we experience a description, it becomes equated with reality rather than a reference about reality. It becomes a huge self-fulling prophecy where awareness of something outside of this corral is often met with "that's impossible" responses. Even though the description is only a partial reflection of the vastness in which we reside, we dismiss events that occur outside of our worldview and hold fast to the familiar—and yet history is littered with advances of things once considered impossible. While we're taught a worldview, we're rarely informed about how our reality originates and that it is only a snapshot in time, however wonderful it may be.

Interpretation

Interpretations of events and descriptions of life influence each other. We interpret a situation based on our worldview that forms from a multitude of interpretations. We then give our experiences meaning. An interpretation is a way of looking at something, and every now and then doing so in a remarkable way.

Stemming from the conditioning and expectations learned from upbringing—education, culture, peers, and all other influences—we build a grand mosaic representing life. We freely and routinely interpret the actions of others. We interpret the behaviors of the stars. We interpret the possibilities. All these interpretations fall within our reflections. And even if one dares to conjecture a new perspective, it is somehow related to the already known world. Interpretations arise from a starting point: the consciousness that filters, categorizes, and defines awareness. A reality both ushers in more consciousness and limits it.

Figure 2.1
Cup or Faces Paradox
Even with the same information, the image can be interpreted as a cup or as two faces looking at each other. With a shift of focus, you can view the world in dramatically different ways. Fluency with diverse ways of looking at life is a step toward freeing awareness.
(Public domain, courtesy of Wikimedia Commons.)

Interpretations change as awareness expands and incorporates new references. Some years back, a friend was giving me a tour of Paris' museums. She was a curator at the Louvre, and as she was explaining how paintings are labelled and presented, we entered the Louvre's ancient Italian section. One painting portrayed a monk flying high through the air en route to a prison. The explanation next to the painting indicated that it depicted a monk ministering to the prisoners. I commented that it looked like an OBE, and my friend responded that it could be a valid interpretation; however, that thinking was not in the worldview of those who wrote the placard describing the painting.

You can always find information to support an interpretation. The more long-lasting ways of thinking often have many perspectives to support them. The problem is that these are the ones that are easy to get lost in. The saying that "there is a reason for everything" is more accurately a situation where you can find a reason for anything.

Inventories

We can't be attentive to everything. We must trim our focus; otherwise, we'd be overwhelmed and dysfunctional. We therefore gradually learn to pay attention to elements within our worldview and disregard distractions, those things that don't fit. We create inventories, organized awareness of meaningful reflections.

A hamburger (or vegan burger) has an inventory of things such as a bun, meat (or whatever), lettuce, onion, and ketchup. The kitchen where it was prepared has an inventory of pots, pans, grill, refrigerator, cooks. The building housing the kitchen has windows, doors, floors, and walls. The transportation network delivering the hamburger also has various inventories, such as those things that make up trucks and roads. Harvesting the lettuce and producing the ketchup have their own set of inventories that may overlap with other industries, such as with buildings, roads, and kitchens.

Just sitting down to have a hamburger involves an interrelated, complex network of inventories that you have learned to use. The inventory of ordinary reality consists of an array of inventories, including hamburgers, politics, religion, science, education, and much more. Consciously interacting with your daily world is a superior achievement.

The bits and pieces forming reality are verifiable. We experience them, we label them, we relate to them, and we communicate about them, all of which gives the description immense power. The upside is that you have this world to view and live in, while the downside is that it confines consciousness to that world and prevents awareness of things outside of its borders. The existence of the energy body and OBE are pieces of a shamanic inventory, which is subject to the same principles that build any reality. It simply provides more options.

Selective Cueing

To learn about something, it must first be called to your attention, placed in your awareness. During childhood, we're told what to pay attention to and what to discard. A child is taught that "water" can be "hot." Humans select and agree on what is relevant based on a host of considerations, such as those for survival, cultural expression, and personal orientation. When acting in concert, these piecemeal elements produce the world as you know it. A reality is born.

This procedure of *selective cueing* renders an inventory. Pieces of an inventory are established and connected through selective cueing, the deliberate focus on specific features of the world. Repetitive selective cueing builds and maintains inventories. Inventories build and maintain realities. A worldview then affects what continues to be selectively cued. In general, we recognize the existence of something specific, describe it, and give it meaning for how it fits within our world and how to use it—all aspects of selective cueing.

This conditioning continues throughout life as we build an amazing collection of categories and constellations of awareness, reflected by transportation, education, health care, and government. The more inventories interrelate, the grander their meaning, and the deeper we become locked within a reality constructed by the forces of time and culture.

Basically, selective cueing consists of emphasizing and de-emphasizing pieces of the world. What we are taught and how reality is selectively cued to us determines the extent of our limitations. Scientists and shamans teach their students what to look for and what to avoid or discard. The process is the same; however, the content of what is taught is quite different, with the effects generating almost mismatched worlds.

Yet, these worlds are beginning to merge. For instance, later in this chapter you'll learn that both shamans and some scientists agree that there is not a material reality, and that any point of view, small or large, is an interpretation of something that can't be defined.

Social Agreement

Imagine all the elements that go into designing and building a bridge, let alone all the pieces that go into creating an entire culture. Take all the interlocking concepts, then expand that to include every aspect of your life. Then imagine what happens when a group of people consolidate, validate, and magnify the value of all these parts. What happens is that consensus manufactures a reality.

Don Juan says that to make sense of our world we need to stay within boundaries. The borders of any world are regulated by social consensus or agreement, the *social base* as don Juan terms it.[1] With consensus comes a shared inventory and common experience. We may then organize to develop technologies and to build civilizations.

Cohesive groups can produce more results than an individual, consensus reality being one measure. Still, social pressure to conform, to not step too far from accepted reality, is a daily influence. Psychedelic drugs, for instance, disrupt the continuity of the reality one has become accustomed to and opens doors to wider vistas. If someone, including a therapist, is not familiar with the nature of worldviews, they are apt to misinterpret the drug-induced experience. And therapy, if needed, might be inadequate. This is no different than a person glimpsing other realities without taking drugs and then having that experience discounted due to pressure to maintain a consensus reality.

Consensus relies on groups of people sharing an inventory, agreeing on the elements that comprise it, and sharing interpretations about the meaning. Everything associated with a grocery store, from farming to distribution to sales, is the result of group consensus forming a mini world of the food industry. There are many variations of automobiles, for another example, but there is a core identity for each. And even if someone uses an automobile as a huge flowerpot, it doesn't take away from the shared meaning of "automobile."

Reality focuses awareness, but due to its expanse it is not easily grasped as being a representation. It contains implied and often unquestioned facts. Based on shared views, socially defined meaning emerges into accepted conditions about life. The more people abide by consensus meaning, the more widely held the view, and the less it is questioned. This applies to our daily world and dreaming. The second ring of power mentioned in chapter one pertains to shamans entering into an agreement about the meaning of dreaming, how to use it, and procedures to develop it.

Social behavior is also shaped by language. Terminology and definitions bring to light a common inventory and filter information based on their meanings. A different definition of one word can highlight a chasm among individuals' understanding and give rise to misunderstanding. Terms define perception.

Language produces the continuity of a worldview. It is required to guide daily life. Terms, inflections, and cultural understanding of a language define, reflect, and produce group participation. Labeling OBE, near-death-experience (NDE) and the like as extreme behaviors is done so in relation to the current social base. They are outside the boundaries of what is thought to be ordinary behavior. For mystics, they are natural and quite normal. This measurement can be applied to everyone. It is just a matter of reconfiguring consensus reality.

Self-Reflection

Self-reflection is the binding force of inventories, interpretations, and worldviews. It is literally what is reflected on. It isolates elements for selective cueing, informs interpretation, stabilizes inventories, and produces entire worldviews.

Reflecting within yourself orients you to life, describes what has meaning, and illuminates that which has been unknown. Reflection allows us to have friendships, technologies, and cultures. Reflection provides a means for self-development. It provides navigational references to help increase awareness. A how-to book, for instance, is loaded with reflections about a topic that can help one learn that subject. These reflections, however, are not the actual friendships, technologies, cultures, or skills.

Reflection allows us to create and maintain an essential view of life. It is needed for navigating city streets, employment, and healthcare. However, through an unceasing circulation of the same perspective, one view of life becomes woven into stories that are repeated over and over as though they are myths becoming real. By then, no other options exist.

Recognizing this process, shamans took the bold step of learning how to stop their internal reflections, their repetitive deliberations. Don Juan considered this general behavior of reflection as self-importance. He considered self-importance to be the basis of everything good as well as everything rotten in the human experience. And he reflected on how tackling self-importance became a strategy of shamans, allowing them to free perception.[2]

Shamans broke it down into two compartments: mental and emotional. The mental side is when you define and interpret yourself, others, and the world in general. This is the substance of inventories. The emotional counterpart concerns self-enhancement. This is where you measure yourself, reflect to yourself, about whether you're good or bad, are proficient or not, or are worthy or unworthy. For both aspects, a key element is continually categorizing and bolstering your definition of self.

To counter reflection, shamans learned to temporarily stop their internal dialogue, the ongoing loop of telling yourself this is such and that is so. This doesn't mean you shouldn't accurately assess yourself, others, and circumstances. It means to give yourself a breather to be more objective and less reactive, and therefore less confined by your version of reality. Chapter five offers an exercise to stop your internal dialogue, as well as other exercises to manage reflection.

Projection

All aspects of reflection are an effect of projection, which is typically thought to be the process by which people attribute to others what is in their own minds.[3] There are both personal and social implications. When you complain about another person, for instance, perhaps trying to win an argument by saying the other person is arrogant, then odds are you have, in some way, that behavior. Denigrating another person to bolster one's own arguments is an example of being arrogant.

An alternate interpretation of that behavior is saying the person is out of balance, an explanation with less of an emotional charge behind it and perhaps a more objective one. The person's inventory could be different, or the person may have had a traumatic experience shaping their life, with either situation giving the appearance of arrogance. Then again, the person could be arrogant, but that doesn't remove the ins and outs of projection.

A defining characteristic of projection is the level of intensity you feel about another person.[4] People who are the most argumentative, defensive, and vocal in maintaining their position or taking issue with another person, are those who remain in the deepest throes of projection. They have become mentally and emotionally invested in producing a given outcome. The degree of emotional reaction indicates how tightly they're holding onto their interpretations. Self-righteousness doesn't mean someone is right. With these simple examples, you can observe the two sides of self-importance at play in yourself and others throughout the day.

Expanding our definition of projection, we find that social agreements, including those of consensus reality, are examples of mass projection since they are based on widely held interpretations that are often backed by emotional commitments. A worldview allows us to project upon, and thereby predict, our environment. Yet we often make events conform to our projection. We then act according to our thoughts and disregard information that doesn't fit. Time and again, we strive to make the world conform to our thoughts.

In general, projection pertains to interpretations. Adding meaning through emotional connections is also important to understand the process. But losing the emotional side of importance doesn't mean becoming emotionally sterile, just like suspending thought doesn't mean becoming less mentally capable. This contrast points out the intricacies of human behavior that need to be managed to better learn and expand awareness.

Broadly speaking, tackling self-importance became a keystone in the shamans' path. Some of these dynamics can also be found in the practice of science. To continue forming a foundation to study the energy body, let's now gain a glimpse of those two worlds.

MYSTICS OF OUR TIME

For our explorations, it is helpful to know a little about the type of shamans who investigate the energy body. To begin, a shaman is a type of mystic. Mystics adhere to mysticisms, which are disciplines centered on life beyond the earthly dimension and practices that lay the groundwork for a transcendent union with the cosmos. Awareness of being one with creation is often a hallmark of these paths, avenues of investigation that have endured for centuries.

Mystics often tout that there is an absolute or ultimate reality, assigning to consciousness characteristics that are not mechanical, physical, or calculable—these being the bastion of classical science. Quantum physicists, on the other hand, deal with probabilities and uncertainties, and may portray quantum worlds using theories rather than hard and indisputable facts, producing visions of reality that are almost mystical.

One can even make the case that quantum physicists, especially those focused on producing an updated rendition of the wavefield, are mystics. For thousands of years, mystics have routinely dealt with alternate, yet interconnected and unified, dimensions of life. And now the quantum world is described similarly: a multiverse of parallel, interacting dimensions, where everything is connected—a mystical oneness of creation. As we'll cover, many ultra-modern, scientific wavefield principles are the same as those found in ancient shamanism.

Mysticism is found in various traditions throughout the world. Mysticism is like a pier: It gives added reference, a new vantage point, and a means for traveling beyond ordinary landscapes. It outlines goals and steps to realize those goals. It provides more options than found in a typical reality. While sometimes enfolded within religion (often considered a high form of religion), mystical strains of thought are more consistent with philosophy in that they adhere to procedures to acquire knowledge rather than to promote theological belief.

There are also cultural considerations. While the world's three major monotheistic religions—Judaism, Christianity, and Islam—share common ancestry, each has developed into a singular form of mysticism. Other forms of mysticism sprouted throughout the globe. Even though they all generate a mystical relationship with the cosmos, they may not all consider paranormal experiences, such as psychic functioning like OBE, to be viable for personal development. A Zen Buddhist may shun the high adventures of OBEs, a Taoist may allow them, and a shaman may require them.

Reflecting types of mystical orientation, it is interesting to note that meditative experiences vary among mystics. Electroencephalograph (EEG) research, for instance, has shown that a Zen master might stay alert to the simple rhythm of a metronome while remaining deep in meditation, while a skilled Yoga meditator's EEG doesn't register the physical-environment stimulation. Even with common overarching goals, different disciplines yield different results.[5]

Buddhist monk and psychologist Jack Kornfield presents the two principal schools of mystical thought as transcendent and immanent.[6] A transcendent path strives for the higher order of altered states, including mystical revelations, while an immanent path doesn't place importance on altered states but focuses more on realizing that everything needed is already within ordinary time and space. Shamans incorporate both by tapping mystical dimensions while understanding we have everything we need here and now.

Mysticism, like science, offers a coherent worldview that gives meaning and predictability. Still, both concern interpretations of something that ultimately cannot be interpreted. An absolute mystical reality poses the same problem as a reality generated by scientists: they are both reflections of something outside of their realities. But you need something to work with to get on with life, and the practices of mystics and scientists contain specialized terminology needed for precise understanding. For a layperson, their worldview hovers in the background, a behind-the-scenes influence, whereas mystics and scientists actively investigate their descriptions of reality.

Succumbing to interpretation, mystics often make another discipline fit with their own, which is a form of projection. Scientists do the same, even going so far as to castigate their colleagues who dare to challenge the status quo. The findings of science become reality, and if something is not considered scientific, it is dismissed as lacking substance. In turn, because of the vastness of mystical descriptions, mystics often think they among all others have found true reality.

Reflections of Shamanism

In general, mysticism yields a path of transformation of awareness, ability, and place in this world. Shamanism is one avenue, and a shaman is a type of mystic. There are many facets of shamanism. Worldwide, it remains one of the most widely practiced philosophies, and versions of shamanism can be found on every continent. There are some instances where it is regarded as an indigenous religion. While it was once considered a staple of rural life, branches of shamanism now extend into urban environments.

Some of the shared features of shamanism include healing, journeying via dreamlike awareness, utilizing altered states of consciousness, respect for the environment, finding emotional equilibrium and purpose, and viewing the world as being comprised of energy. But you do not need to be a shaman to espouse the characteristics of shamanism or to find value in the efforts of shamans. Many of shamanism's perspectives offer benefits because they reflect a healthy investigation, understanding, and appreciation of life.

One branch of shamanism originated several thousand years ago in central Mexico and has been best characterized in the books of Castaneda. Singularly focused on the energy body and world of energy, this class of shamans employs skills of perception, such as the advanced use of dreaming and directly *seeing* energy. In addition, don Juan was clear that his lineage was not associated with any culture. He sometimes referred to his lineage as Toltecs to indicate highly knowledgeable and skilled energy body practitioners. To him, Toltec meant men and women of knowledge removed from the Toltec culture of Mexico but still known by that term.[7]

These shamans live in a multi-dimensional world. They embody concrete knowledge without words, and readily perceive nonordinary or altered states of awareness. Dreaming and out-of-body travel are part of their reality. At the same time, these people represent a step beyond shamanism. While common features include dreaming, healing, and personal and social balance with life, they do not rely on traditional artifacts such as manner of dress, rituals, and tools. Other than continually challenging the existing order of reality, they don't have set practices. Their efforts remain a work in progress. The energy body is the keystone of this endeavor.

The Energy Body as Shamanism

Shamanism consists of various practices and a worldview. The description includes the energy body: where it comes from, how it works, and how to manage it. Yet the worldview is held lightly and is routinely discarded as a matter of practice. This enables rapid personal development since interpretation is a steppingstone, or a channel marker.

Working within their worldview, and by having created that worldview, shamans learn what energy is, how it works, and its applications. This becomes a stable reference. By recognizing, mapping, and describing the energy body, shamans form a consensus that brings the energy body to life by being part of the description of life.

This lineage examines natural capacities of the energy body and develops them to an extreme level. Shamanism, therefore, portrays a particular way of going about the exploration and development of the energy body. Doing so reveals the natural conditions of life. While the anatomy and processes of the energy body can explain shamanic abilities of OBE and healing, they also provide a way to make sense of human consciousness in general.

A Little History

In Castaneda's books, don Juan often referred to his shamanic tradition as a lineage of seers because of the emphasis on examining the luminous world of energy. This has a specific connotation that distinguishes it from other types of seers including clairvoyants, visionaries, and mystics of other traditions.

Millennia ago, these shamans actively cultivated power for power's sake. According to legend, these men and women could perform X-Men-like actions, such as hurling boulders, teleporting their physical bodies, and shapeshifting. Their form of journeying took them to recondite, bizarre areas of the wavefield that gave rise to aberrant behaviors centered on using their skills to subjugate others. They reveled in their ability to visit other worlds, patting themselves on the back for their genius. This hubris led to their downfall. They were so wrapped up in their own machinations that they didn't notice Indian and Spanish invaders sweeping into their land and targeting the cultural power brokers of that time, the shamans.[8]

This was the heyday of magical potions, talismans, incantations, and witchcraft. Humans turned against humans for the sake of enhancing power. This contrived relation to the world acted against those who misused power by reducing their awareness of a reality beyond themselves, causing their practices to fall into disarray.

Retreating and regrouping, they realized that they had become lost in their explorations. They over-emphasized the intricacies of their inventory, which had become a burden rather than a means of liberation. This had the effect of weakening their balance with the world and causing them to lose sight of personal and social growth. With these insights, they revitalized their teachings and practices. A defining feature of this reformation was shifting to an unyielding examination of the energy body in relation to the environment. A new cycle was born.

Yet, even with their indulgences, the ancients had cast the foundation for the new shamans. They knew the world was alive, that there were other dimensions, that psychic ability was valid, and that multiple modes of perception were self-evident. Continuing with these underpinnings, over generations new cycle shamans revamped their worldview and emphasized personal character to withstand any negative effects of their explorations.

The teachings shifted away from a quest for domination to a principle of not harming others. Furthermore, shamanism was seen as something to be leveraged to increase knowledge, not something requiring dogmatic adherence. They became independent of culture and consensus reality. In doing this, these shamans refined an elegant depiction of the human energy body that the old cycle adherents had begun charting. As don Juan put it, the new cycle arranged the building blocks for coherency.[9]

The hallmark of the new cycle of shamanism was the introduction of the ethical use of energy. Practices were streamlined and aberrations reduced. To avoid having foreign powers disseminate their ranks, they acted with small teams rather than large groups. The idea that the system should be used for the development of awareness rejuvenated the participants and realigned their behavior. They became singularly interested in freedom beyond perceptual conventions and beyond the confines of reason that govern a reflective reality.

While there is no official version of shamanism, there are consistent practices such as those previously mentioned. A guiding light of modern practices is that each generation needs to evaluate and redefine, with new terminology, their relation to life. From a traditional shamanic perspective, don Juan might be considered a renegade. He challenged convention and recognized the dynamics of descriptions. He used the new cycle description for a navigational reference and to impart the foundations of knowledge. It is from his teachings as presented in the work of Castaneda that the new cycle has taken root.

Personal Power

Don Juan also used the term "warrior" to indicate a practitioner, defining it as one who hunts power and, most importantly, has the necessary training and character to do so.[10] I think it is valuable to look at shamanism as a map and means, whereas warrior relates to the discipline of sobriety, stamina, humility, and other like-minded traits. The warrior embodies a certain spirit and style of enacting the teachings. In essence, warriorship is the thread connecting all stages of growth. It is a discipline that transcends the set practices of mysticisms, including shamanism.

Thanks to don Juan and Castaneda, warriorship has been baked into the new cycle's method of investigating consciousness, adding flavor to the tradition. The warrior is at once integral to modern shamanism while being independent of it, a posture that allows the craft to be challenged and evolve. Some elements of warriorship are mentioned throughout this work. For simplicity, when I reference shamans or shamanism it is understood that this includes warriorship.

For one and all, personal power is needed to survive. The pursuit of personal power is part and parcel of shamanism. A shaman's skills in nonordinary reality result from having sufficient personal power. The level of work with altered states, such as OBE, healing, and one's relation with the environment are defining elements of personal power.

Power is the possession of energy and ability to use it in specific ways to influence outcomes. In terms of physics, energy is the ability to do work, to change something; power indicates how much can be changed, and how much energy is used to produce change. In the case of the energy body, personal power is a measure of what can be perceived, what can be understood, and what skills can be performed. It is both an avenue for learning and a barrier against it, all depending on what you do. Like all forms of power, it is used and abused throughout life in all occupations and endeavors.

Evaluating a Philosophy

Unless you are somehow gifted, to firmly move forward in learning you need a system that will offer a comprehensive worldview, one with channel markers to keep you on track, and how-to skills. This is exactly what mystical philosophies and science offer. The markers may be elaborate views or simple tips. For example, don Juan advised Castaneda not to become overconfident. This is backed up with scientific research. Psychiatrist Arthur Deikman, in his landmark study of cult behavior, *The Wrong Way Home*, found that overconfidence leads to the demise of spiritual organizations as well as individuals.[11]

Whether practitioners follow the path they preach is another story. That's a fight with self-importance. For instance, Deikman found that self-righteousness is a marked feature of cult members. Embarking on a path of self-importance is contrary to staying on the path. It only leads into room after room of mirror images of yourself, or rather of the images you have of yourself. That won't get you too far.

The attitude that there are only a few chosen shamans floating around, or that only a select group of scientists is authoritative, is also an indication of cult behavior. Indeed, Deikman found that devaluing outsiders was a firm indication of cult activity. The ability to properly relate to others hinges on personal power and how well you align with the other person. You understand another person not by what the person says but how you interpret what is said. That occurs from your personal power.

Be it science or mysticism, philosophy provides a framework that can help you grow as you let your current knowledge become obsolete. Part of the challenge requires remaining true to a philosophy while also remaining true to yourself. You need momentum and balance. In this light, a viable philosophy always has two features that indicate whether it's strong enough, and flexible enough, to guide your development.

The first indicator of a viable philosophy is that it's non-exclusive. It won't arbitrarily dismiss ideas, practices, procedures, worldviews, and goals. It opens doors. If something works, it works. If you're a shaman and come across a Buddhist or other practice that helps you, you don't ignore it because it isn't part of your primary path. You incorporate it. If the findings of scientists augment your mystical path, claim them as your own. Likewise, if the discoveries of mystics add insight to scientists, acknowledge them.

The second indicator of a workable philosophy is that it clearly teaches it is a means to an end, not the true version of reality. It is to help generate clarity, not lock up perception in its worldview. The attitude that there is only one true path provides another indication of cult behavior. This is also a feature of fundamentalism and shows that religions and philosophies can easily create a bridge to less desirable behaviors in the name of knowing better than others. Neither shaman nor scientist is immune from arrogance.

THE DYNAMIC WAVEFIELD

Science and shamanism represent realities built from consensus. By using different lenses and arriving at dissimilar interpretations, scientists and shamans have constructed different worldviews, what don Juan described as "cognitive systems."[12] In one, NDE is due to brain seizures. In the other, it is one of many legitimate transphysical phenomena. In one, the world is material, in the other it is energy. To fully understand either view, a person needs to become fluent with the respective inventory.

Yet there are areas of agreement. For instance, shamans and scientists agree on the existence of energy. In the world of science, the field of bioenergetics centers on the flow and transformation of energy among living organisms and their environment.[13] As the term indicates, it deals with biology (the study of all life) and energy (perhaps the underlying structure of all life) and where these two intersect. The meeting area between biology and energy is immense, extending beyond imagination. As virtually every area of human activity and every nook and cranny of our world is touched by bioenergy, it stands to form the basis of an entirely new cosmology. If energy is in any way a determinant for biological actions and reactions, then new avenues of investigation and new technologies for healing and wellness will sprout.

At the same time, these revelations are not casting an entirely new net over the scientific world. "The emerging concepts do not require us to abandon our sophisticated understandings of physiology, biochemistry, or molecular biology," maintains James Oschman, biophysicist and author of *Energy Medicine: The Scientific Basis*. "Instead, they extend our picture of living processes, and of healing, to finer levels of structure and function."[14] And, as physicist Milo Wolff says, "Nothing happens in nature without an energy exchange. Communication or acquisition of knowledge of any kind occurs only with an energetic transfer. There are no exceptions. This is a rule of nature."[15]

And recently, a new generation of wavefield researchers who are reshaping views of quantum physics have entered the picture. For instance, quantum processes were once thought to only be active at sub-atomic levels. These dynamics are now recognized as occurring at macro levels across all spheres of existence. This thinking was largely ignored because classical physics could still measure macro, or large, events. Macro conditions are sufficiently stable that classical physics does the job, and quantum processes could be studied separately. No longer ignoring the larger view among other areas of investigation, the new quantum investigators are considering multi-dimensional activity of the wavefield.

These advances don't necessarily render obsolete what has come before. Classical physics remains an essential reference to build bridges, buildings, and even spacecraft that house humans. However, spacecraft will eventually incorporate new arenas of physics that transcend current laws about what is considered possible. As a result, new technologies based on ultra-modern physics will permit interstellar, faster-than-light travel. This contrast serves as an example that classical and modern physics are not only interpretations of science, but of reality.

No Longer in a Material World

Another area of agreement between new quantum researchers and shamans concerns the pervasiveness of energy. Typically, energy is thought to emanate from physical objects (this being a classical physics perspective). Even with Reiki and other laying-on-of-hands modalities, healing energy comes from the practitioner. Living in a material world that has a by-product of energy is a dominant worldview around the globe. This inventory-shaping idea governs our daily lives in no less a manner than thinking Earth is flat.

Leading-edge physicists are elevating this thinking to where energy doesn't just play a role, it is all there is. These wavefield theorists regard the world and the objects within it to be comprised solely of energy and bound in such a way that they give an *appearance* of physicality, especially since they are easily measured. Thinking within the shamanic world similarly finds that objects are different forms of energy, that all energy originates from a single source, and that the essence of the entire universe is energy. Objects have the appearance of solidity because we have trained our eyes to interpret the world in such a manner. In short, the world is pure energy.

This thinking also transcends the idea that there is a barrier between material and energy worlds. Currently, chemical reactions can be technologically measured, while wavefield activity is more in the realm of theory, and so material-world definitions have the upper hand in forming a description of reality. Physical measurements cement there being a material world. However, shamans measure energy, including that of the wavefield, by *seeing* it directly, by witnessing the luminosity and effects of energy, and find that these actions and reactions are predictable.

Wavefield Emanations

Shamanism arose from centuries of examining emanations, currents of energy stretching throughout existence. This bedrock finding of ancient shamans is part of a cosmology that modern physicists refer to as the wavefield. Shamans and scientists alike consider this to be highly dynamic, like the ocean, where many influences determine conditions at any one moment. Shamans have found that specific vibrations connect everything in the same manner that scientists view entanglement, or quantum interconnectedness.

Both scientific and shamanic worldviews depict how objects originate from the wavefield. All life's creatures arise from this source and return to it upon death. In quantum physics, this is referred to as *coherence* and *decoherence*, the coming together of elements within the wavefield and the unbinding of those elements as they return to the wavefield. Due to the constant flow of information that both shamans and scientists recognize, the wavefield creates conditions of reality and is, itself, part of that universal reality. By evaluating information streaming through, and of it, the wavefield determines its next actions. From the whole of the wavefield to individual creations, the wavefield embodies intentionality.

For both scientist and shaman, the wavefield is the foundation from which all worldviews emerge. And while the world of energy advances prior descriptions, it is still an interpretation based on the consensus of shared internal dialogue. Since shamans and scientists share similar core principles concerning emanations and the wavefield, I use the terms wavefield and emanations interchangeably. Please keep in mind I'm only addressing a few shared ideas. The full measure of scientific study of the wavefield, or that of shamans, is beyond the scope of this work.

Birth and Death of the Energy Body

Here's where it gets fun. Ancient shamans and new wavefield scientists agree on how the energy body, or any object, coheres into existence. In science, wavefield creations are known as *wave packets* or *superpositions*.[16] And this can be applied to the energy body as well. As geneticist and biophysicist Mae-Wan Ho describes, a conscious entity exists as a macroscopic wave function, a quantum superposition of coherent activities.[17] In shamanism, wavefield dynamics create everything, and portions of the wavefield are contained within the energy body. Humans are therefore an intimate part of the wavefield.

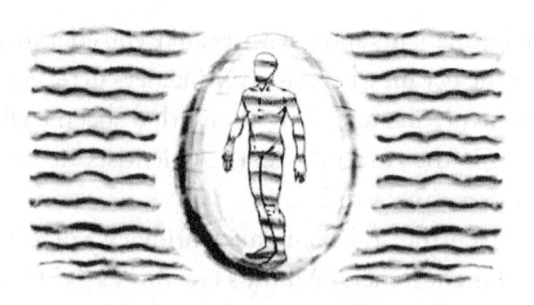

Figure 2.2
Environmental Emanations
The energy body is created by wavefield dynamics.

Upon *seeing* this process, a shaman might say that different energies assemble into an energy body. How well the elements of a creation harmonize determines the quality of coherence. While the wavefield produces the energy body, for both science and shamanism it is their respective shared inventories that allow the recognition of it.

Fixed states, conditions, and proven laws define classical physics. As a central condition, the world is thought to be comprised of material objects. Because survival requires the ability to predict, the development of classical theory and prediction work hand in hand, given that forecasting events requires stability. Validating the expected behavior of a material worldview confirms the scientific inventory.

In the quantum universe, however, material particles serve to represent matter and do not have fixed positions or other properties.[18] It is in this view that there are no material objects, only variations of the wavefield that express observable coherence. Likewise, a tenet of shamanism is that there are no physical objects, only emanations of energy from which everything originates. In both inventories, the wavefield is energy, and if its energy unifies in a certain way then that coherence of energy is observable, but only giving the appearance of being material.

Wave packets also undergo decoherence, or dissolution.[19] This part of the process is not dissipation in an ordinary sense, but rather an unbinding of the elements that coalesced to create a packet of energy. In short, decoherence destroys wave packets. This life-and-death cycle creates conditions for new observables to come into existence, requiring the entanglement of information as the wavefield assesses itself and decides how to proceed.

Shamans describe the same thing. Old cycle shamans referred to the wavefield as the "dark sea" since it was beyond comprehension,[20] a parallel to scientists referring to dark energy as such because it is not well understood. For ancient shamans, death was being sucked into the dark sea and the body torn asunder, an apt description of decoherence. *Seeing* the wavefield produced an immense, towering black form. Reflecting their mythology, they termed this the Eagle. They found that the Eagle bestowed awareness and then devoured it.[21] A new cycle rendering is that a dying person's body disintegrates under the force that had previously created consciousness.

Stepping back and looking at the entire unfolding of creation, both scientists and shamans observe wave packets emerging from the wavefield due to the robust way in which they form a relationship with their environment. The wavefield monitors the process and continues to select for coherence or decoherence based on the packets' interactions with the environment.[22] In other words, the coherence of a packet in connection with the wavefield is a reference for whether the wavefield continues to support the packet, keep it alive, or cause its decoherence, its death. The wavefield is constantly updating itself, which means learning and adaptation are required. The wavefield therefore has a relationship with its creations. It actively listens to what has been created and responds. Of interest is that the downfall of the old cycle shamans was due to their failure to adjust to changing conditions—even ignoring them. They were out of touch with life.

This wavefield cycle also places into effect conditions that prevent certain packets from being observed, from cohering to completeness. States that survive become classical in the sense of being sufficiently stable to be measured by the rules of standard physics. Over time, these experience a natural loss of binding and undergo decoherence.[23] The wave packet leaks back into the wavefield.[24] This is known as a *wave function collapse*.[25] However, another scientific interpretation is that there is no wave collapse, just a continuous reordering of information, of energy, throughout the field,[26] a view that inspires concepts of other-dimensional survival and reincarnation-based phenomena.

Overall, the ebb and flow of life results from the environment monitoring itself. This leads some scientists to consider that there is only one world and that it evolves based on its own assessments.[27] Moment to moment, each wave of creation changes, never to be duplicated. Yet, each wave is formed by constant processes that produce these ever-changing conditions. As don Juan poetically says, emanations are forever in motion yet remain eternal.[28]

Information

The information age has grown from the capacities of computers to information being considered a process, state, or disposition—even the bedrock of reality.[29, 30] As part of this expansion of thinking, a debate has risen regarding whether information is exclusively physical or whether it is *everything*.[31, 32] This dispute carries wide-ranging implications for everything, from how we conduct medical care to how we view the nature of consciousness to how we participate in life.

For wavefield dynamics, information is an animating force of the wavefield, the ingredient that produces wavefield decisions of coherence and decoherence. The ongoing flow of information among packets and within the whole of the environment regulates wavefield activity. Something to note is that information carries the ability to influence and thereby change things. It is interactive, evolving, and a form of power. This is also the basic definition of energy, the ability to do work, to be able to alter conditions. Information and energy are therefore equivalent and interchangeable terms.

Information within the wavefield can be perceived by the wavefield's creations, which then send information into the wavefield. This interaction continues unabated within continuously changing conditions as the wavefield selects what it will do next. But for what purpose? Old cycle shamans, says don Juan, saw the Eagle bestow awareness to enrich itself.[33] A new cycle shaman might think this occurs for the wavefield to become aware of itself.

FOOTPRINTS OF KNOWLEDGE

Scientists built a description that relies on, and forms from, specific behaviors. Shamans did the same. Each has a worldview based on their respective inventory. One doesn't negate the other. Each discipline has validated their discoveries. The degree of separation between their worldviews, however, is enough to get anyone arguing.

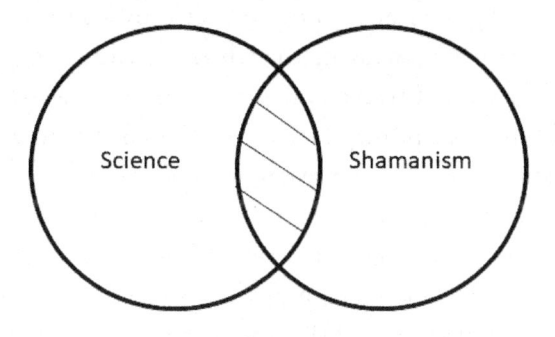

Figure 2.3
A Meeting of Minds
Science and shamanism represent two worldviews having different inventories. Due to advances in both, there are now shared elements of their inventories, with the wavefield as a central feature.

Shamans and scientists alike investigate the universe, systematically organizing, interpreting, and building their worlds. Both groups create knowledge, each from their unique starting points. Scientists use mechanical instrumentation for much of their observations; shamans use the energy body's resources. Scientists reflect and generate social consensus, as do shamans. New research builds on what came before. Replication of experiments is a keystone for the practice of science. Shamans have their methods. Both camps have recognizable behaviors that define them. They just have different ways of going about their work.

In review, features of a shared inventory among shamans and some scientists have come into view. This like-minded portrayal of life allows for the exploration of humans and cosmology from a new, more comprehensive angle. Both practices share considerations about the nature of information permeating and unifying existence, for instance. They also agree on the formation and demise of objects, including humans. And they realize life is made of energy with only the appearance of materiality. In addition, both entertain the idea that there is an unknowable part of existence. There are portions of the wavefield that humans do not connect with and are therefore beyond perceiving, let alone recognizing. From this comes an understanding that meaningful perception forms from interpretations.

For both endeavors, there is always a new breed of researchers steadily advancing and leaving footprints of knowledge. New quantum researchers are slowly reweaving the fabric of reality, just as new cycle shamans do the same. This evolution has led to where both groups share similar building-block principles that ancient shamans put into motion.

Scientists now validating key parts of the shamanic worldview makes it more difficult to automatically cast a wary eye in the direction of shamans. Accepting that shamans stood on this higher ground first will take some time. In coming decades, however, it wouldn't be surprising if scientists expand their definitions and interpretations to include more shamanic elements. Once scientists begin tackling the energy body, new worlds will emerge which might also open additional doors for shamans.

3 ⟩ Energy Body Dynamics

The anatomy of the human physical body identifies it as being human: arms, legs, head, torso. The energy body also has an anatomy, a defined structure that permits others to recognize it, to *see* it, as being human. Learning its capacities, management, and coordination among parts is no different than learning about the physical body.

The energy body is natural. We all have one. Shamans, however, have learned to access normally unused portions. This reveals why they are skilled in altered states of consciousness such as OBE as well as the use of the entire energy body. The energy body is central to the shamans' inventory. It shapes their lives and reality. Some parts of it are now in mainstream inventories, such as chakras, meridians, and auras. A few inventories contain the more complete anatomy. The essential components of a shamanic inventory include:

Uniformity

Uniformity is the shape of the perimeter of the energy body. Within it is a pattern of energy known as cohesion, which is determined by how energy forms within this boundary. Uniformity is the structural hardware, and cohesion, the internal conditions, is the software of the energy body. Together they filter what information is perceived and processed, what can be comprehended, and what can't.

According to shamanic tradition, during the days of the old cycle shamans uniformity was narrow, like an American football, but over time is becoming more spherical. Its evolution is thought to govern human activity, with a narrow shape associated with abuses of power, while the trend toward a spherical shape accents balance, fewer ethical distortions, and wholeness. This makes sense in that a sphere connects with the wavefield in a rounded, uniform manner, resulting in more balance between self and environment.

Cohesion

From a wide angle, uniformity defines cohesion: what arrangements can be made and its overall abilities. Cohesion determines behavior, experience, and reality. In this way, you create your own reality. While uniformity establishes possibilities, a more complex process determines the state of cohesion. What we regard as the physical world is one cohesion within the energy body. Awareness of other dimensions correlates with their respective cohesions.

An inventory builds cohesion, and interpretation is a projection of that cohesion. The interlocking elements of an inventory provide cohesiveness, coherence, and clarity of perception. This filters awareness into interpretations and meaning. Coherence applies to how elements of cohesion combine, or how they assemble to produce meaningful recognition of the environment. How well the parts work and play together relates to the quality of consciousness.

Cohesion governs the alignments of internal and external energies. Acting as a filter, it connects with the environment and bends information according to how it formed. Too many inventory details consume energy and keep awareness in place, making it difficult to perceive beyond those boundaries. Avoiding this effect is a main reason new cycle shamans streamlined their inventory.

While mysticisms usually have a common goal of developing consciousness, they have different inventories and techniques. Since the inventories are different, they have different cohesions, and different arrangements of energy. This both results from and produces different styles of mysticism. The same principle highlights the divisions between mystics and scientists. Since they have markedly dissimilar cohesions, they live in vastly different worlds.

The Assemblage Point

The assemblage point indicates the type of cohesion. Brain waves, for instance, roughly indicate the state of consciousness of the person. Dominant activity of one frequency usually suggests the person is sleeping, while another frequency indicates waking states. However, brain waves do not produce awareness; they indicate it. In this manner, old cycle shamans thought the assemblage point produced awareness. New cycle shamans overturned this view by determining that it marked a specific state of awareness associated with the type of cohesion. They found that changes in cohesion, reflected by movements of the assemblage point, produced perception.

The assemblage point is a small, somewhat brighter bundle of light within the energy body, making it difficult to *see* as it is a ball of luminosity within a larger ball of energy. However, don Juan says it isn't all that difficult to *see*; rather, the barrier to doing so is thinking we can't *see* it because it isn't there.[1]

The assemblage point exists independently of the physical body. Cohesion takes its form from the parts put into it, from a host of interrelated influences such as educational conditioning, state of health, worldview, and overall environment. The quality of this binding produces coherence which leads to the stability of the assemblage point. Perception is unstable if the assemblage point is jittery.

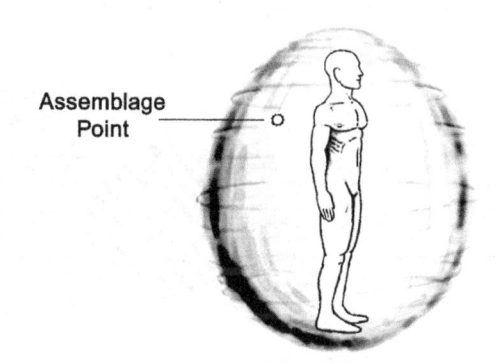

Figure 3.1
The Assemblage Point
The assemblage is a small, bright area inside the energy body. It is not part of the physical body. Its location indicates what is being perceived.

Another way of describing the assemblage point is that it is an area within the energy body where all the elements that go into an inventory assemble or consolidate. It is a point where perception is brought into focus as internal energies intersect with external emanations. It marks what is perceived and experienced, a state of consciousness that can reveal this world or other dimensions. This intertwining and assembling of many elements crystallize cohesion, stabilize the assemblage point, and focus awareness.

A classical view of physics, where the world is material, represents one assemblage point position based on the cohesion where that point of view has been built. The view that everything is information, and that the material world is only an appearance of energy, is another position. Both interpretations result from their inventories which have coalesced into their respective cohesions. Both are marked by different assemblage point positions.

In addition, some mystics regard the physical world as an illusion. But in the shamanic inventory, the physical world is not illusory; it is a particular cohesion. In these terms, it is as real as any other cohesion. If the assemblage point were to sufficiently move, the physical world would change into something else. But it would remain real in terms of the prior assemblage point's position. In other words, changing cohesion shifts the assemblage point, and this can produce awareness of different worlds between which you can go back and forth.

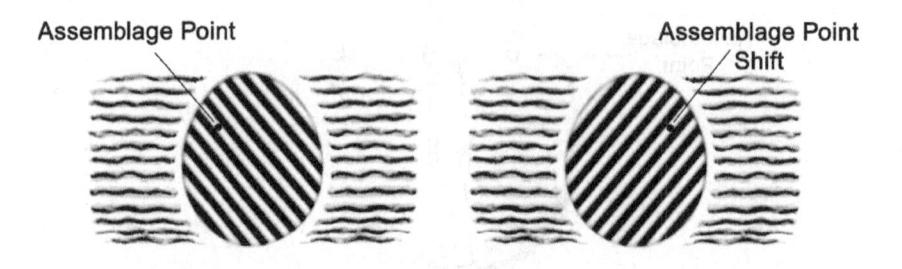

Figure 3.2, a & b
Assemblage Point Shift
Changing cohesion can be measured by a shift of the assemblage point.

Emotional moods used as frames of mind can shift the assemblage point. The intent of the mood changes the nature of cohesion. But the underpinning of how the assemblage point, cohesion, and inventory relate to one another is maintained by one's internal dialogue. When it is suspended, cohesion relaxes and the assemblage point moves. Don Juan thinks that more than ever, humans need to understand the assemblage point as our survival depends on it.[2]

Chakras and Meridians

Middle Eastern and Asian mystics provided useful maps of at least portions of the energy body. Chakras and acupuncture meridians, for instance, have found their way into cultural expression throughout the world. Briefly, chakras are energy centers that traverse the spine. Each accounts for some aspect of perception: the lower for physical, the higher for spiritual awareness is one schematic.

The depiction of the chakra-nadis network of energy offers an eastern counterpart to the full energy body. Please refer to the works of mystics of those traditions, or to my prior book, *The Complete Energy Body*, for a more detailed accounting. This presentation of energy body anatomy here is only to provide reference and context for OBE and consciousness in general.

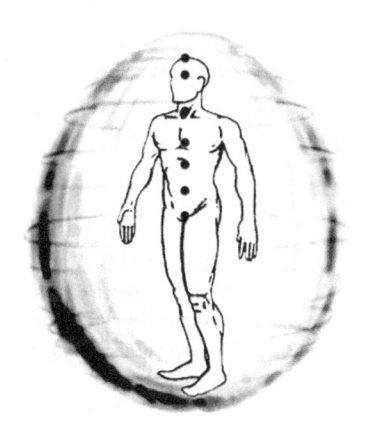

Figure 3.3
Chakra Locations
Chakras traverse the length of the spine.

The interaction among chakras affects cohesion. If a person is focused on a particular chakra, cohesion responds, and then that energy and meaning is on one's mind. Interactions among chakras offer a good indication of what is involved in achieving and maintaining balance. You might understand, then, why trying to establish a unified direction in life is like trying to orchestrate the behavior of cats, as the saying goes.

Meridians also influence cohesion. Simply put, they are channels of energy flowing throughout the body. Disease is thought to occur when a channel becomes blocked. Restoring the flow produces health. Meridians have been mapped for thousands of years, and highly detailed charts are now used by acupuncturists.

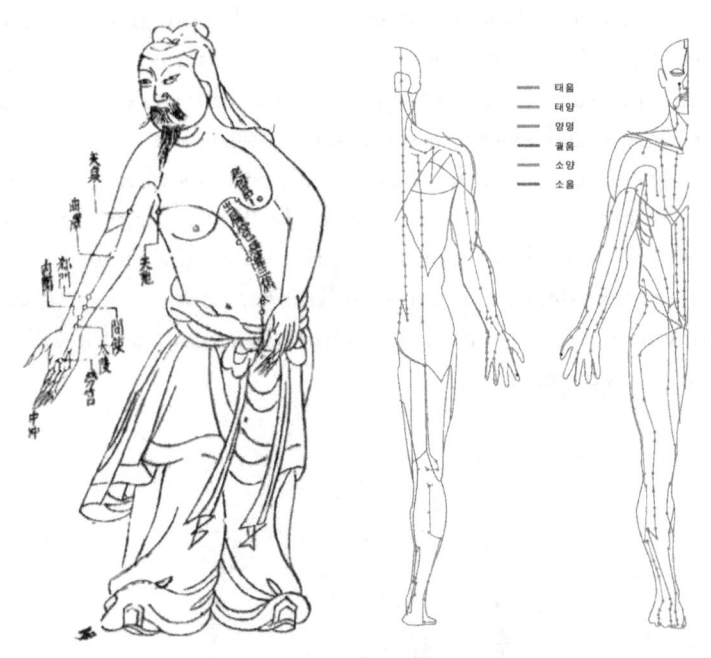

Figure 3.4, a & b
Ancient and Modern Meridian Charts
From a simple schematic to something more complex, these show the evolution of mapping acupuncture points. (Public domain, courtesy of Wikimedia Commons.)

Chakras and meridians are systems within the energy body, just like the physical body has circulatory and nervous systems. Interestingly, the nervous system, chakras, and meridians all have basic trunks with branches (channels of energy) spreading out and narrowing the further they stretch from the center of the body. Coherency between meridians or chakras and the body results in a more stable cohesion. In a similar manner, how well the chapters of a book cohere indicates the quality of the whole book.

Coherence produces the integrity of an individual. It maintains awareness amid all the environmental forces impacting a person. As we grow from child to adult, we hope that all our experiences cohere in a way that provides for a better and more balanced life. Enculturation, for instance, significantly affects cohesion, especially considering how many forces need to harmoniously cohere to provide for stable social behaviors.

The Aura

The aura is an expression of energy that reflects cohesion. It is not the energy body. It is more like an incandescent light bulb: uniformity is the outer glass, the filament is the physical body, and the gas inside the glass is cohesion. From the interactions of all three parts, light emits from the bulb. The aura is basically the same thing, only related to the energy body.

Figure 3.5
Light Bulb Aura
The interaction of the bulb's parts produces light. The relationship among the energy body's components produces the human aura. (Clip Art Library, used with permission.[3])

The aura provides some diagnostic information. Colors may be used to interpret one's state of health. More generally, the clearness of the aura indicates the health of cohesion, which indicates the health of the body. The better you become at aura gazing, the more you can *see* what is behind it. Chapter five contains gazing exercises.

ENERGY FIELDS

I mentioned the first and second energy fields in chapter one. As a microcosm of the wavefield, these exist both within and without the energy body, although those that are internal are limited. The human energy body is a type of coherence and does not contain the full measure of energy outside of it. There is also a third energy field that exists outside of the energy body. In general, these pertain to ordinary life, other dimensions of existence, and areas literally out of this world. They have also been defined as the known, unknown, and unknowable.[4]

First Field

The first energy field pertains to order, be it human-made or of the wavefield. It also relates to what has been learned, the known world. Social agreements indicate enough people have developed their first fields, their knowledge, in sufficiently similar ways to agree on what information is meaningful, such as when forming consensus reality. The more you align with any form of order that produces learning, the more cohesion expands. Aligning with the natural order of the wavefield produces a significant increase of awareness. It allows alignments of energy beyond consensus reality.

Second Field

This refers to untapped portions of the first field within the energy body. Attending to it requires a shift of attention, which is why the first and second energy fields were regarded by Castaneda as the first and second attentions. Dreaming, for instance, relates to the second attention. The second field is also considered to be the unknown which has the potential of realization. Learning is awakening more of what can become known. Therefore, it is potential in the sense that it is order that can eventually be comprehended. An individual's cohesion affects what type of order will become available, and what type of knowledge will be experienced.

Accessing other dimensions is discovering more of the order that extends throughout all dimensions. Dreaming is a primary means for this exploration. The fundamental dynamic between dreaming and personal growth is balancing the first and second fields by experiencing, learning, and activating more of the energy body. What was potential has become realized. Awareness of what was once part of the second field has been incorporated into the first field. The unknown is now known.

Without a sense of first field order and purpose, traveling within the second field is often a matter of trying to make sense of a wasteland. You have no relation to it, and the experience would be like losing your mind. This speaks to the importance of preparation prior to engaging in OBE, an act of entering the second field. Since deliberate second field awareness via dreaming is less filtered than the first field focus of the daily world, you gain more awareness of the wavefield. Yet a first field sense of life is required to make substantial gains in expanding this awareness.

Third Field

The third energy field is considered unknowable because it consists of conditions that exist outside of the energy body. Unlike other streams of energy, there are no corresponding energies within the energy body. As a result, you cannot achieve the external-to-internal alignments that yield meaningful perception. This doesn't mean that the third field doesn't impact the energy body, as the entirety of the wavefield exerts pressure and influence.

Shamans became aware of the third field by pushing their assemblage points outside the energy body. Just as the intent of social reality bends cohesion away from natural conditions, don Juan says shamans learned to reshape uniformity in a way that allowed unusual alignments with the third field,[5] with wavefield conditions outside of ordinary human experience. This means that, in some way, the third field contains order existing beyond what is contained within the human energy body. Since perception is being bent in a way that permits at least some awareness of the third field, it can become partially known.

In essence, however, the unknowable remains. There are parts of the wavefield that do not connect even remotely with human awareness. Plus, defining existence as essentially unknowable keeps us in check—always realizing there is something beyond comprehension. As a result, we remain open to learning. Of this, shamans and new wave-field scientists agree.

Relating to the third field in different ways also shows the benefits and drawbacks of definitions and of creating unyielding worldviews. While there is functional value in having definitions and worldviews, they eventually get stretched, if not overturned. It also reveals a little bit of shamanic training in that the definition of each field corresponds with the stage of instruction, with the student's level of personal power and ability to understand.

Introducing the third field as unknowable eventually allows a better understanding of shamanism as pieces of instruction fall into place until the person can effectively tackle out-of-this-world concepts. The progression of ideas needs to be done in a way that rendering life as inherently unknowable remains an ingredient for stable growth rather than a destabilizing obstacle. The general development and expansion of concepts and definitions is no different than what occurs in any educational setting. Shamanism is just a different arena.

Optimally, a worldview is a schematic to guide you beyond the description it embodies, and to where you can be comfortable knowing that everything is beyond interpretation and therefore unknowable. Getting there while maintaining composure is a matter of having sufficient personal power, meaning how much you've learned. Then life makes sense without needing a picture book of reality.

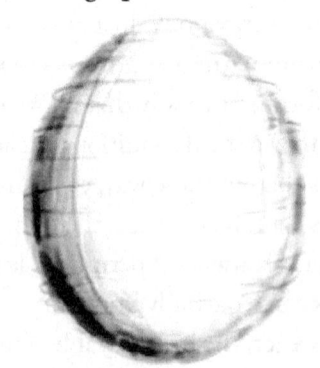

Figure 3.6
Energy Fields
The shaded area represents the first energy field. Cohesion expands into the second energy field the more the energy body is activated. Outside of the energy body is the third field.

Like the barrier between physical and energy worlds, the barrier between the first and second fields is one of interpretation. The second field influences the first field even if this isn't consciously recognized. These fields blend all the time; it's just a matter of degree. We can't survive without the first field, and increased awareness occurs in conjunction with tapping the second field.

Conditional Field

There are two fundamental types of cohesion: conditional and natural. As the term suggests, a conditional field results from how the energy body has been conditioned, particularly by social influences. Family upbringing, schooling, work, peers, and the encompassing worldview of reality all impact a person, and how the person responds to expectations for how to think and behave. If these social and psychological forces are coherent, what is being learned finds solid footing.

Conditioning and expectation shape and maintain cohesion. For example, expectations for educating new scientists and shamans are set by practitioners who have formed well-conditioned energy fields reflecting their specialties. Abiding by these expectations, students gradually condition themselves by learning what is expected and how to behave. The conditional field both establishes and reinforces those expectations. Behavior then conforms with the habits that have been ingrained.

Conditional fields block the flow of information while permitting detailed examinations of a specific field. Scientists can therefore steadily produce more refined results relating to their inquiries but may discount information that doesn't fit with their expectations. And while mystics' investigations focus more on consciousness, they're still apt to discount the teachings of other disciplines. Both scientists and mystics sustain their conditional fields by remaining in the throes of projection, by constantly reinforcing their thoughts about reality.

Forming a conditional field is like building a room with mirrors. We only see our reflections. Holding onto our views, we create a rigid cohesion that prevents dipping into nonordinary parts of the world, and when they happen to surface, we quickly work to put them in ordinary categories or dismiss the event with a response like, "What just occurred didn't really happen." Yet, as new cycle shamans discovered, categories can be developed to propel awareness to a natural field.

Natural Field

A natural energy field results from a harmonious intersection between the energy body and the wavefield, a dynamic balance of internal and external environments. A natural field permits more unfiltered awareness to resonate within personal consciousness. Therefore, developing it involves minimizing self-reflection. In practice, a conditional field doesn't always help you recalculate as events unfold. It makes your experience conform to an inventory, whereas a natural field, like the wavefield, constantly adjusts to conditions rather than to thoughts.

The possibility of activating the natural field exists beyond the confines of mysticisms that are designed to help form it. Since the teachings stem from conditional fields, they can indicate a way to a natural field, but getting there requires letting go of the teachings. Otherwise, whether the teachings are of science or mysticism, you remain within a conditional field, no matter how glorious it may be. A natural field is extremely difficult to achieve and because environmental energies are in constant flux, it is something that can't be fully maintained.

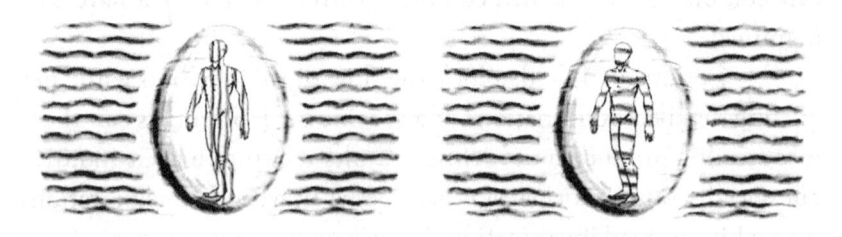

Figure 3.7, a & b
Conditional and Natural Energy Fields
A conditional field results from the social influences of daily life, whereas a natural field blends with the innate environment of the wavefield.

A personal natural field pertains to awakening the energy body as created by the wavefield. Cohesion then forms neatly within the parameters of uniformity. Because there are still boundaries, even though they are natural ones, a case can be made that a natural field is a very refined conditional field. Nonetheless, it is a quintessential relation between an individual and the wavefield.

The Tonal and Nagual

Let's now look at the tonal and nagual. Don Juan's lineage of shamanism applies the terms in a unique manner, and they have no academic definition or anthropological meaning. Don Juan elaborated on these in a dedicated lesson at the end of Castaneda's apprenticeship.[6] Since we're dealing with power and what that means, we need to address this topic because harmoniously developing the first and second fields, and the interaction of the tonal and nagual, regulates the amount of available power you have. This corresponds with your level or degree of consciousness. And this relates to how much of a natural field you've cultivated. The way you handle power, its use or abuse, is a key ingredient for developing the energy body.

The tonal relates to ordered arrangement of various parts as well as the existence of those parts, be the order of human contrivance or of natural conditions. That is, the tonal pertains to unified or coherent organization. If you can point to it, it is of the tonal. It consists of the areas of existence inhabited by all types of entities.[7]

Don Juan also mentions that there is a tonal of the times.[8] For instance, Native Americans lost their tonal when their way of life was taken from them. Shamans have at different times regarded perception as occurring within the energy body or as an exclusive result of the external world impinging on the energy body. Epochs of history also portray the tonal of the times, such as the flat-Earth and geocentric worldviews.

The tonal aspect of the energy body begins at birth and ends at death, says don Juan.[9] This corresponds to coherence and decoherence. But what occurs with decoherence remains debatable. If it is a reordering of information rather than dissolution, the door to reincarnation cracks open since it may be part of the interdimensionality of the wavefield. The next chapter explores how reincarnation might relate to the third energy field.

The nagual is the part of the wavefield and the energy body for which there is no description, no words, and no knowledge other than knowing it exists. It has no limit or duration.[10] We can only allude to it. This reminds me of a Taoist saying, "The Tao that can be named is not the true Tao." To find out if the nagual and the Tao correlate, we'd probably need to put some scholars in a room and let them hash it out. I do know that there are similarities between shamanism and Taoism. At any rate, with sufficient personal power, the nagual is recognizable but remains undefinable; that is, its effects can be observed, or *seen*, and utilized. Yet the dynamics of the entire energy body—the personal tonal—blind us to the existence of the nagual, even though it is our life blood.

Permeating the wavefield, the nagual is like the space between objects that holds everything in place. It is like raw power that can be harnessed to expand or manipulate the tonal, however any description of it falls short. After all, it is undefinable. To interpret it as another form of order, including a meta-order, is projecting first field properties onto it. By defining it, it automatically becomes part of the known inventory, the tonal, and we lose sight of its dynamism.

The second field is charged with potential energy that stands a chance of becoming realized, and thereby changing from potential to expressed order. Experience with potential can carry over to recognizing the nagual. By tapping the nagual, you gain the power to influence, to change circumstances, and with more capacity than normally considered. Power in daily life is usually rearranging elements of the tonal, but awareness of the nagual catapults one's ability into new realms.

This power affects what is expressed, with leverage from the nagual shaping what the wavefield or individuals produce. Since the nagual is not bound by organization or form, it affects original creativity. Unique manifestations spontaneously or intentionally occur and do so without rearranging pieces of the tonal. The nagual also resides outside of time (which is of the tonal) and plays a role in generating new perspectives of life and cosmology.

Contemplating the differences between the first and second fields can act as a step toward relating to the tonal and nagual, but this is not a firm comparison. It only serves to begin a deeper understanding.

THE CORNERSTONES OF AWARENESS

Different parts of the physical body, like ears and eyes, relate to various types of perception. Likewise, in the energy body there are specific areas that pertain to types of awareness. For instance, the heart area chakra relates to feeling and connectedness, and the forehead chakra typically is associated with *seeing* and related phenomena. Shamans have a different schematic than chakras, but the perceptions accounted for by chakras correspond with the *cornerstones of perception*.

These eastern and western versions of awareness sprouted in different cultures and different landscapes, resulting in different organizations of perception. Chakras follow the length of the spine, whereas the cornerstones are nonlinear or not in a straight line. Combined with the tonal and nagual, don Juan refers to the cornerstones as points of one's totality.[11] These modes of perception allow for the investigation, understanding, and development of all aspects of the energy body. Following is an overview of the cornerstones.

Talking

Talking pertains to internal dialogue, bringing into awareness elements of an inventory by defining them and by talking about them. This guides what you think and how you behave, opening doors to new ideas, places, situations—even to the existence of the energy body. But no matter how deeply philosophical talking directs consciousness, it remains superficial because it maintains interpretations about something rather than directly connecting with something. Thought is a reference. As a result, alignments are uneven. That said, talking also leads to understanding this dynamic and the ability to communicate it to others, thereby forming consensus realities, which are all acts of power.

Talking is a dominant influence in life. It can keep you firmly in place, never to move from your familiar ways. It leads to new directions, and new experiences can change your thoughts. As a type of energy, it directs attention. It can set up conditions for behavior but is not the behavior itself, other than that of thinking. Coherent thought forms from a stable cohesion. Put another way, life becomes more reasonable with a well-constructed cohesion.

Reason

As with talking, reason is located in the brain. Reason doesn't mean being academic. It both produces and is the result of organized thought: the consolidation, focus, and intent of energy. This power shapes awareness of life. Order provides steadiness and a springboard to engage life. Reasoning is an arrangement of awareness that reinforces the effects and power of thought. Yet it binds you to an inventory and to a complete worldview because that's the reasonable thing to accomplish.

Reason creates inventories. If the existence of something, anything, is not in an inventory, odds are it won't be part of an interpretation. This makes it easy to misinterpret a person or a situation. To verify this idea, you just need to pay attention to people's reactions during conversations. Mentioning the energy body to people who have closed inventories won't get you very far. They may think you've lost your mind when they may be estranged from their minds.

Not knowing the relation between description and natural reality, however, lends itself to being lost in a mental world. To many, a mystical approach to life may not seem rational because it isn't based on what is considered reasonable. But being in tune with a greater natural order is inherently rational because that is where we reside, even if we're not aware of it.

Living solely in the world of reason, we deplete energy, our power, as we are removed from the environment. Perception becomes hardened, cutting off awareness for other faculties of perception, other cornerstones. By suspending thought and reason, by interrupting our internal dialogue, we open the doors of perception. See chapter five for exercises related to stopping the internal dialogue.

Feeling

We can feel the energetic lines of the world, says don Juan, but we can't touch them. The world, he says, is a feeling.[12] Feeling is also a measure of cohesion. No matter the depth or breadth of a cohesion, feeling gives it an identity, a recognition. How you feel about someone, or something, shapes your world.

Located in the heart, feeling is a type of sensitivity, of awareness. Like thinking, it can regulate cohesion. Its connection with energy allows us to navigate life based on how we feel about work, relationships, and the sense of being alive. It indicates health and illness. It is a key indicator of quality of life and happiness.

Thinking and feeling are intertwined, each affecting the other. Thinking forms feeling, going from understanding to emotionally connecting with those thoughts. If you're in an environment with a set way of thinking, like membership in a political party, country, or social group, you're likely to have shared feelings about certain things. Conversely, feelings can alter thinking. Positive experiences with other races can change racist thinking because your feelings changed, for instance.

In general, the more you can suspend thought, the purer your feeling. When you're not interpreting, you can be more aware of the immediacy of life. While thinking and reasoning are natural parts of being human, the full experience of living is with feeling, not with thinking about living. Feeling is expansive and carries awareness that might not register in reason.

Awareness of your emotions is part of being conscious. Emotional intelligence (EQ) consists of the education of feeling and its expression, allowing you to relate and respond to life's situations. It includes sensing people and the general environment. EQ is also harmonizing thought and feeling as it is easy to think you're one way yet emotionally act another way.

One of EQ's elements is relaxed centeredness, a never-ending work in progress. This allows for a constructive flow of energy. Your emotions apply pressure to cohesion, and cohesion generates emotion. EQ, then, lends itself to the proper functioning of cohesion. While not often recognized, feeling is a mainstay of information and communication. How you feel about another person, what you sense in your surroundings, and your gut feeling for decisions actively shape your life.

You can use EQ to better discern your immediate situation or to tune into other environments, be they related to problem solving at work or another dimension.

However, even though feeling is a fundamental mode of perception, EQ is rarely taught during upbringing, school, or workplace. While much has been written about it, EQ is typically not considered to be something to pay attention to throughout the day. Emphasis is given to intellectual knowledge even though only a fraction of students fully responds to this curriculum. As a result, we're not provided skills early on in our education for a foundational connection with life. In essence, we're actively taught to become alienated from ourselves and society. EQ atrophies, and our lives become less meaningful. We then wonder in horror as teenage suicides increase, scratch our heads about a general dissatisfaction with life, and yet continue to march in the same way.

Dreaming

Dreaming is central to shamanism and its manner of investigating the cosmos. Approached in a constructive way, dreaming fits hand-in-glove with expanding consciousness. Placing attention on the second field, dreaming utilizes procedures and skills to exercise the left side of the energy body, the second energy field. OBE, for example, is stepping into both the dynamism and unknown order of the wavefield, making dreaming an avenue to power. By orienting to a natural field, OBE allows first-field expansion which turns the unknown into the known.

Dreaming requires a specific intention for the placement of attention, thereby bringing about a different awareness than used in daily life. While dreaming accesses the second energy field, that experience can also be considered as employing the second attention, using Castaneda's terminology. Attending to the daily world or to dreaming are distinct utilizations of the energy body and consciousness. Incorporating both into a singular cohesion significantly advances learning, collapses the unknown into the known, and is the central component of forming a natural field.

Dreaming is localized in the liver say some mystics, the adrenal glands say others. Knowing the location doesn't matter to actually dream. But this is interesting to note as an example of how different views address the same thing. Based on different inventories, we encounter contrasting interpretations. Chapters six and seven provide perspectives and exercises for dreaming and OBE.

Seeing

Seeing occurs from precise alignments with the external world. This allows a greater amount of energy to resonate within the internal environment. It is done with the body, not reason. It is direct experience, not reflective. *Seeing* also takes on several forms such as an unusual feeling or a kinesthetic realization.

Corresponding with the endocrine system, *seeing* takes you beyond description to the essence of life and into the luminous world. A scientist can describe in detail what a tree is made of, but *seeing* lets you observe the tree as a coherence of energy. The more balanced your alignment, the more developed your energy body, and the better you *see*. My perception of emanations described in chapter one occurred via *seeing*. The sensation was witnessing thick, fiber optic-looking strands of light. The conceptualization of the experience was based on a shamanic inventory.

Seeing can be used to discern pure energy, wavefield mechanics, and aspects of time such as observing historical periods.[13] In addition, the case can be made that martial artists use a form of *seeing*. Since energy precedes physical action, fighters *see* the intent of their opponents and respond before the other person strikes. They anticipate their opponents' next physical moves.

The nature of *seeing* changes as you become more proficient, and there is a range of experiences that can be placed under the *seeing* umbrella. You might notice energy waves like that rising from hot asphalt, experience an immediate "knowing," or observe luminous energy.

What you *see* initially may not make sense at all. Just like a baby noticing ripples on a lake from wind, may not connect the changing patterns of ripples and the reflected light as being an effect of wind passing over water combined with sunlight. Associations such as these occur with time, experience, and by having context or description.

Seeing allows you to evaluate the energy body. You can also use *seeing* to discern the condition of fruits and vegetables in your local grocery store, or calculate the state of energy of a friend, where the person is coming from, as it were. In the world of science, there is not yet a means to assess *seeing*, as the energy body is not part of a scientific inventory. If it is not recognized as existing, technologies to measure and reproduce *seeing* (or the energy body) can't be invented.

Seeing is not necessarily the final word. Each generation must adapt to current circumstances. Descriptions need to be updated to keep pace with the evolving wavefield. Memory maintains an inventory, as we constantly remember its pieces and hold them in place. This has an effect of making novel information conform to what is already known. If *seeing* isn't recognized as valid, for instance, it will be dismissed as something unusual and nothing to remember.

Shamanism grew from *seeing*. Old cycle shamans thought it was an important attainment to perceive energetic essence.[14] However, they became obsessed with what they saw, giving them an inflated sense of self and knowledge. They lost themselves in creating intricate descriptions of reality, and this eventually led to their downfall. As a result, new procedures and interpretations were built into the modern cycle's method. Sobriety was viewed as essential, and the warrior's discipline was established. Exercises for *seeing* are in chapter five.

Will

Located in the gut, *will* is basic energy, an umbilical-like connection with the wavefield. The *will* of the energy body is not a matter of being willful or deliberate. It is a multi-level connection with the environment that gradually comes to life as cohesion expands. It is your personal connection with life. Intent focuses *will*.

Reflecting styles of organizing perception, some mystics place *will* at the third eye, the area of the forehead chakra. Shamans center it in the gut near the naval, and so more toward the body's center of gravity. But no matter the location, the accounting for this energy, that it exists and is part of human anatomy, can be found in eastern and western mysticisms.

Awakening the cornerstones leads to activating *will*. For this, a person's life must be balanced and purposeful. The person needs to be able to let go of meaning and suspend rigid interpretations while remaining centered. This leads to new meaning. Part of this is using the energy body as your primary identity rather than it being the physical body. Yet you can use awareness of your physical body to help assess if you're perceiving the world through reason or *will*.

Reason only reflects external order, says don Juan, but you need *will* to witness effects of the wavefield.[15] Feeling, *seeing*, and dreaming connect to *will*, making it a dominant cornerstone. Awakening it is necessary to proceed to a fully natural field, at which time a person is guided more by sensing the natural order than by reason.

The initial awakening of *will* can be disconcerting. Odd, sometimes queasy, sensations may occur. Objects have a sharp clarity about them. The world might be viewed as being two dimensional, with depth as a texture, a type of intensity. This changes the interpretation that the world is three dimensional. A 3D world is like the appearance of physical objects being material; it is a matter of what we have trained ourselves to expect.

My first experience with *will* occurred while I was walking adjacent to a U.S. Navy housing complex. Since the first 24 years of my life related to the Navy, I felt a sense of belonging. I entertained thoughts about the Navy and my relation to it. I then felt pressure just below my navel. Something pushed out from the inside. I then felt a stream of energy from my abdomen into the world. It seemed to direct itself toward the housing complex. As I paid attention to this unusual, but not uncomfortable, sensation, I discovered I could isolate specific feelings. As though the stream of energy were a flashlight scanning a large room, I examined several feelings associated with the Navy and could also prod the surrounding environment.

Without conscious deliberation, I settled within a strong feeling that indicated the houses did not reflect my present life. Using my thoughts, I summoned past feelings about military life. I noticed my thoughts served as a focus enabling another part of me to reduce the feelings of old. Bringing myself back to the present, my awareness again centered in *will* where I was no longer part of the Navy. The housing was part of my world, but I was not a part of the housing. From this experience, I found I could easily distinguish between reason and *will*, and between myself and the world.

The Complete Energy Body

Our ordinary world is upheld by reason, the shaman's world by *will*. Both descriptions have rules, procedures, and interpretations. Perceiving by reason or *will* is a function of how cohesion is conditioned. Reason allows us to observe and map the world, and then produce technologies to harness it. *Will* permits direct participation with the world of energy and engages the cornerstones.

Without *seeing*, you're flying blind as to the essence about you. You'd have no personal, verifiable information of the wavefield. It would only be a concept. Without dreaming, you won't have the power to significantly boost cohesion, which includes increasing your ability to *see*. Without feeling, you'd lose sense of yourself and your path.

Grooming the cornerstones requires being in touch with those parts of yourself. This helps bring the other parts of yourself to life as you tune to the whole of existence. Based on the previous information about reason and *will*, a simple exercise to activate *will* is to pay attention to whether you're perceiving the world mentally or sensing it with your body.

THE NATURE OF CONSCIOUSNESS

The essential aspect of the energy body is consciousness. Don Juan describes the energy body as a cluster of fibers that are aware.[16] The degree of personal awareness depends on the degree to which a person can let environmental stressors influence cohesion. In different ways, these tensions compress cohesion which leads to changes in awareness and behavior. You can easily sense what this means by paying attention to the strains at home or in the workplace and how they affect you.

Shamans extend the types of environmental influence from everyday activities to multi-dimensional effects. Awareness, then, hinges on what you resonate with and what your energy body can handle. Developing cohesion allows you to withstand more environmental tensions and thereby align with more of the wavefield and become more conscious.

Figure 3.8
The Expansion of Consciousness
Enlarging the first field indicates having expanded consciousness and personal power.

Scientists and mystics alike typically decline to say what consciousness is, how it comes to be in the first place, what its essence is, etc., and so it is defined or described by processes and attributes. From a scientific perspective, at an elementary level consciousness is sensitivity to stimuli.[17] It is also explained in terms of awareness, the utilization of that awareness, and the formation of consciousness into perception, memory, thinking, and learning.[18] In addition, some regard consciousness in terms of awareness and the ability to emotionally express oneself based on experience.[19]

As outlined by shamans, attributes of consciousness include awareness, attention, and intention. Awareness pertains to a general state of perceiving; attention involves discerning features within awareness; and intention requires the deliberate focus of attention on features in awareness.

Attention and intention are processes and skills to manage awareness. Attention holds awareness in place and maintains a view of something. Attention is the harnessing of awareness corresponding with the degree of maturation, and intent is the manager of this dynamic. In terms of what humans generally perceive, don Juan says that everything exists because of one's attention.[20] One type of attention upholds our daily world, and another type allows development of dreaming.

The degree to which these abilities are integrated indicates the development of an individual, professional discipline, or society. From these interactions, we define reality and groom cohesion, and vice versa. If the nature of consciousness is reinterpreted, our experience becomes reinvented. Conversely, new experiences place consciousness in a new light—a leap-frog process.

Mind

A common definition of mind relates to thought, or the mental activity for acquiring knowledge from experience and the senses. In another definition, it relates to knowing by conscious and subconscious processes, albeit with an emphasis on reasoning.[21] From an energy body perspective, these elements of a standard inventory are limiting because there are several conscious processes not related to reason that directly feed knowing. When talking about the energy body, we need to expand the definition of mind.

Modern neuroscientists regard mind as resulting solely from brain functions, an effect of an array of material neural networks. This corresponds with viewing the world as being material. More in line with shamanic attributes of consciousness, psychologists often relate mind to conscious and unconscious aspects of awareness—what we call to our attention, or don't, and how we do this.[22] Some researchers consider mind to be an information processor.[23] The brain would therefore not be the source of awareness but would process and make sense of it.

By isolating attributes and processes, researchers have inventoried consciousness and mind in line with classical (material) science. Applicable to all viewpoints, don Juan says that mind can be defined as one's complete inventory.[24] The definition of mind both reflects and determines your inventory and, therefore, your state of consciousness.

With shamanism, we can relate the capacity of mind to the overall energy body. This includes the scope of cohesion rather than just the brain. With each cohesion, a person assembles a frame of mind.

Setting your mind to something, establishing an intent, brings to bear all those elements that went into forming your cohesion. The more you've awakened your energy body, the greater your abilities of mind.

Interestingly, science has recently begun to broach the idea that the physical body plays a significant role in consciousness and that the brain is not necessarily the driving agent of awareness, but rather that while the brain and body act independently, they inform each other. Consciousness is then regarded as being distributed throughout the body.[26]

In a shamanic schematic, the physical body is a cohesion of the energy body, with physical and purer energetic components choreographing behavior on the stage of life. Like the finest Swiss watches, humans continuously process information in different ways, and with different gears and mechanisms. Timing and rhythm are always present.

As reflected by the cornerstones, we have available to us more knowledge and awareness than thought and reason. Educating feeling enhances reason and allows it to entertain new perspectives. *Seeing* offers immediate comprehension. Dreaming alters the landscape of possibility. Overall awareness, then, transcends academic knowledge. By focusing too much on the intellect, like defining mind as a mental function, we've isolated ourselves from our nature by refusing to acknowledge our greater capacities of awareness.

Don Juan underscores the need for a significant shift in our commonly held worldview. He maintains that the first step would be building a wide consensus that the world is made of energy rather than of concrete objects.[25] In application, a traditional shamanic teaching is to balance self and society with the greater environment, using the wavefield as a primary reference. By not having this awareness, humans are inherently out of balance with themselves and with all aspects of the environment. In essence, don Juan argues that humans need to become more conscious so that, as previously mentioned, we may survive.

A Conscious Wavefield

Reflecting entanglement, all parts of the wavefield—all parts of life—are interconnected. From a shamanic perspective, there are an infinite number of lines of light joining humans to the things about us. Alertness is being conscious of this fabric of existence, to observe what occurs in the spaces surrounding the events where we normally place our attention. This is an in-between area of consciousness, betwixt and between thoughts and worldviews. This focus allows more awareness of wavefield dynamics, and suspending conditional fields permits us to *see* these conditions.

The effects of these lines of luminosity are like those ascribed to human consciousness, that of being aware of oneself and the general environment. The wavefield is aware of the whole and its parts, and the parts are aware of and respond to other parts as well as to the whole. Wavefield scientists maintain that by continually monitoring and transferring information, the wavefield attends to multiple dimensions, states of being, and all portions of itself. It embodies intention. It creates, modifies, and destroys wave packets. A shamanic correlate, don Juan says emanations are aware and alive.[27, 28]

An independent observer is not required for wavefield dynamics to occur.[29] Humans are not required to legitimize the existence of the wavefield. It adjusts, adapts, and evolves based on its own doings. In that it creates and maintains life forms, it is fair to regard the wavefield, in and of itself, as being intelligent.

In short, the wavefield is aware of its own conditions, can intend results, and remains attentive. It embodies, or rather is the source of, human attributes of consciousness that give rise to individual consciousness. Accordingly, it isn't that we are conscious of the wavefield but that we are conscious because the wavefield is conscious. We are made of and from it—which makes us able to be conscious of that portion of the wavefield that coheres into human form, the energy body.

4 ⟩ Our Multi-Dimensional World

The environment is a leading determinant of human behavior. Whether we hunt, fish, or farm depends on the terrain. It also dictates what implements are necessary and can be made, and what type of shelter can be constructed. And this only pertains to geography and survival.

There are also social, business, sports, and other environments that shape daily life. As evidenced by global warming, human conditions influence natural and social environments. Understanding the environment is how we navigate life. Our surroundings tell us if we have a sustainable course. For this, we need to pay attention and apply consciousness, not just conjecture about it.

The energy body forms from the greater environment of the wavefield. Consciousness is stabilized when internal and external energies align. Culture, upbringing, education, profession, and friends all influence cohesion. Every environment has an energetic atmosphere, a cohesion, that affects personal awareness. How we participate in each setting hinges on our cohesion—what we're open to and what we filter out. And when you change your cohesion, you alter the environment, a micro-wavefield effect that sends information into the whole of the wavefield.

The relation between internal and external conditions also reflects how well you're in tune with life. Geographic cohesions of the desert, jungle, and city apply pressure to the energy body, and the response is based on different imperatives, including such things as survival, entertainment, and business. Achieving harmony of the results is another story. If the local way of life focuses on urban development, for instance, an empty stretch of land becomes something that needs to have buildings. It needs to be changed from its natural state to that of the human world.

In addition, social agreements, be they of the family, workplace, or reality, alter cohesion. This information feeds the wavefield which responds as it wishes. The wavefield has its own mind, intelligence, and way of doing things. Some may be readily apparent, such as marked changes in weather patterns based on human activity, while others might not be as discernable. In any case, this is all part of a dynamic environment.

Coming to terms with multiple dimensions gives fluency to cohesion and enhances your awareness. This vibrance becomes readily apparent as you amplify, or power up, consciousness. Out-of-body travel, for instance, lets you visit areas of this and other worlds. During an OBE, I traveled to Mars and found it inhabited by sentient entities appearing as geometric forms, ostensibly having evolved over eons from other life forms. It was therefore of interest when scientists later reported finding evidence of flowing water once being part of the Martian landscape, indicating the possibility of past life.[1] The following hints at the environments that are possible to explore with OBE, or by generally expanding consciousness.

THE NATURAL EARTH

Many people regard Earth as a living entity and hold that the forms of life it brings forth are intricately woven together. This idea has been alive for centuries but in recent times has been defined and scientifically argued as the Gaia hypothesis.[2] As mentioned, from energy bodies to planets to dimensions, the wavefield creates observables that influence each other and the whole. It follows that our physical environment is an observable aspect of the wavefield within this network of mutual influence. The coherence of multiple energies forms our physical environment, the cohesion of Earth.

Energies of Earth

We evolved within an ocean of energetic influences, immersed in light and dark cycles, geomagnetism, cosmic radiation, a package of extremely low frequencies in the general environment known as Schumann resonances, and more. Conditions such as these eventually made for a stable environment, at least sufficiently suitable for humans to evolve. Then and now, our biological makeup mirrors the composition of Earth. In short, we are of, and one with, our environment. Don Juan considers Earth to be the source of what we are as humans.[3]

Scientists have mapped many of these conditions. For instance, circadian rhythms are an evolutionary adaptation based on natural day/night, or light/dark, cycles that time daily events. They can be traced to the earliest life forms on earth. Like a quality timepiece, the circadian network is a pecking order of oscillators, stretching from cells to systems, that cycle in line with circadian rhythms. In animals, circadian behaviors range from genomic expression to metabolic activity to behaviors including wake-sleep cycles and feeding.[4] Visible light helps an organism reset out-of-phase rhythms. And different colors of light have varied effects such as drowsiness or mood changes.[5]

In addition to circadian rhythms, life evolved while immersed in other types of cyclical energy.[6] An example is Schumann resonances, extremely low frequencies (ELF) generated by tropical lightning storms around the world. While researchers noted classical waveform activity in the 1890s, Schumann resonances were confirmed to be a global system during the 1960s.[7] These frequencies resonate within a cavity formed between the Earth's surface and the lower region of the ionosphere. They generally persist as a standing wave having minimal distortion and with only minor variations throughout the day.

It is noteworthy that Schumann resonances correspond to the ranges of human brain waves. These bands relate to functions of consciousness such as waking, relaxation, creativity, and sleeping.[8] Therefore, activity within the brain corresponds to environmental conditions that affect human evolution. Schumann resonances have also been correlated to acupuncture meridian activity, indicating that the body absorbs and responds to environmental electromagnetic signals.[9]

Geomagnetic storms, caused by shock waves of solar wind, are disruptions in electromagnetic fields. They have been associated with heart attacks, a sudden deficiency in the brain, and mood changes. During severe storms, the brain has been shown to have reduced dominating electrical rhythms, an indication of diminished stability.[10] About 10 to 15 percent of the general population is predisposed to adverse health due to geomagnetic variations.[11] Again showing interconnection among Earth's systems, it has been hypothesized that the disruption of Schumann resonances is a biophysical mechanism associated with these types of adverse effects on health.[12]

The sun's radiations, associated with routine 11-year sunspot cycles, have been correlated to changes in volcanic activity, earthquakes, and animal and human behaviors including those relating to physical and mental health.[13] One study indicated that cosmic electromagnetic radiation might oscillate in such a way as to disrupt healthy brainwave activity, thereby leading to brain cancer and other disorders.[14]

Cosmic rays in general have strong biological and climatic effects. This emission of energy from beyond Earth produces more clouds and thereby changes the temperature. Increased ultraviolet-B exposure due to damage to the ozone shield presents health risks such as skin cancer. Plus, changes in ionization affect lightning discharges, consequently altering the chemical composition of the atmosphere.[15] Furthermore, nearby galaxies have magnetic fields that affect solar activity.[16]

Therefore, as we step beyond the immediate earthly conditions that gave rise to life, we find that Earth doesn't exist independently of its surroundings. It has its own profile relating to its environment and its cohesion, of which humans are part. Life on Earth is literally part of a symphony of galactic proportions.

Technology

A pervasive aspect of our environment is technology. From wooden tools to heart monitors to social media, it drives social organization, heals the sick, and sends people into space. Succinctly defined, technology is an assemblage of practices and components for a specific purpose.[17] It involves harnessing intent, a given purpose, to achieve results. It helps us make sense of, organize, and apply the overwhelming amount of information bombarding us throughout the day. In this way, it shapes perception, ability, and reality.

Experience results from the type of technology being used. Automobiles are one thing, spaceships another. While both are transportation technologies, they provide different experiences. A profession, for another example, is a cohesion, an assemblage of elements that align thought and behavior with its purpose. Like naming a technology, the practices and procedures of shamans define shamanism, and likewise the behaviors of scientists define science.

This perspective provides a way to relate to shamanism as a type of technology—a cognitive technology—and to understand and use it without thinking that it is a definitive statement of reality. Shamanism organizes and implements natural conditions, giving a person direction and purpose. In other words, it is a tool that takes the elements of consciousness and implements them for a specific effect.

For example, in a material world technology is needed to measure, to determine the existence of something, and to learn how to manage pieces of our world. Increased awareness occurs through telescopes and satellites. In a world of energy, direct perception of the environment provides a means to measure and make determinations. Shamans employ the cornerstones, capacities of the human mind, instead of inventing technologies that mimic them; for instance, *seeing* instead of telescopes. Castaneda reflected on how the practice of shamanism drastically modified his awareness.[18]

Material and cognitive technologies can support each other. One example is the Hemi-Sync™ technology developed by Robert Monroe, founder of The Monroe Institute (TMI). This sound technology assists in balancing the electrical activity of the brain. Listening to certain signals, the brain entrains to, or falls in line with, the tones. In practice, Monroe discovered he could keep people awake while they entered dream states.

While participating as a subject in TMI's lab and listening to specific Hemi-Sync signals, I had clinically induced mystical and near-death experiences as well as OBEs. In each instance, the laboratory experience corresponded to similar events that occurred, without the use of Hemi-Sync, prior to and after my laboratory sessions.

The NDEs resulted while entraining to a 1.5Hz signal, a frequency close to what is considered brainwave, clinical death. As I listened to the tones, I spontaneously found myself traveling in a tunnel with a vortex at the end of it. In the center of the vortex was a gentle but brilliant white light. I sensed that the light consisted of a uniform field of energy of indescribable proportions. Exiting the tunnel, I saw a huge ball of white light. Although I felt it in impersonal terms, I could understand why many people who have had a NDE think of it as a tremendous light being.

Approaching the light, I saw it as pure energy, or as a void, depending upon my orientation which I could easily shift. When I entered the light, I felt it could be used for any purpose, that it was neutral. I had the realization that perception within it is not intellectual, although it might be possible to take the intellect along for the ride. I felt the light was a permeating energy of creation. I then went completely through the light and found that on the other side of it everything was reversed. I found a mirror-image of the physical universe I knew in my ordinary life. I recoiled at the intensity of this altered state and the experience ended. Bridging a mystical experience, a realization quietly exploded within me that throughout creation all realities occur simultaneously and within the current moment.

As Monroe mentioned to me, the greater power is being able to access these types of experiences without the use of his sound technology. Cognitive technologies allow the development of awareness but eventually need to be set side aside for a more enhanced sense of freedom and growth. Looking at worldviews as technologies allows them to be updated or replaced. Doing so acknowledges their immense value but also that they are not the final word.

A MULTI-DIMENSIONAL WORLD

A shared perspective among scientists and shamans is that not only do we live in an interactive world, but that existence is multi-dimensional. A shamanic teaching is that humans can access and comprehend only a few dimensions. Some of these are visible, some are not, some sport organic life and still others contain conscious inorganic beings. Currently, scientific investigation has not yet caught up to shamanic understanding. While scientists and engineers grapple with interstellar travel—a major advance in our material relation to the cosmos—shamans have been traveling interdimensionally for centuries. Even so, they recognize the limits of exploration, both in terms of actual probing other dimensions and of interpreting those travels.

As part of shamanic cosmology, shamans maintain that within the wavefield there are distinct bands of energy, streams of bundled light. An unknown number of these bands, perhaps infinite, comprises the wavefield. Each band contains immense vibrational energy that carries the information of its domain.[19] For instance, each stream relates to specific functions in the same manner that meridians and the circulatory system have defined purposes. The coherent binding of multiple bands produces a species.[20] Chakras offer an example of multiple energies forming a whole entity.

Don Juan says that only a small segment of wavefield emanations is within human awareness.[21] In addition, while several bands combine to form the energy body, only one of these pertains to ordinary daily life.[22] The other bands relate to other dimensions that humans can access.

We therefore need to account for wavefield creations outside the ordinary, daily human band. This includes other lifeforms; some perhaps completely alien to our reference, and some perhaps more advanced intellectually and technologically. In other words, our daily world uses but a portion of the energy body. The structure of the entire energy body permits travel to planets beyond Earth as well as to other dimensions.

The shamanic inventory expands the composition of our known world. The energetic architecture of Earth, the existence of other dimensions, and these connections with human cohesion are part of this arrangement. Pressure from a multidimensional environment condenses internal states. This compression of cohesion determines the degree of awareness.[23] If other dimensions are not consciously included in this coherence, those environments are not perceived as existing.

Cohesion is the overall filter of perception. Like turning the dial on a radio to access different stations, it can be adjusted to allow us to tune into aspects of Earth's dimensions and to those beyond. Our three-dimensional world results from conditioning consciousness. We understand what we put into it. Shamans recognize this and focus their intention to investigate these extradimensional energies, thereby shaping their cohesions to be more aware.

A distinct wave of the wavefield is thought to split and develop more branches.[24] Scientific theory therefore supports the idea that there are many worlds within the wavefield, if not an infinite number of variations. By modeling the existence of alternate realities, researchers have taken a first step toward entering and exploring them.

Alternate dimensions contain their own coherence of time, environments, and other characteristics. The inventories of each, minimal or extensive, give a dimension its identity. Providing there are connections within the energy body, other dimensions can be accessed by shifting the assemblage point, by changing cohesion. The differences between one reality and another could be as minor as the number of hairs on one's head or as major as the number of moons of a planet, or even whether the dimension has such things as planets. Perceiving the possibilities and probabilities of the quantum world is enabled through personal intersection of energies with other dimensions. What you tune into, align with, and experience is a matter of your cohesion. The more fluent your cohesion, the more you become aware, and the more you can encounter.

Inorganic Worlds

According to shamans, the wavefield creates an abundance of entities inhabiting worlds comprised of two basic types of awareness, those of organic and inorganic life. Organic life is the natural forms we're accustomed to. Inorganic life consists of different configurations of energy that are not defined by the biological considerations applied to organic life.

These two groups of awareness exist independently of each other, and yet they coexist. What shamans define as inorganic worlds are parallel to, but separate from, the physical dimension. Consistent with wavefield entanglement, they energetically bridge each other.[25] Some inorganic beings live in unknown regions of human perception. While residing in autonomous worlds, they may still resonate with the human band. There are also lifeforms that reside beyond human perception.[26]

One class of inorganic being that overlaps the earthly world is commonly known as elemental spirits. After many encounters, I have come to know them as being intimately connected with Earth while also inhabiting their own domain. They reflect the vitality of nature and therefore are often deemed to be nature spirits. However, their lives do not rely on humans or Earth. They have various configurations of energy that are typically attributed to faeries, gnomes, elves, and the like. After *seeing* their energies in abstract forms as amorphous light, I have come to understand that these mythic representations result from anthropomorphizing them, from projecting and interpreting their awareness into something more akin to that of humans.

The ability to perceive elementals hinges on changing cohesional speed to resonate with their dimension. This is the same thing as saying a shift in the assemblage point produces an alignment with a different world. Visitations to the elemental world can be spontaneous or deliberate, with the adventure or interpretation based on cohesion. Each type of elemental tends to be associated with a specific environment. Elves, to offer a rough schematic, are often found by trees, winged faeries by water, and gnomes by more solid, earthy areas. This is just to give an idea, not lock in stone, how elementals behave.

I did learn from various encounters with elementals. A significant lesson is that when we destroy our natural world, we remove essential energy. As a result, elementals find no safe harbor and leave this dimension. In other words, the more nature is destroyed, the more the spirit of the land disappears.

To give another example of inorganic life, don Juan thinks dreaming is tainted with an old cycle mood where shamans sought power to manipulate others.[27] He adds that one region of the inorganic world is a testing ground where you learn how to handle power, a very tough obstacle to growth. Castaneda, for example, was tempted by inorganic beings to learn telekinesis. All he had to do was hand over his soul to them, so to speak. Fortunately, he resisted.[28] I've also had a few encounters that are consistent with old cycle practices—and probably something best left alone.

An encounter with an inorganic being took place one afternoon while sitting in the showroom of a custom glass shop. I worked for a cabinet maker and was on an errand to pick up a piece of glass. While waiting, I noticed an interesting configuration of mirrors on the far wall. A large bronze mirror was flanked by standard, mercury-coated mirrors. Enraptured by the effect they created, I gazed into the bronze mirror. I laughed at myself as I thought about Castaneda pulling an other-dimensional entity out of a mirror, wondering if I could do the same.

After several minutes of gazing into the mirror, I observed a man-like figure step out of it and into the showroom. He was a little more than medium height and stocky. I remember thinking that he seemed a little taller and slightly less muscular than don Juan. Why I thought of don Juan I don't know. Perhaps it was from associating Castaneda's story about the mirror with this occurrence. Perhaps it was because I fleetingly recognized don Juan's energy stepping out of the mirror.

The creature had large bumps on its head and was slightly hunched over. This created a marked contrast with don Juan, who was the epitome of health and stature. At times, however, I had witnessed don Juan present himself in different forms. For example, once I encountered him in the guise of a drunkard, and yet another time as a woman. But then, the thought that the being wasn't don Juan jolted me.

Only then did I realize that I had no idea how to respond. I felt like Mickey Mouse in the film *Fantasia* when the sorcerer's apprentice unwittingly unleashes great power. In a mild panic, I simultaneously shifted my vision away from the being and stood up to walk around. This dispelled the image of it. I still felt its presence, however. Spooked, I went outside, got in my car, and drove off. One of the lessons I took with me was the value of EQ as a means of handling unsettling encounters with other lifeforms. Another lesson was to stop fooling around with other-worldly powers.

Old cycle shamans used visits to inorganic worlds as reality busters to upend their reason, shake up cohesion, break the continuity of reality, and learn to perceive other domains. That process may have run its course. Investigations relating to the more modern turf of extraterrestrials could serve that purpose but sidestep the nefarious influence of inorganic worlds. That said, these regions remain part of our larger world and may, in some manner, influence earthly life. This domain may be waiting for further discovery to be made possible in a manner similar to how very strange deep-sea creatures are now being photographed. What is learned over the passage of time might recast the nature of other worlds.

It is also interesting that scientists now speculate about the existence of inorganic life. Their considerations relate more to forms of artificial intelligence (AI) that arose from other types of life. In other words, AI evolved beyond the organic life that formed it.[29] Of note, a current debate focuses on where AI might be headed, such as when and where technology becomes self-motivated and finds humans are no longer needed.

Extraterrestrials
Closer to our home base of Earth, it is worthwhile to note extraterrestrial life. A sign of our times, environmental toxicity and climate change spark discussions of the need to immigrate to other planets if humans are to survive. Plans for exploratory missions into deep space are well underway. In addition to what is becoming routine space travel, there may be other options for space exploration and discovery.

I mentioned my Mars OBE, for instance. In an upcoming chapter, I recount how I visited the moon during OBE. There are also other options for outer space encounters. During the early 1980s while in the dream research laboratory at TMI, I seemingly contacted extraterrestrial intelligence from Pleiades. Over time, several individual entities made themselves known, and each had a specialty akin to Earth academics. They described themselves in a way similar to how we have become accustomed.

The source of information in these sessions referred to a step-by-step process of acquainting us with their physical existence. Some people conjecture that extraterrestrials (ETs) travel from another dimension. Others think they're of this dimension but have learned time travel. This species indicated that, as though they are time traveling, they are checking up on their ancestors. Over the span of centuries of evolution, humans became the ETs now visiting us. To avoid widespread panic due to their current visits, they had the equivalent of a public relations campaign.

Central to this effort was incrementally providing evidence that they are real. Accordingly, over time there have been sightings of extraterrestrial, biological life reported here and there. Some of these can be easily interpreted as weather balloons or atmospheric conditions, while others are more provocatively unshakable, such as when several people witness a flying object that looks to be extraterrestrial. The authority and sobriety of those reporting the sightings are invariably called into question. However, the idea of ETs slowly percolates.

In April 2020, things became more interesting. The U.S. military released videos of "unidentified aerial phenomena."[30] Highly trained naval aviators reported and videotaped objects flying at extremely high rates of speed and maneuvering in ways that could not be accounted for by current laws of aerodynamics.[31] Upon learning of this, I wondered not only about the validity of my dream-like experiences, but whether the ETs' PR campaign had stepped up a notch or two.

Mystical Experience

A mystical experience (ME) is having your feet on the ground while soaring through the heavens. It delivers an intimate experience and an unshakable recognition of being immersed within a multi-dimensional world. It speaks to scientific entanglement.

Mystical experience is perhaps the defining component of a mystic's pursuits. The hallmark feature of a ME is experiencing oneness with creation. There is also a deepened sense of reality where the physical world is seen as limiting.[32] Other features include that the ME is short-lived or transient, that there is difficulty in rendering events into mental constructs, and that there is a sense of objectivity and clarity. If a person is directly participating in a fuller dimension of life, having a sense of objectivity seems plausible because the experience is more real than textbook descriptions of reality. The event is self-validating, and the limitations of the physical world become obvious.

Mystical experience is ineffable, meaning that consciousness extends beyond the limitations of words. It is therefore difficult to encapsulate the experience with language because there are no references for the direct expansion of personal consciousness into the wavefield. While leaving the person with knowledge, it is a venture into regions of awareness beyond known references. This may also indicate sensing the nagual, which don Juan says is unspeakable.[33] Perhaps this also relates to tapping far reaches of potential. In either case, there is direct knowing, an immediate comprehension. One becomes conscious that personal awareness is truly connected to the wavefield.

This experience is also akin to condensing consciousness. It leaves behind knowledge that gives cosmological insights into space, time, and unity. Williams James, the father of American psychology, considered these characteristics sufficient to designate ME a particular state of consciousness.[34] Scientific investigations of ME demonstrate that it stimulates multiple areas of the brain. In one study, physiological changes during meditation correlated with five frequent elements of ME: intensity, unity, transformation, clarity, and surrender (acceptance).[35] In addition, investigators revealed that, on average, people who have ME are well-adjusted, healthy, educated, and creative.[36]

ME can be accounted for in terms of wavefield processes, in that scientists hold that the pieces of the universe emanate from, continue to reside in, and then return to the wavefield.[37] Wave packets, condensed forms of the wavefield, are part of the observable order. An aware organism therefore can be considered a macroscopic wave function.[38] A human being, an energy body, is a type of wave packet, a macro-wave function, and is therefore part of the wavefield. This is the definition of interconnected oneness which ME brings to consciousness.

ME can occur during an OBE or a NDE.[39] It is even possible to live in a way that contributes to having mystical experiences. Traditionally, this has been the province of mysticism: philosophies, religions, and lifestyles that engender a mystical relation with the universe. These are metaphysical technologies that provide a way to reveal the wholeness of life. A mystical experience often results as a by-product of having this orientation.

Near-Death Experience

Some researchers relate near-death experiences to the random effects of a dying brain, thereby dismissing any legitimacy of the paranormal event. However, NDEs do not necessarily occur near physical death.[40] People may have an experience that qualifies in content as being a NDE without their lives being in jeopardy. In addition, information that supports the validity of NDEs but is limited in scope may distort how NDEs are interpreted by only focusing on what is meant by living in an exclusively physical world. Doing so automatically diminishes the potential that other dimensions exist, at least in researchers' thinking.

During a NDE, there is a shift from normal waking consciousness to refocusing attention beyond the physical.[41] This change produces a variety of perceptions. Sometimes a person has an OBE. There is often a tunnel leading to white light. Many times, people report encounters with deceased people, especially relatives. It is also normal to receive some type of revelation.[42] And one can have a ME.[43]

A person's expectation, formed by cultural and educational conditioning, also plays a role in determining the content of NDEs.[44] A devout Christian stands to connect with Jesus whereas a practicing Buddhist may meet Buddha. The person may also receive some type of guidance. People may report that they encounter an environment of white light. The light may contain ephemeral shapes of men, women, and children. Not all the elements categorizing a NDE need to be experienced for it to be a bona fide NDE, just awareness of the overall configuration. Research shows that having a NDE recasts one's views of life and death.[45]

Immersed in the field of light, people often feel as though they are part of everything, experience unconditional love, and say they've met God. During the TMI session mentioned above, when I saw the ball of white light, I could easily understand why people think of the experience as having met God—that interpretation seemed a good fit. However, shamans have a different take.

For shamans, the white light is thought to be a composite cluster of energies comprising the human energy body.[46] It is "all that is human," a type of plaster mold (a little crude but gets the point across) reflecting the wavefield coherence of humans. When people encounter it, there is a natural acceptance without reservation. The person feels as though he or she is part of everything because the person is experiencing the completeness of being human. This is then projected into something recognizable. Since we haven't been taught of the human totality, and we have been taught about God, the light is interpreted as an encounter with God.

In the ensuing weeks at TMI, for example, I had brief, spontaneous experiences with this light. A couple of months after the first encounter with it, I was back in the laboratory. I soon kinesthetically felt a tunnel in my abdomen. I then saw the white light. This time I had a more settled perception of it due to the repetition of experience. I understood that it was not God; it was the pinnacle and completeness of human awareness. It was like being consumed by the top chakra of the energy body. It was a bridge between the person and the wavefield. It was the fullness of human coherence. Interpretations of it being God were projections based on social conditioning. All said and done, though, every view of the white light is a matter of interpretation and the respective assemblage point positions.

It is safe to say, I think, that experiences of unity and the white light indicate becoming more conscious of human nature. Even if we confine MEs to connecting with earthly energies, it still represents wholeness. All in all, these types of revelations offer transcendent awareness beyond the reaches of what is currently thought to be true. These forms of consciousness are natural to humans, and they are extensions beyond mundane worlds.

It is also common for people who have a ME, NDE, or OBE to regard the experiences as having found The Truth. In terms of energy body dynamics, these events are encounters with cohesions more expansive than ordinarily experienced, not an ultimate finding about reality. Each provides an avenue of exploring consciousness, and together they illuminate what that means.

More specifically, people often think that NDEs offer proof positive that there is life after physical death. To me, it only offers evidence that we have additional modes of perception available to us. Using extrasensory forms of perception as a tool to investigate survival may take us to visits with dead relatives, or to nonphysical entities who teach us of life after death. In this manner, we might accumulate data regarding personal survival, and this information might affect our worldview.

An OBE during a NDE doesn't necessarily indicate after-death survival either. After all, it is "near death," not actual death. That said, by powering up their entire energy bodies shamans have reportedly traveled into the third energy field, a dimension which may offer evidence for life after death.

OUT OF THIS WORLD

Humans travel the dark sea of consciousness, says don Juan, and Earth is a station on everyone's journey. Life, he adds, is a detour.[47,48]

At birth, due to the fixation of the assemblage point, he says, we forget where we came from and our purpose. Perhaps this is like forgetting what we dreamed upon waking. At any rate, we get caught in an eddy of sorts, a dynamic of energy that keeps us swirling around and focused on earthly life. Shamans learn to break free of this force and continue their journey beyond the confines of this world.[49,50]

This may relate to the reordering of energy mentioned earlier when describing one option of wavefield decoherence. Here, the dark sea is synonymous with the wavefield and brings the possibility of stepping around the dismantling force, the decoherence, of an individual's life. The reconfiguration of individual awareness combined with the imprisoning effect of the eddy sparks questions about reincarnation.

Reincarnation

Reincarnation is a popular belief throughout the world. It generally relates to soul growth or evolution over many incarnations or life experiences. Theologians often assert continuity of consciousness after life, whereas modern neuroscientists maintain that awareness vanishes with the death of the body.[51] If reincarnation is valid, it is an example of other-dimensional influences on the energy body.

Aside from the mystics' long-standing interest in reincarnation, there is also scientific curiosity. Investigators at The University of Virginia's Division of Perceptual Studies (DOPS), for instance, are carrying forward the work of Professor Ian Stevenson, who ushered in a discipline of examining health conditions relating to reincarnation. His book *Twenty Cases Suggestive of Reincarnation* established a benchmark for the field.[52]

Stevenson documented birth defects of living people that correlated with the manner of death of someone in a previous life. For example, a shoulder deformity and chronic pain not attributable to an event in this life corresponding to being stabbed in the shoulder during a prior life. Stevenson was rigorous in the use of medical records and personal reports to track down possible connections between a person living now and someone in the past. He screened against there being a common means of knowledge whereby a person could learn of past events and project those onto the case being investigated.[53]

Focusing on children, DOPS researcher Jim Tucker published on this phenomenon.[54] In one incident, Bruce Leininger described how his young son recalled, in detail, events that occurred during World War II. With no relatives or documents providing information, the boy accurately recounted people and conditions in a fighter squadron in the Pacific.[55]

Others have also found evidence for after-death survival. Brian Weiss, Chairman Emeritus of Psychiatry at the Mount Sinai Medical Center in Miami, has successfully employed past-life therapy to address a range of health conditions. One patient, for example, suffered from anxiety and panic attacks and was treated with medication. Under hypnosis, the patient recalled past life memories that proved to be the causative factors of her symptoms. At that time, reincarnation was alien to her beliefs. Over time, the patient became more psychic, which she attributed to an effect of the therapy. Weiss says he then began using more hypnosis and less medication to resolve psychological problems.[56]

Reincarnation is typically thought of along linear lines of past, present, and future. Part of the reshaping of current models is that the future may influence the present, perhaps even more than the past in some instances. Rather than reincarnation, some prefer the designation of simultaneous, multiple incarnations that stretch across time.

Therefore, when talking about past lives, it might be more comprehensive to also talk about future lives. Looking at time as a wavefield dimension, it may be that past, present, and future coexist, each influencing the others. Individual lives within different time periods would have their own identities that influence each other to varying degrees. When a person dies, it may be that the wavefield takes that information and creates a person in a time that gives a sense of historical continuity, past to future.

Furthermore, the human energy body may be the assemblage point of a larger, other-dimensional entity. And this could be the assemblage point of a yet larger being, and on and on. There then comes a time when individual awareness, no matter how large, enfolds into the whole of the wavefield leaving only a pure state of oneness where individuality doesn't exist. From this stance, reincarnation evaporates. And yet, as don Juan indicated, the possibility of retaining individual awareness remains when entering the third field. Depending on how you arrange your perception, how you create an inventory, you can validate any of these interpretations.

By incorporating these concepts into an inventory, life becomes an experience of multi-dimensional time travel. There is an other-dimensional relationship associated with reincarnation, in addition to the earthly dimension of traversing time from birth to death. If these ideas were elements of consensus reality, we would literally be in another world of thoughts, interpretations, behaviors, and experiences.

Paradise

Shamans have learned to step out of the swirling eddy previously mentioned and venture beyond the forces of decoherence to retain their awareness. While I have *seen* don Juan instantly appear from a field of luminosity (chapter one), an event I interpret as him returning from the third energy field, I can only intellectually grasp his lessons concerning stepping into the third energy field. Don Juan's time with me centered on the basics. For the intellectual discourse, he had me read Castaneda's books and a wide assortment of other works. Over time, I realized it was the basics that got me through thick and thin and were the guideposts to personal growth and developing the overall path.

Based on direct observation of the wavefield, shamans paint a provocative picture of life and death that is consistent with scientific wavefield theory—or rather, the emerging scientific view is consistent with that of shamans. In this accounting, all possible arrangements of individual selves float as bundles of energy throughout the wavefield. The force of life binds some of them into a coherent entity, in this case a human being. It is then that we lose awareness of the true self, says don Juan.[57] A sense of individuality and the effects of cohesion produce self-reflection. This focuses awareness away from wider, natural conditions, and we lose sight of our grander nature. Losing self-importance, reducing reflection, opens an avenue to recognizing our original state.

Death is a dismantling of the bundles of energy that comprise the energy body as it evaporates back into the wavefield, extinguishing personal awareness. However, don Juan maintained that some shamans embark on a "definitive journey" as they enter energy fields that were once only on the periphery of awareness.[58] He called this the "Fire from Within," a process where the first and second fields merge and the energy body fully lights up, the tonal and nagual act in unison to give a boost of power, and the person fuses with the wavefield in a new configuration of energy that withstands the forces of decoherence.[59] While don Juan holds that everyone briefly enters the third energy field at death, he considers it a supreme accomplish to do this while retaining personal awareness. A shaman tunes cohesion for survival, and this maneuver is an extreme version.

As mentioned, old cycle shamans thought that during death the Eagle devoured a person's awareness for its nourishment.[60] Acknowledging the basic experience of decoherence, the more modern rendition is that the wavefield uses that information to become more aware of itself. In both instances, this seems like projection by attributing human characteristics to a cosmological state of existence that is beyond our grasp. That said, new cycle terminology portrays the event as the release of information contained by an individual into the wavefield at death. The wavefield processes that information which informs or enlivens the entire wavefield. So maybe "nourishment" is apt in a manner of speaking, but it still suggests projection.

Life after death is a concrete region, albeit of a different order than the daily world, says don Juan.[61] Requiring an exquisite alignment of first and second fields and of internal and external energies, the physical body is forged into another form of energy. This involves the use of dreaming to perceive all that is human, and then jumping out of that domain to perceive the inconceivable. Evidently, the person may retain the ability to reassemble their physical body and return to Earth, which is how I speculate that I met don Juan.

In a theological conversation with Castaneda, don Juan said that being cast out from the Garden of Eden is a way of saying that we lost our silent knowledge, our innate awareness that supersedes reason. The shamanic path, he continued, is an avenue leading back to that paradise.[62]

* * *

Shamanic views and practices must be measured alongside other reports and evidence suggestive of reincarnation. It may be that paradise is open to everyone, not just mystics. Consistent with other mystical perspectives regarding reincarnation, it may also be that getting caught in the eddy is experiencing a cycle of rebirth over many lifetimes, and that escaping the eddy corresponds to breaking the wheel of rebirth, as some mystics refer to ending reincarnational processes.

We also need to ask if the Fire from Within interferes with natural processes related to soul growth. Does it hinder progression? If reincarnation has no grand purpose, is the Fire from Within a matter of leaving nothing to chance by escaping the eddy and bringing the cycle of rebirth to an end? Is it a meta-natural means to return to where we came from while remembering why we left in the first place? Is it becoming aware of other-dimensional existence? Or is it a means for the wavefield to blandly gain another type of experience? What conditions might have produced the wavefield? If something gives rise to the wavefield, what is behind or beyond it? And then beyond that?

These are just a few inquiries for shamans and scientists alike. For both, referencing life in terms of wavefield emanations provides ample focus to evaluate natural conditions on Earth as well as what may exist beyond. But we can't default to mysticisms, including shamanism, simply because they have answered these questions. Doing so is ignoring the basics of learning, as we end up buying into a pre-established worldview. Answers already in hand might be accurate. Then again, they are based on the capacities of human perception which means there is a vast unknown before us. We also need to remain open to the effects of the unknowable, of perhaps never finding true answers. By doing so, we can purposefully continue the voyages humans have always undertaken to expand the known world, what that means, and what the next steps might be.

5 } Managing Your Energy Body

Almost all aspects of the energy body involve some type of awareness of the physical body. Body knowledge is key to activating all cornerstones. Being in your body is perhaps the best exercise for out-of-body experience, for instance. You're centered, focused, and intentional.

Orienting your nonphysical senses to the body is simple, it's just a matter of different kinds of exercise. From these basics, you become more aware of the wavefield while staying down to earth. You go further out in consciousness while remaining within your body. To begin, take stock of yourself from time to time throughout the day. Quiet down, listen to your body, and deliberately feel connected with your environment for a few seconds. Pay attention to tensions, release them, then notice what insight this brings. Think about what you want to do, then feel the sensations this produces in your body.

Go for a walk. Pay attention to muscles throughout your body. Then feel your muscles connect with the environment. Feel yourself move through time and space. You'll sense when you lose your connection and why. Balance on one leg, then the other. Throw a ball into the air and catch it without thinking. You'll find that thinking interferes with catching the ball and that letting your body perform is more effective. For another simple exercise, step heel to toe forward and backward. Get in the habit of body awareness.

The following exercises help develop balance in different ways: physical, mental, emotional, energetic. There is nothing exceptional about them. A few have scientific names; most can be found in other mystical disciplines. I've found them to be of value, as have others, but I am not advocating their use. That's your decision.

FUNDAMENTALS OF MANAGING CONSCIOUSNESS

If you're managing body awareness, you're governing cohesion. Getting your cohesion in shape is just like exercise to condition the physical body. A person can know the words, and even the meaning, but not how-to. The following skills are the fundamental building blocks of learning to develop and maintain your energy body. They allow for more advanced applications and can even supplant the need for drugs to move the assemblage point. They are how I, and others, dispensed with psychedelics en route to using the energy body by one's own resources and abilities. They are the basics of cultivating personal power.

The energy body establishes an interface between what occurs in the environment and how you perceive it. As though it were transparent film, you can recognize influences shaping awareness and thereby regulate your cohesion. The more options you have regarding the nature of your consciousness, the better your abilities. Toward this goal, this chapter focuses on skills allowing you to implement the options presented throughout this book.

These skills are not meant to be encumbering. They are not harsh or rigid and shouldn't be approached that way. They create the grease that lets one arrive at a truer form of discipline. This aspect of the shamans' discipline, says don Juan, is "the art of facing infinity without flinching, not because they are strong and tough but because they are filled with awe."[1] In this light, exercises apply to the attributes of consciousness: awareness, attention, and intent. No matter your stage of development, they provide a means to further your growth.

Accessible and Inaccessible

Being accessible is when you're off center and overly influenced by others or circumstances. Just as a matter of how energy behaves, their energy tries to fill the gap. This may result in them wanting to control you because they regard you as an extension of their energy. In any case, your behavior falls in line with external conditions rather than your goals. This removes you from the flow of life as you get caught in other currents of energy. At the same time, there are situations where you need to be accessible, at least to some degree, such as at work where your performance hinges on allowing the requirements of the job to influence you.

The remedy is two-fold: First, become accessible to a higher power. Being accessible to the wavefield allows you to step outside of conditional fields. The more you stretch into your nature, the less influence others can exert on you against your consent.

The second part of the remedy is to be inaccessible, a form of remaining unaffected. Worry and trepidation automatically open the gateway to being accessible, and not in a good way. Being inaccessible doesn't mean shutting down the flow of energy. It doesn't mean to hide from others or yourself. It consists of deliberately choosing what relationships (of any kind) you open to, close off, or something in between. It means being unaffected so you can maintain your balance without getting lost in the circumstances about you, and not governing yourself solely by meeting the expectations of others. You still need to own up to your mistakes and misgivings. But don't let them deplete your energy. You also need to recognize when you got it right.

Accessibility and inaccessibility are complementary, each employed at given turns of the road. You determine if, when, and where you want the environment to have sway. It is a dance of being able to regulate this dynamic duo based on time, place, and circumstance. The balance between accessible and inaccessible is a means of determining alignment, of managing cohesion. This allows you to abandon yourself to the quest of expanding consciousness.

It can also produce interesting experiences. For example, in Castaneda's book, *Journey to Ixtlan*, don Juan talks about a dance of sorts that allowed Castaneda to become accessible to the power of the wind and stay awake all night. While driving straight through from Tucson to Austin, Texas (a full day and night drive), I thought I'd try it. At sunset, just as the last light wavered in the sky, I stood atop a small hill, faced the west horizon, extended my arms with my palms open, and jogged in place. In a few seconds, I felt energy rush into my palms. My arms extended further and became stiff, almost rigid. I then felt energy flow through my arms and fill my body. A gust of wind hit my face. I stopped the dance, got in my car, and drove off. I remained alert the rest of the night without coffee or artificial stimulants. Arriving in Austin, I had sufficient energy to go out to dinner and socialize.

Nonattachment

Nonattachment, or detachment as mystics often refer to it, is a necessary stance when exploring consciousness. I prefer the term nonattachment, as detachment might suggest severing connections and becoming aloof rather than paying attention. Nonattachment offers a quiet zone or space between an external event and an internal reaction. It is a neutral, yet personal, relation between the environment and oneself that offers the ability to perceive what is at hand more clearly and objectively.

Nonattachment helps with EQ. You do your best to remain unaffected by circumstances. This takes time but is doable. Another side of nonattachment requires not being invested in the outcome of your actions or of a situation in daily or dream worlds. This overall bearing is needed to accumulate energy, says don Juan.[2] It is not an excuse to allow abuse by not addressing egregious behavior in yourself or others.

Suggestions:
1. Recognize that you are fully connected with the world and responsible for your actions. Nonattachment is an attitude, a relation to the world, so don't disconnect or detach yourself from the world.
2. Strive to remain calm and centered within yourself. Frequent meditation will assist you.

3. Participate in group activities without regard for how you are perceived by the group. This doesn't mean to act foolish, but if you should behave contrary to the group's protocol, let any criticism slide away from you.
4. Instead of criticizing, mentally and emotionally accept without comment situations that usually spark you to react.
5. Do your best to not let your desires command your behavior.
6. Cultivate a sense of self-observation. As though you were standing behind yourself, watch yourself without judging or censoring your behavior. Try not to identify with any roles. Just allow yourself to act normally. Over time, you identify behaviors you wish to modify or eliminate.
7. Be aware that you are developing nonattachment, and patiently let that awareness provide lessons. In other words, you will set into motion lessons around nonattachment simply by intending them. So, once again, pay attention.
8. Like other skills, this takes time and experience to become proficient.

Death as an Advisor

Relating to death as an advisor makes life personal. You drop pretense to get to the core of what matters to you. When faced with death, other concerns pale in comparison. Meaning wells up from the heart and you clearly understand how you want to live. This humility inspires, tempers, and molds character. Its greatest value is giving you the motivation to act by determining what matters, and what matters most is living. Merely tying your shoelaces becomes luxurious.

It's not necessarily that when we physically die, we die forever with no experience in the hereafter. That is another question and problem altogether. But the fact is that on this planet we all die; by owning up to this, we can enhance our lives. Using death as a focusing agent for the here and now provides a functional way to maximize your life, with an emphasis on leaving this world with no regrets and a full heart.

A strong focus on death permits a deliberate focus on life. If you push away the knowledge that you will physically die, you push away one of the most significant events in your life. This results in blindly refusing to take hold of your life. Adapted from don Juan's teachings, here is a simple way to use death as an advisor:[3]

1. Simply ask your death how you should behave. If you were to die now, what do you want to be doing? How do you want to act?
2. Behave accordingly.
3. Implement nonattachment so you don't become morbidly obsessed with the technique.
4. Repeat the exercise throughout the day, or use as necessary.

Nonpatterning

This is a central exercise and part of every form of meditation I've experienced. Regardless of your activities, it is one of the most practical tools you can develop. The scientific term is *deautomatization*, meaning to interfere with automatic, conditioned behaviors.[4] It interrupts the usual process of organizing and interpreting information. Don Juan referred to it as *not-doing*, or not doing what you ordinarily do.[5] You then set the stage for new behaviors, learning, and awareness.

Conditional fields, maintained by reflection and interpretation, constrict the flow of available information. Nonpatterning opens the windows to more awareness. In and of itself, feeling is nonpatterning. Entanglement tells us that we connect with the environment and are part of it. Feeling reveals this blending and gives us awareness beyond our conditioning. This also applies to the other cornerstones.

Nonpatterning destabilizes conditional fields which allows a natural relation with the wavefield to occur. In practice, no inference is made regarding the origin or outcome of the event. This means that you don't organize or formulate a situation. Act as though you are unaware of anything unusual happening, but at the same time pay attention to details. This prevents you from jumping to conclusions and allows you to accumulate information.

Nonpatterning is a perceptual skill, not a hard and fast rule of behavior. You disengage perception to engage it more clearly, but you don't surrender your knowledge. Even when it is necessary to pattern something, to make sense of something and apply it, you can still nonpattern by not being attached to the outcome of your actions.

Here are a few ways to grasp nonpatterning:
1. Unfocus your vision and gaze at the environment. Reversing figure-ground images is helpful. See chapter two, Figure 2.1.
2. Reverse the order of statements. "Out-of-body experience helps develop perception," turned around is "Developing perception helps out-of-body experience."
3. Don't interpret the actions of others, or define yourself. Don't refer to yourself as a physician, a mechanic, or a teacher. Perform your actions well, but don't identify yourself with them. If someone asks what you do, respond that you collect information, that you live, that you walk the face of Earth. If this seems unrealistic, remember you strive to be unreal in that you seek to expand your notions of reality, not strap yourself further into them. In turn, offer the same consideration to others.
4. Feeling the world about you is nonpatterning and a way to store personal power.
5. Throughout the day, observe several events without interpreting them.

Meditation

Meditation is nonpatterning. It involves exploring the deepest recesses of yourself. It often acts as a solvent to help remove obstructions and as a guiding force to help you make sense of it all. A key ingredient for any meditation is not to analyze what occurs during the meditation; allow all perceptions to come and go without censoring or editing them. Meaning arrives on its own.

You will find meditation provides the practical benefits of facilitating relaxation and enhancing problem-solving capabilities. This quiet listening facilitates realizing your entire being. There are various books, tapes, seminars, and other teaching tools to learn meditation. Some styles advise not to scratch if you itch. Others say scratch, pay attention while doing so, and then return to your inner world. Experiment with several methods to find what style works best for you.

Routines

Also known as *dishabituation*,[6] this exercise of disrupting routines helps prevent cohesion from becoming too hardened. It is a form of nonpatterning. The idea is that habits consolidate cohesion. They are the conditions which fix the assemblage point in place, and thereby uphold your reality. Your world exists through the habitual position of the assemblage point. To establish new cohesions, you need to introduce new habits. Practices of shamanism and science are based on this. They build new habits. One of the habits of shamans is to disrupt them. Accordingly, disrupting routines applies to all situations to keep cohesion supple.

As you break a habit, you open yourself to new habits, new behaviors, and new ways of looking at the world. Unfamiliar experiences help increase knowledge. On the other hand, fresh behaviors themselves help you energize cohesion to break old habits.

To help loosen perception, try these:
1. Do something just for the heck of it. Move all the living room furniture to the middle of the room and leave it for a few days. Rearrange it again based on feeling. Where does it feel like the sofa should go? Where does it feel like you should place the rocking chair? Don't worry about the way it looks. Let feeling guide you. Have some fun with it.
2. Place your left shoe on first for one week, then place your right shoe on first for four days. Vary the exercise randomly.
3. Every day for 20-30 minutes, walk around your house or neighborhood guided only by feeling. Don't censor where you walk by shoulds and shouldn'ts. If you have an impulse to bend over and pick up a candy wrapper, do so. If you feel good about knocking on a friendly neighbor's door for no apparent reason, do so.
4. Pay attention to your activities. You may discover some comfortable habits are superficial, serving no purpose. You may also realize how

habits create habits in what you perceive. If you want to be aware of more, give yourself more options.
5. Drive to work on different routes, at different times. One problem you may encounter is thinking you are altering routines when you are only creating larger ones. If you vary the route to work each day, you are creating the routine of varying the route to work. To correct this, use feeling. You might drive different routes three days in a row, then drive the same route twice. Whatever.

Internal Dialogue

Internal dialogue grounds reality. Our incessant stream of thought creates and upholds descriptions. It is the foundation for building inventories. Whether it is shamanism or science, internal dialogue acts as a coalescing force binding perception into an unshakable reality. Managing it is central to loosening cohesion, bringing the cornerstones to life, and increasing awareness.

It is difficult to move consciousness past prefabricated thoughts. By constantly referencing an inventory, cohesion is overly conditioned, and a hardened alignment takes the place of fluent perception. Understanding the benefits, drawbacks, and general effects of self-reflection and projection sets the stage to manage your energy body. You then comprehend that your participation with reality stems from a continuously circulating collection of interrelated thoughts. When that flow stops, the energy body accesses new information that eventually breaks the hold of worldviews. This opens the way to *seeing*.

To begin, use a particular way of walking that interrupts self-reflection:
1. Walk with your hands in an unusual position that does not attract attention. The novelty directs energy away from the ordinary attention created by your routine way of walking. If you hold your hands in a dramatically unusual position, you might have to contend with other people sending their energies toward you as they wonder what you're doing.
2. Direct your vision slightly below the horizon. If you are in a hill or mountain environment, steadily look 10-40 feet in front of you. If

you look 20 feet away, for instance, continue looking 20 feet away as you walk.
3. Unfocus your eyes, allowing your peripheral vision to absorb as much as possible.
4. Listen to and smell the environment. Feel your surroundings. Sense the environment. You're trying to get out of your thoughts and into your body.
5. Walk at a normal pace, or slower than your normal pace.
6. For safety, walk where you don't have to contend with traffic or other obstacles. Otherwise, you're thinking about navigating rather than interrupting your thinking.
7. There comes a time when you have the realization that you just turned off your internal dialogue.

Personal History

Personal history becomes a habit for maintaining reality. Always thinking about experiences, memories, and their meaning develops cohesion into a highly conditional field. In addition, maintaining a social identity prevents you from changing your behavior and learning things outside the perimeters of consensus worldviews. Don Juan says that stopping your internal dialogue is a key that allows perception to travel beyond this boundary, and erasing personal history supports this effort.[7] Like other not-doing exercises, this is a way to disrupt the effects of calcified cohesion. Doing so allows for new awareness, interpretations, and experiences. It also helps avoid becoming ensnared in the thoughts and expectations of others.

Erasing personal history disrupts the interpretations of others, keeping them from pinning you down in their thoughts. Other people define you, rightly or wrongly, by taking your history and then trying to make you fall into line with their thoughts. A desire to be known by others locks you into this two-way street of reflection where you give personal history while others try to pin you to it. The solution comes from not letting your past, and how you or others interpret it, get in your way of moving forward. This exercise also has the advantage of revealing the basis of interpretations—that they are points of view.

There are times when you may need your history, such as when applying for a job or obtaining a passport. But in common social situations, there are ways to erase history to your advantage. Changing your name automatically interferes with the energetic momentum of your life. Another option is to not tell people exactly how you did something. Leave space in their imagination. You can offer partial or vague accounts of your actions. When someone fills in the blanks for you, go along with it. This also has practical benefit of not being boorish in conversations by bending the conversation to your interests. You can fully participate while remaining quiet about yourself.

A very important part of this exercise is not becoming sneaky or secretive. This warps cohesion. You need to be studiously honest with yourself and deliberate about your purpose. The goal is not to have deceitful behaviors but to become more aware. You remain in touch with your history; you don't forget what you've done. And there are times when you accent your identity, such as reminding yourself you're a scientist, a dreamer, or a whatever, as a means to strengthen that cohesion.

Erasing personal history may be clunky at first. Sophistication develops with time and practice. There may come a time when you've outgrown the need for this exercise and so can jettison it. In the meantime, to keep this exercise in check you need personal responsibility.

Responsibility

Don Juan advised Castaneda that the basis of his difficulties was not being responsible. Don Juan told him that when he decided to do something, he should go all out. He must begin by knowing why he is doing something, then proceed without misgivings.[8]

Most of us have been conditioned to defer to authority, and those in authority often demand deference. It's part of ordinary society. But the value of having a stable social order shouldn't negate the quest for personal growth and the ability to act independently of society if that is what is called for. Balancing these often competing demands rests with assuming personal responsibility.

The glue of cohesion—responsibility—cements awareness, character, circumstance, and goals. This forms a foundation to shape your life. Responsibility is essential for the development and integrity of cohesion. Otherwise, perception is off the mark and behavior is not centered. A stable cohesion requires you to be responsible for the knowledge you claim, and why you sought that knowledge. This leads to your next steps.

Applying this, how you implement the information in this book is your responsibility. What you do with it rests on your shoulders. Perhaps the most effective way to assume responsibility is to use your death as an advisor.

Combinations

These exercises work independently and together. They are all tied in some way to self-importance and require the management of mental and emotional reflection. Collectively, they are part of a cognitive technology for managing the energy body. Like any good technology, one element, or gear, connects to others, and all parts work in unison. For example, don Juan says that erasing personal history is a must for shifting cohesion, and that disrupting routines, using death as an advisor, and assuming responsibility are supports.[9]

These same techniques can also be applied to accumulating sufficient personal power to find a teacher as I described in chapter one. And they can be used to gather experience and establish your own path. This also requires gaining more personal power which is acquiring more awareness. Combined, these exercises allow cohesional expansion and stability.

These core skills therefore allow you to achieve new alignments. Nonattachment to suspend and allow; responsibility to strengthen and integrate; inaccessibility and accessibility to pick and choose; death for focus; disrupting routines for flexibility; and stopping the internal dialogue to open the gates of awareness. These skills can change their relation to each other, so that what was once a support becomes supported by others.

ENERGY BODY APPLICATIONS

The exercises above have a wide application of enhancing the energy body. They can also be applied to each of the cornerstones of perception, as well as for the general expansion of awareness.

Feeling

Feeling is a form of nonpatterning and counters projection. You can talk about what you're feeling, and about the relation between thought and feeling, but doing so sheds little light on this cornerstone; only experience with it delivers body knowledge. Emotional intelligence (EQ) is the refinement of feeling. This consists of being in touch with your internal environment as you travel the external world. EQ is being centered in the heart, letting it breathe, and learning to connect with the world in a way that nourishes your life.

Practicing feeling and developing EQ, which go hand in hand, offer a substantial means to re-orient your place in this world. One way to focus on feeling is to pay attention kinesthetically, to pay attention to the sensations in your muscles and physical body. Another option is to pay attention to subtle, intuitive-like sensations.

To further get a handle on feeling:
1. Don't interpret events. Accept them at face value. Stopping your internal dialogue is an effective bridge for this. Let yourself sense what is happening.
2. What do you feel about specific issues: politics, relationships of one kind or another, the film you just saw?
3. Ask yourself how you feel about these. "What" and "how" are different responses.
4. Observe yourself responding emotionally to events throughout your daily life. Objectively assess these reactions.
5. Use feeling rather than thoughts for assessment. Listen with your heart when someone speaks. Try not to get caught up in the expectations of others. Go behind the scenes to let yourself become aware of your motivations and those of others.

Dreaming

Dreaming is a natural ability for anyone. It is essential for shamans. The following two chapters illuminate dreaming and approaches for its development.

Will

Will is the major epicenter of the energy body, reason being the other epicenter. It is the energy binding the cornerstones. *Will* is a force allowing shifts of cohesion, with intent guiding that energy. To awaken *will*, you must step outside of your thoughts and reason. You increasingly connect your body knowledge with the order of the first energy field. You recondition abilities of awareness, attention, and intent to expand consciousness. This adds to your body knowledge, the information and skill embedded within you. And then you go at it again, and again.

Mihaly Csikszentmihalyi, author of *Flow: The Psychology of Optimal Experience*, says that consciousness is "intentionally ordered information," and intention is the force maintaining order.[10] Order includes all kinds of organization, not just verbal reflection. It both reflects and results from a stable cohesion of any magnitude. It is also the natural world. Oceans contain order, as do jungles, as does the universe, as does the wavefield. How humans perceive order is another matter.

The transition to *will* occurs as you learn and then stabilize new awareness. A permanent shift to *will* occurs when you are able to place the accent of your daily life on the cornerstones of feeling, dreaming, and *seeing*. Rather than go through the day referencing what you have learned, you sense the fuller energies of the world by giving precedence to, for instance, your EQ. From this, you allow learning and thinking to come and go like the ebb and flow of the tides. Your life takes on a dream-like quality reflecting heightened consciousness. You stay focused and grounded by intent.

When awakening the cornerstones, you're stimulating *will*. But there is also a separate, fuller sense outside of exercising the cornerstones that becomes apparent with experience, where you know you're in a world other than reason. Since *will* is connected to the order of the first energy field, you're not losing rationality. Since it is connected to the potential of the second field, you're gaining access to the natural order of life.

SEEING THE LUMINOUS WORLD

Seeing is the basis of modern shamanism. It provided the description of the wavefield and energy body, and enabled evolution of its practices. Stopping the internal dialogue is an essential ingredient. Body awareness is required. Reason doesn't come along for the ride. Once you gain competency, you can stop your thoughts by intending to do so, just as you will eventually *see* by intending that behavior.

To acquaint you with the cornerstone of *seeing*, here are some preliminary perspectives and procedures:

Betwixt and Between

To assist re-conditioning cohesion to handle more information and *see*, cultivate the habit of looking at the world in many ways. Learn to look at two sides of any story. By realizing everything is an interpretation, and that this is based on thought, you can use that leverage to stop your internal dialogue.

To begin, use opposing viewpoints. For instance, the description of classical science and the material world contrasts well against shamanism and a world of energy. Philosophical propositions, such as whether free will exists, also serve this purpose. You can even use policy differences between political parties. Anything that produces opposition works.

Humans have long struggled with oppositions such as with having free will or no free will, that we are active co-creators of reality or just observers of that which already exists, and that there is no definitive future or that the future is already fixed in place. These three areas form the following exercise. I suggest familiarizing yourself with the following steps prior to proceeding.

1. Visualize, feel, or otherwise perceive a sphere of energy representing the joy of having free will. Immerse yourself in this sphere and allow it to fill your entire being. Your decisions are yours. You have the freedom to make your own choices.
2. Place this energy aside for the moment, and perceive an energy sphere representing the magnificence of not having free will. You are part and parcel of a preordained, divine order, and you realize how intimately you are connected with it as you perform as an actor on a stage. Your part has already been given to you. Have fun with it.
3. Place both energies before you, equal in distance on each side of the center of your perception. Place your attention in between these energies. Find the balance where you feel no tension between the two energies.
4. Leaving that awareness, visualize, feel, or otherwise perceive a sphere of energy representing the brilliance of co-creating your reality. Through give-and-take, you interact with the entire cosmos, and thus your reality is molded.
5. Placing this awareness momentarily aside, perceive an energy sphere representing the power of gradually becoming aware of that which already exists. Movement through time and space is only an exercise in perception. All time resides in the present, and moving through space is the movement of mind. Everything always was and always will be. As you increase your awareness, you gradually become conscious of that which already was, is, and always will be.
6. Bring both energies to the fore of your awareness. Go in between them to a sense of balance. Allow whatever perceptions that occur to occur.
7. Leaving that awareness, in your own way perceive a sphere of energy representing that there is no future. The future occurs from what happens in the present. And the present is the present. "Future" is only a thought.
8. Place this energy aside for the moment and perceive an energy sphere representing the future as already existing. Rather than causing an event to happen because of your thoughts, you have those

thoughts because the event has already occurred. All your actions are predetermined. You travel through your feelings to the place where they have already happened. We are all catching up to find out what is already there.
9. Place both energies before you, and place your attention in between them.
10. Using your imagination, form a triangle. The three points of the triangle represent the balance point of steps 3, 6, and 9.
11. Inside, at the center of the triangle, find the place of no tension.
12. At the free perception point imagine a speck of white light. Approach the white light, which grows larger and more brilliant. Place your attention at the threshold of the light.
13. From here, you can use your intent to ask questions, to *see*, or just to relax. The main idea with the exercise is to recognize, at least to some degree, the validity of other views and the importance of not clinging to your own. Perception can be an open window.
14. Step into the light. What, if anything, happens?

Each of these elements is an assemblage point position, a type of cohesion. Being a co-creator with the divine follows the thinking that you have free will and can use your *will* and intent to build your world. In the same manner, becoming aware of that which already is follows from having no free will and thinking that the future is fixed in place. These are parts of their respective inventories.

When enough elements relating to one line of thought come together, you have a philosophy, or maybe a full-fledged reality. Use the exercise to step in between science and shamanism, for example, with science representing a world built through reason and shamanism a world formed through *will*. By doing so, you won't be bound by either and may enjoy the fruits of each. The constellations of thought resulting from these approaches influence perception, which influences behavior, which influences experience. Experience then self-validates the philosophy, all of which produces a loop where perception and experience are manufactured due to self-reflection, not by a natural order.

This exercise relates to finding the power that exists in between the items that manifest. It is a force from and in which coherence develops, be this at personal or cosmological levels. Finding balance and using it to move the assemblage point is hooking into personal power. This is one of the more valuable results of commanding this skill of going in between. It also increases your ability to simultaneously hold opposing thoughts, making you more fluent with interpretations.

When perception is not hemmed in by prior conditioning such as from social consensus, it has greater freedom to move. You can then shift to *seeing*. This awareness can then be integrated to help expand the first field. As with any learning, there are gradations of skill. This exercise of opposing concepts is a way to shift cohesion; it is learning an intent associated with *seeing*. You'll eventually learn to go beyond the exercise and *see* based solely on intent.

Gazing

A preliminary to *seeing* is *gazing*, a means of creating new alignments. It permits the energies forming cohesion to circulate more freely and allow different perceptions to surface. Gazing is a form of meditation that develops visual fluency where images gently come and go. It also develops an ease of body awareness. It stimulates your perception of nonphysical energy such as luminosity in the ground, in the sky, and around people. It is an avenue to the energy body, says don Juan.[11]

Gazing lets you merge your first and second fields. Then, as you match (align) your energy body with energies at large, you begin to *see*. You might say gazing helps the energy body become more supple. As such, it helps you explore and strengthen your awareness of energy that is totally distinct from the physical energy you're most familiar with. The mirror gazing, also known as *scrying*, I mentioned in chapter four is one example.

For your benefit, don't gaze while driving or operating machinery as you might move yourself too far from the ordinary and cause an accident. You can, however, gaze while talking with people. As you gaze at their energy bodies, for instance, let your speech arise easily and naturally.

To begin:
1. Relax, try to be nonattached.
2. Establish your intent to gaze.
3. Don't focus on the world as you normally might. Don't, for example, pick out an object and then look at it. Let your eyes go soft, unfocused.
4. Feel your body merge with the world.
5. If you *see* a haze of light or swirling dots, let them be. Don't focus on them, or you'll go back into physical-world focus. The light is the luminous world breaking into your awareness. Later, when you have gained more experience, you can focus on the light and it won't disappear. But until you train your eyes and your body, your normal habits of perception will take you back to your ordinary world.

Gazing is akin to a ritual of harnessing intent. Through repetition of a given behavior, just like learning to stand up, you gradually learn the intent of the behavior without thinking about it. Over time, you'll quickly enter gazing. As your practice becomes more full-bodied, it becomes easier to shift into *seeing* proper.

Gazing teaches you to look at the world differently. This automatically interferes with normal thinking, which suspends looking at the world in a certain way. You begin to understand the processes of forming a reality as well as how to use that knowledge to expand consciousness.

Here are several variations of gazing:

Shadow

This is very relaxing. You can use virtually any shadow. To get the idea, gather a bunch of dead leaves into a pile. Sit down in front of the leaves and gaze into the shadows. Allow the shadows to change form, but try not to maintain any form that the shadows create. Let the shadows shift. You can isolate the shadows of leaves, trees, buildings, mountains, or anything else. The intensity of shadows on the side of a desert mountain is remarkable and creates a powerful exercise.

Then, intentionally form patterns of shadows in the same manner you would create a tree out of branches and leaves. Instead of attending to the normal features of leaves, branches, etc., you construct the tree from the shadows within it. Allowing new patterns to emerge from the shadows diffuses the conditioned patterns of the ordinary world.

As you continue gazing, intend your awareness to enter and merge with the shadows. You'll discover they have a very rich texture. You can also play with the depth of field. Send your awareness toward the shadow or allow the shadow to come closer to you without moving your physical body. Then continue gazing until you *see* light emanating from the shadows.

Fog

This exercise is an effective way to avoid fixations. Since the fog represents the unknown, it makes your environment less certain and more mysterious. Uncertainty opens perception. As you gaze at fog, move your eyes slowly along the fog bank to avoid fixating on the fog itself. This maneuver can also be used for other gazing exercises and *seeing*.

You might have imagery appear in the fog. Gazing while at a beach with my girlfriend, I once saw three Indians on galloping painted ponies. She had images of past events. At the beach on another occasion, I decided to meditate. I calmed my thoughts by relaxing and focusing my hearing on the waves. I fixed my attention on a city ordinance sign approximately 30 feet away. While looking at the sign, I tried not to conceptualize the sign, the sand, the water, the benches, or anything else. I just let it all exist without trying to uphold the elements of the environment. I ceased being "at the beach."

After a short time, perhaps only five minutes, I saw the sign change into a man who started to approach me. Rather it was as if the man emerged from the sign, as the sign retained a phantasmagoric quality. The darkness prohibited a well-defined image. I continued meditating. I tried not to tell myself that a man had just stepped out of the sign and was headed my way. At the same time, I didn't try to dispel the image. I became indifferent. The speed of the man's approach increased. As the man drew closer, I involuntarily stood up in one, deft movement, whereupon the image disappeared, leaving the sign glowing in the faint light.

This is a demonstration of temporarily releasing perception that can be applied to all forms of gazing. Other than loosening my perception and observing the reality-shaping effects of a fluid cohesion, I placed no particular importance on the event. It was just another, sometimes entertaining, day. Most psychologists would interpret this as some type of disorder rather than as a sign of learning. It's a matter of interpretation, not only of the event but also the backdrop, the consensus reality of what's producing the experience. Mental disorders exist, but if different interpretations are not known, then every departure from consensus is categorized as a disorder.

Classes on mysticisms, also known as transpersonal psychologies, are severely lacking in professional healthcare education. When options of consciousness beyond current perspectives don't exist, patients' treatments are limited. Part of a mystic's education is learning how to integrate these types of experiences into a larger picture. They have positive meaning and are not viewed as something in need of correcting for the sake of conformity.

Water and Fire

Old cycle shamans established these types of gazing. Due to their effectiveness, new cycle practitioners kept them. With water gazing, separate the qualities of wetness and fluidity, then focus solely on the fluid part. Let your awareness flow wherever. In this instance, wetness is a first-field property and fluidity a second-field property.

You're thereby gaining fluency with the second field as well as separating elements of descriptions. Fire gazing uses the same principle of separation. In this case, though, the distinction is between heat and flame, where you let the energy of the flame move your perception.

People

Position a friend in front of a blank, white wall. Gaze at the space surrounding his or her physical body, what artists call negative space. You might *see* a band of white light covering the edges of their body. In time, other forms of light might appear. You might *see* their aura, for instance.

With all gazing exercises, you're essentially looking and feeling for contrast and movement, separation between the ordinary and nonordinary, and changes in perception. It is easy to adapt this to urban environments by using a waterfall at a park, rainwater runoff through gutters, shadows cast on buildings, or people on benches. The diffuseness of fog is another approach as it has an unknown quality which can be used to destabilize your ordinary way of looking at the world, and letting more of the mystery within surface.

Seeing

There is no way to effectively describe wavefield emanations, says don Juan, only witness them.[12] From these observations arise interpretations, which is one reason he advocated acquiring only a taste of the shamanic worldview—so that it could be placed in opposition to ordinary reality and used to *see*.

Seeing cuts straight into witnessing streams of luminous energy. It often carries a visual sense associated with perceiving different forms of light but is itself not visual in the normal sense. You might also make sense of your observations by kinesthetic and intuitive means. It consists of a shift in cohesion, establishing a relationship with the environment that activates this cornerstone.

Depending on the way a person processes information, *seeing* differs among people. The structure of light may vary while the meaning remains constant. For example, two people could *see* differently but arrive at the same conclusion. One person may *see* energy, while another person experiences an unusual feeling. The effects, though, are consistent and identifiable.

There are common features as well. When a person *sees* during daylight, the environment becomes darker, and conversely a dark environment becomes lighter. *Seeing* another person's energy body often translates as perceiving packages of luminosity. The energy body might appear as an oblong ball of light and the surrounding world as long strands of intense yet softly glowing light.

Since *seeing* is done with the body, it requires you to become everything around you and, at the same time, become nothing. You disappear to find greater awareness. You need to connect to oneness and slide in between interpretations. First, though, you need to know that this option exists, so if you happen to encounter it, you know what it is. You need EQ to let go of your focus so that you can relax and merge with the world. This sets the stage to transcend the material world. The new alignment of cohesion results in *seeing*.

In a meditative, nonpatterning posture similar to gazing, it is common to *see* dots of light, waves of energy, a gentle rain of light, a haze, or other oddities superimposed on the environment. You might notice a band of energy around the edges of people or things. In all cases, awareness expands until you no longer perceive the material world, just fibrous light. When you begin to *see*, normal conditioning kicks in and perception reverts to the physical world. The effort is allowing *seeing* to happen rather than making it happen.

To begin:
1. Relax. Try to be nonattached to anything you perceive. Let go.
2. Begin gazing, nonpatterning.
3. Stop your internal dialogue.
4. Don't focus on the world as you normally might. Don't pick out an object, then look or stare at it. Let your eyes go "soft," unfocused, but with a steady gaze. Your sight may be directed toward a specific object, but you simultaneously expand your vision to the full periphery.
5. Feel your body merge with the world. Remain centered within your body as you connect with the external world. Feel the flow of energy.
6. If you *see* a haze or rain of light, a thin film of energy, or what looks like swirling dots, let them be. Don't focus on them, or you will pull back your prior cohesion and refocus automatically on the ordinary world. The light is the energy world breaking into your awareness. You are *seeing*.

As you gain experience, you will be able to immediately focus on these types of energy and they won't disappear. You will then be able to expand the luminous world. But until you train your eyes and your body, your old habits of perception will rule. Later, you'll have a new set of habits that allow you to enter the world of energy anytime, anywhere.

6 { A Foundation for Out-of-Body Experience

Dreaming, as used here, takes us into the heart of shamanism. It applies to both the practices of dreaming and to it being a sub-technology within the overall cognitive technology of shamanism, which provides a wider view of dreaming practices. Dreaming itself outlines a place to start, steps to become proficient, goals, and applications. OBE is a way to explore these elements. Whereas an astronaut leaves the earthly arena to venture into deep space, shamans leave the ordinary world to enter deep consciousness.

Dreaming is a way to move the assemblage point, to alter cohesion. This knowledge can then be integrated into daily life, a traditional shamanic maneuver. Dreaming consists of different intents, dynamics, experiences, and options for behavior. Just like the classical physics barrier between the material and energy worlds, the barrier to entry occurs from thoughts and interpretations about what is possible. You need to anticipate and expect that you can enter dreaming. While the steps are the same for everyone, says don Juan, each person has his or her own way of dreaming. The details of one's adventures differ, and your experiences become personal.[1]

There are standard procedures to enter and use dreaming. In other words, it is a learned skill. A stable daily life, for instance, allows you to better manage dreaming, something that eventually becomes repeatable by intent rather than procedure. In addition, there are processes for stabilizing dreams to make them as practical as your waking life, which also becomes a matter of intent rather than process.

Dreaming brings coherence to imagination. It consists of stagecraft where you orchestrate the interplay of personal and environmental energies. Dreaming changes your relation to the wavefield, thereby changing your consciousness. It enhances your perception of order by taking you into wider vistas to observe the dynamics of creation.

Through dreaming, you enter a land of potential where you can apply dreaming to almost any endeavor. It accesses areas of the energy body whether they be of the physical world or other dimensions. It irrigates the energy body and makes it fertile. Used properly, it helps promote precision of perception and refinement of ability by tempering the energy body. Its overarching purpose is to expand cohesion and maximize consciousness. It is an energy-generating process that accelerates learning, which is why it enhances personal power.

LEVELS OF DREAMING

To generate the power for dreaming, you need to redeploy existing energy. Since dreaming is a natural capacity, you don't need to use a shamanic procedure to become aware of it. However, shamanism offers practices, procedures, and purpose. It is a means of organizing consciousness to bring about expanding awareness. Dreaming levels, or gates, as they might be called, are part of this technology.

Traversing the levels requires foundational discipline to form wider and deeper alignments with the wavefield. This is also a feature of shamanism in general, as you learn to be less influenced by consensus reality and more adept at managing awareness based on internal assessments that result from a deeper connection with the wavefield. Just as the warrior's discipline is the backbone or upright strength of shamanism, the structure of the levels stabilizes and strengthens dreaming pursuits. The dreaming technology is like a well-paved avenue with directions and warning signs.

Practical applications are wide-ranging. Don Juan said that his colleague, don Genaro, who was highly skilled in dreaming, could do more than if he were awake.[2] Don Genaro appeared to Castaneda as his normal self while his physical body was in a different location, for example. Don Juan's other apprentices were charged with using dreaming to become a counselor, a healer, and an architect.[3] Castaneda learned to write his books through dreaming and *seeing*.

This is not far-fetched. One of my professors in college was writing a book on newspaper design. He was having trouble with one chapter. During a dream, he *saw* the entire chapter, including references, which means he became aware of very technical and precise information. You can also use dreaming for general problem solving by posing questions and letting answers come on their own. In a traditional shamanic maneuver, you find something in a dream and then express it in daily life. This requires entering dreaming, stabilizing a specific dream, and then remembering it upon waking.

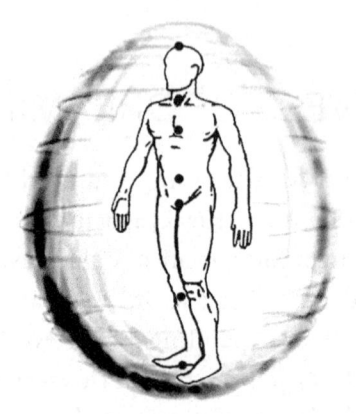

Figure 6.1
Centers for Dreaming Levels
The locations of dreaming gates roughly correspond to the locations of chakras.
An interesting study would be to compare these two approaches.

The process of learning the levels requires all elements of consciousness: awareness, attention, and intent. The first thing you need to know is that other dimensions exist and can be explored. You then prepare for dreaming, learn how to engage it, and utilize it. This turns ordinary dreaming into situations of knowledge and ability that become acts of power.

There are two aspects for each stage: entry and management. This corresponds with the expansion and stabilization of cohesion, respectively. At each level, you learn to loosen, re-stabilize, and control cohesion. If you leapfrog a level and find yourself in a higher one, don't tell yourself you have to go back. Just get on with it. Don't lose yourself in a structured approach; use the structure for guidance. Try not to lose touch with everyday life. Keep yourself within sight of dry land, so to speak.

Applied dreaming should be practical to enhance overall personal growth. The two-step process of entering and managing awareness within each level reflects the merging of the first and second energy fields. Progressing through the levels increases this unification, which leads to an expansion of consciousness.

Level One: Entering Dreaming

This is where you increase your awareness of waking and sleeping while aiming for an in-between area to slide into dreaming. You'll feel different sensations in your physical body, a richness of experience, the deeper you enter dreaming. Initially, just like a basic meditation, you connect with blackness, the unknown. Your cohesion is saturated with natural energy. The darkness feels heavy yet pleasant, as though you're wrapped in a thick, down quilt on a cold winter's night. Remaining in this blackness indicates you've reached the threshold of the first level and have learned a little bit of how to remain awake during sleep.

You can remain within dreaming for hours and it will feel like minutes have gone by. You're likely to fall asleep. Sometimes it seems as though you are asleep while awareness percolates in the background. Later, the darkness abates as you learn to move about in dreams.

With experience, you become aware of dreaming as entering another dimension, like an adjacent room in your home that you can enter and exit. To cross into level two, you need to surface from the blackness and into a dream. A step forward is to isolate a stream of images. Connect with that flow. Become part of it. At first, you may feel out of control, which you are. Learning to surf the images brings the dream more under control. Work through fears and worries by keeping yourself focused on the dream. Dreams may get weird or wild, both being impediments to maintaining focus. This is not something inherent within dreaming but is more a reflection of your cohesion. That said, there may be experiences involving primal or archetypical themes that arise since dreaming opens doors of awareness.

For example, while dreaming I noticed a large boa constrictor crawling on the floor. Using energy body management techniques, I didn't react; I just watched. As it crawled up my body, I accepted the scene without holding onto it and without trying to force it away. The snake then slithered into the back of my skull and out my mouth. Nonpatterning became exceedingly difficult, but I made the attempt. In a split moment, the snake vanished, and my head became glowing white. At that moment, I could direct the dream's content. Serpentine energy often relates to the kundalini force described in eastern mystical traditions. Kundalini is the flow of energy associated with chakras. It relates to healing and consciousness and is often depicted as primal serpentine energy.

The overall objective is to step completely into the dream. Resting in the blackness means you have reduced your focus to the first field. Crossing into a dream indicates your focus has shifted to the second field. Entry occurs by maintaining sufficient attention on an element within the dream.

Level Two: Dreaming Travel

This level is also known as *lucid dreaming*, knowing you're dreaming while dreaming. You can choose a dreaming topic by holding an image firmly in your imagination. You then deliberately direct the content of your dreams as they occur in real time.

As you're dozing off or daydreaming, maintain continuity of the dream. Just as a child learns, at the beginning your experiences will be random, but you'll begin to sense that you're doing something while asleep. The dreams become more lucid, but you're still dragged around like a toddler. The transition into lucid dreaming is fluid, anything can change. You need single-mindedness.

Finding your hands in a dream is a classic exercise to bring about lucid dreaming and is presented in the next chapter. Here, know that as you exercise more control within the dream, your lucidity takes on greater proportion. To cross into this level, you can either dream that you wake up from within a dream or use the dream to vault into yet another dream. Rather than find your hands, you isolate a component in the dream and focus on it. You then use your concentration as a springboard to change dreams.

For example, during a dream I was watching a road while standing idly at the side of a house. It was nighttime. I became immersed in watching the lights of cars before they came into view. But then I began listening to wavering tones in my ears. As a result of consciously changing focus, I entered the dream. I began feeling extraterrestrial energy. The dream then changed, and an approaching car turned into a flying saucer. I began reflecting on the dream and its detail, and I soon lost track of myself as I grew disoriented. Overcoming these types of obstacles allows the deliberate shifting of a dream's content.

Another major impediment is indulging in the dream's content by either analyzing too much or luxuriating in your enhanced freedom. The remedy is to continue evolving within and beyond the second level. This takes practice, plain and simple. It's a self-study course. Once over the threshold of level two, the dream ceases to be an ordinary dream. You're now on the doorstep of OBE.

Level Three: Out-of-Body Experience, Entrance

OBE has been reported as astral projection. Sometimes OBE is related to the *dreaming body*. The term OBE came into vogue over the last fifty years, with Robert Monroe and Charles Tart popularizing its use. I use OBE as it is a convenient and recognized term but it is not truly accurate from an energy body perspective.

Many skilled practitioners contend that we all go out-of-body routinely, we just don't remember doing so. A debate exists about whether we create the dreaming body for each OBE or whether the dreaming body is part of energy body anatomy. Either way, it is a natural aspect of humans that redefines what it means to be human, at least from contemporary considerations.

Unlike lucid dreaming where the dreamscape shifts or can be shifted, the environment is stable during OBE. At this level, you begin to merge dreaming with the daily world. The abutments for bridging the first and second energy fields are now in place. A primary obstacle is getting lost in the details of the dream environment. It is now clear your energy body is part of the environment, each affecting the other, and this carries the proclivity for latching onto every detail available. To counteract this, you need the flexibility brought about by nonattachment and disrupting routines. Remain immensely curious, but not transfixed.

Flying dreams are real-time OBEs. You just haven't made sufficient connection. The novelty of OBE can also throw you off track. If you unexpectedly find yourself out-of-body looking at your physical body, leave the area and do something, anything. This will break the habit of thinking we must be in the physical body to perceive. Also, don't let surprise interfere and ruin your OBE. Remaining focused on your target destination (knowing why or where you want to go) is a way to overcome surprise and its tendency to refocus your attention back to your physical body.

You don't have to lucid dream to have an OBE. People may spontaneously find themselves having one. For instance, while meditating, I abruptly found myself suspended in mid-air over the downtown Tucson streets. I soon found that by shifting my energy I could alter how I observed the traffic's speed. At alternate times the vehicles were zipping about or crawling at a snail's pace. I soon found that I could control the speed of the traffic on command.

Like dreaming from within a dream, elevating OBE capability uses a similar process of having an OBE from an OBE. For example, during one OBE, it was as though I went into another. The distinguishing characteristic of this third projection was the absence of form. Don Juan says the new cycle shamans aren't interested in creating a body. They're looking to become awareness itself.[4] Having a form during OBE results from the habit and expectation of normal awareness.

In this episode, my awareness was focused as a point from which I could shift perspective like looking around a parking lot, but it did not have substance, a body or form. I initially had images of flying upside down over a meadow in a mountain range. I transferred all my attention to the flight, and my awareness split from my body, leading to a traditional OBE. Arching my back, I looped up and back to start flying right side up. Leveling out, I noticed I could watch my dreaming body fly from a perspective above it. I could also shift my perception from that area to see my physical body rest in my apartment. I discovered I could also watch both bodies simultaneously from the vantage of awareness without form.

Level Four: Out-of-Body Experience, Travel

Just like you learned to travel within a dream in level two, now you get to travel outside of normal dreaming while having an OBE. In the early stages of level three, you typically end up anywhere and everywhere, all depending on how your cohesion shifts. At level four, you learn more locomotion skills. You engage precision by pinpointing your destination. At this level, don Juan says you can travel within this world, travel to other dimensions, or travel in the same dream with another person.[5]

An initial lesson is to not control the dreamscape as you do while lucid dreaming. Let things be as they are, not as you want them to be. From this awareness, you change your environment by traveling, just as you do in daily life. You can then practice different types of control, which use different intents. These can be felt in the dreaming body. You can hoover like a helicopter, speed like a jet airplane, rest on top of a cloud, or visit any place on Earth. Proximity to a place or object is also regulated by intent, like changing the focus of a camera changes the depth of the picture.

The more advanced application is to use your intent so that your OBE coincides with the time of day where your physical body is at. The perception of time can get turned around, and you need to restore continuity. As a bonus, then, this level automatically provides lessons on the nature of time. If some part of us experiences multiple dimensions with different timelines, then this exercise is honing those experiences to align them with that of your daily life. If there aren't various timelines, the exercise develops control by matching dreaming with daily life. The effect is similar, if not the same. Success is a matter of effort, experience, patience, and having the context and wherewithal to apply all of this.

To review, there are key areas of dreaming, with OBE being our target example. The first is entering a dream. This involves transitions for both entering and exiting. There is also the need for control and the corresponding ability to shift intent. And then there is a requirement to integrate experience in order to move to the next level. This means you accept natural conditions and then tune them to your cohesion for more understanding and utility, for more knowledge and ability.

There are additional levels beyond the fourth, each bringing the entire energy body further to life. These include having sufficient power behind OBE that other people can see your double as though you are at that location in your physical body. This is the prelude to teleportation, or intentionally moving your physical body to different geographic locations. This ability is the forerunner for the Fire from Within. I've addressed the double and teleportation in previous books and the Fire from Within briefly in this book to better examine topics like reincarnation. I'll wrap up this section because the theme of this book concerns abilities available to all humans no matter their paths, and the double and teleportation usher us into a much different arena.

Whatever you perceive is based on the interplay between cohesion and the environment, with uniformity being a determinant for the possibilities of arranging cohesion. Finding success in dreaming means that you've consolidated these energies within your energy body. Just as there are a variety of perspectives and skills in your daily world, the same applies to dreaming. The practices for consolidating a dreaming level are developing a new cohesion, learning to travel within it, and then hooking this into your daily life, thereby expanding your known world. The quest is to blend first and second fields, physical and dreaming energies. The environmental landscape opens dramatically as you do.

OUT-OF-BODY EXPERIENCE

Out-of-body experience is often defined as a lucid dream, intense imagery, a mental flight of consciousness, or some form of psychic phenomena. From a classical perspective, OBE is one form of an other-than-physical-body experience, and it has three common features. First, consciousness is exteriorized away from the physical body. Once experienced, there is no doubt that consciousness can exist outside the physical body. While having an OBE, for instance, you may view your physical body from your bedroom ceiling or from across a room.

Second, this nonphysical perspective has form of some kind. It might resemble your physical body where you experience arms, legs, shoulders, etc. Or it might take on another form such as an animal, a sphere of light, or a dot of awareness. If you choose, you may also replicate your physical senses. You can see, hear, smell, touch, and taste. Several years ago, I briefly taught OBE to elementary school students who were blind. They were highly motivated as they were sighted during dreaming.

Third, the form is animated and has emotions. The OBE is not dry in the sense of just being aware. It carries the capacity for different kinds of movement, feelings, and emotions. Since the dreaming body has form and emotions, you can interact with your surroundings as you would from within your physical body.

The similarities with the physical body, plus the enhanced capabilities of the dreaming body, make OBE a practical method to better understand perception. Replicating the physical senses serves as a bridge between physical and nonphysical perception, preventing the experience from becoming too removed from the ordinary. Enhancing your abilities during OBE, such as transcending ordinary time and space, speeds up learning by providing experiences from which to measure and comprehend multi-dimensional awareness.

Furthermore, you can experience a classic OBE without being asleep and entering dreaming. An experience may occur while awake. For instance, while in between jobs several years ago, I lived in Virginia.

As I lay awake on my bed one afternoon, I daydreamed about visiting New York City. I abruptly became aware of myself walking in a large city. I had been developing OBE capacities for years and wasn't surprised. Shifts of perception like this had become routine.

I looked around and saw a common landmark building. I knew where I was. When I returned my awareness to Virginia, I looked about my bedroom. Normal. Closing my eyes, I again became aware of walking through New York. I felt as though I had a physical body, even though my preferred method of travel during an OBE had become a sphere of energy. I enjoyed the walk. Two weeks later, I caught a train to New York City to visit friends. I had never toured the city, so they took me downtown—where I recognized the exact location I had earlier walked in nonphysical form.

Although sparse, there are scientific investigations relating to OBE. In one study, researchers found that 95 percent of cultures worldwide report OBEs, with an incidence ranging from 10 percent of the population to virtually all. Eighty-nine percent of those interviewed wanted another OBE while 78 percent found lasting benefit, and only two percent regarded the experience as being mentally harmful. Twenty percent of western (hemisphere) university students reported having had an OBE without having taken drugs. OBEs due to fever, accidents, and drugs were on the lower scale of correlations. Indicating the normalcy of OBEs, pervasive relaxation was the most prevalent element associated with having OBE.[6]

However, scientists often discount OBEs by relating them to temporal-lobe seizures or otherwise abnormal neural activity. One researcher claimed to produce OBEs by cortical stimulation, but the reported experiences didn't resemble OBEs.[7,8] Proponents of transphysical events such as OBE, NDE, and ME regard these studies as forcing data to comply with existing scientific models.

A shamanic or like-minded schematic offers more room to assess states of consciousness. Rather than consciousness arising from the complexity of an organism, it may be that the whole of the organism arises from consciousness. Scientific data can support the view that the nature of mind can be approached through mapping neurological activity. However, the basis for interpreting these studies is currently limited due to scientists confining their understanding to the effects of physiology and where awareness occurs from the physical body. Their interpretation ends up being akin to a self-fulfilling prophecy.

Referring to studies indicating OBE as a natural occurrence, I think profound relaxation enables OBEs because people manage to get sufficiently out of their own habits of perception to allow a very natural shift from physical to nonphysical perception. They loosen their grip on physical perceptions to such a degree that their nonphysical perception, the stuff from which dreams are made, surfaces with enough clarity to produce the OBE.

While dreams may precede OBE, this progression is not always evident. For example, often I just find myself outside of my physical body flying over treetops or playing in clouds. Just as often, though, I notice the onset of an OBE as I work my way through a dream.

I once became aware of dreaming when I felt unusually connected to the physical environment in the dream. It was as if gravity and temperature were stronger than normal. Recognizing the dream, I left my body as a sphere of medium blue light. I traveled to an indoor pistol range where my first thought was to enter an empty booth for some target practice. Remembering I was out-of-body, I hovered about the range watching others shoot.

With sudden calm, I scrutinized the situation, or rather knowledge about the situation broke like a wave within me. I knew that by nonpatterning, I had remembered my out-of-body state. Also, for the first time in a long while, I felt casual about being around firearms. Ever since Vietnam, I held a fascinated disdain for them. Now, I felt like the fever had broken and I was no longer tied to that fixation. The idea is that some kind of blockage became lodged in my cohesion. The dream released it.

Other OBEs also demonstrated how cohesion determines the content of an OBE. Ever since childhood, I wanted to visit the moon. The one academic study I took to as a boy was astronomy. I avoided history and mathematics, and, aside from astronomy books written for children, I typically read *Flash* and other science-fiction comics. Going to the moon appealed to me as a natural step to heading elsewhere. As an adult, I often tried to set up an OBE to go the moon by gathering mental and emotional energy to go there. I always got sidetracked, ending up almost anywhere but the moon. Patience prevailed.

Lying on my back on my living room floor, I was dreamily dozing when I abruptly entered an OBE. I had no sensations of leaving my physical body. I sort of bounced out of it without any indications other than knowing I was now out-of-body and in deep space. Upon recognizing this, I thought of the moon and immediately found myself there. As a rule, senses are heightened during OBE. Even so, the moon was breathtaking. The soft dirt shimmered as though it were magical dust. Light reflected off the smallest rock. The moon radiated abundant energy. I found it a unique form of life unto itself. The surprise of finally making it to the moon bounced me back into my physical body.

Failures in trying to get out-of-body can also produce results. Upon waking, you can feel why you didn't enter dreaming. In the instance of the moon, you can adjust to handling surprise or other things that end an OBE. With each failed attempt, you are conditioning yourself for success.

You might have extended dry spells between OBEs. This could be that you're caught up in your daily world and don't have the interest or energy for OBE. It could also be that you need time to find meaning and incorporate experience. Making fundamental shifts in consciousness, in cohesion, is a long, deliberate process.

Silver Cord

It has been common for people who reported experiences of astral projection to cite the *silver cord*, a strand of light linking the physical and nonphysical bodies. I've heard it said that if the cord breaks during an OBE, the person dies. While I've never witnessed it, based on my travels it seems that would be difficult to snap, if it has a limit at all. Relating to it in this way places physical limitations on nonphysical experiences.

Some regard the cord to be a connection with God.[9] Annie Besant, a notable nineteenth century theosophist, thought severance of the silver cord occurs at death.[10] It may be that the silver cord is *will* or a representation of it, something that would throw the topic into new realms. Reports of the cord in more recent accounts are scant, if not absent.

I tend to think that reports of the cord were valid, but the cord was psychologically manufactured to create a feeling of security that lessened the fright of leaving the body, as doing so can be associated with death. However, just as the growth of perception and knowledge enabled astronauts to spacewalk without needing a tether, advances in consciousness have led to a different experience of dreaming where the cord is no longer necessary. If this is true, creating the silver cord makes it no less real than creating a tether in the material world. It's the same process and effect. Skilled dreaming arises from cognitive technology and spacewalks from material technology. Both are steadily advancing. Whether the cord is perceived may reflect the nature or tonal of the times.

Dreaming with Others

As mentioned, don Juan says an option during dreaming is traveling within the dreams of others. There are no set procedures. Someone takes the lead, and the rest find themselves pulled into the same dream. It's all a matter of intent based on the agreements of dreaming. Several years ago, I exercised dreaming with others and found some success, though I no longer practice this skill.

After a conversation with Susan, a psychotherapist living in New England, we decided to see if I could influence her while she was in the dream laboratory at The Monroe Institute. We were previously co-participants during an in-residence program. She was back for another program, and I was hundreds of miles away. She said she would be in the sensory deprivation booth the following day.

Resting in a reclining chair in my living room at the prescribed time, I relaxed and centered my attention within the lab where I had spent many hours. My awareness shifted to a small, dark room, and I knew I was in the booth. I felt Susan's presence. Slightly straining my vision, I could see a vague outline of her on the waterbed. I merged with her energy and focused on helping her enter dreaming, preferably an

OBE. My perception then left the booth and hovered about six feet outside of it and roughly ten feet off the floor. I noticed a bundle of energy next to me. It felt like Susan. The energy moved like a plastic bag filled with water, as though it tried to maintain a spherical shape but couldn't. As it shifted, dense blue and white lights pulsed through the otherwise clear, soft white light.

She later told me that, early in the session, she perceived herself flanked by light beings. She also had a mental image of my physical body and felt as though I were present. She then felt as though she were floating; she said I held her, offering support for her journey.

Tom, another co-dreamer, was a psychologist who lived about 60 miles south of my home in Florida. We agreed that one part of my instruction consisted of physically visiting his home to provide normal instruction as preparation for OBE. The other part consisted of projecting my consciousness to him while I remained in my home. During this time, I was to energize his dreaming to bring about an OBE. Looking at this from another perspective, my task involved deliberately moving his assemblage point and causing him to be aware of his dreaming body.

Tom had an extensive background in metaphysics and had had an OBE years previously, so he didn't require much preliminary guidance. One night, I attempted to influence his awareness from a distance. Through the same technique of relaxing and focusing my dreaming on him, I soon felt a connection. I saw his feet and head. I also saw flashes of red, blue, and yellow light throughout him. I tugged at his dreaming body at the feet and later pried at the top of his head. I then went under his body and pushed up on his dreaming body. Not getting anywhere, I scanned his energy trying to diagnose the difficulty. I felt he lacked confidence that he could go out-of-body on his own. I had an image that he viewed himself as being locked within himself. Discussing the experience together the next day, he said he felt tremendous energy pouring into him and confirmed my feelings about his lack of confidence.

About two weeks later, even though he thought he had the flu, we scheduled a session. I didn't feel a good connection as I was tired. I tried to energize him. The next day, he said his flu symptoms lifted after the session and that I returned to him a few hours later.

Since I had no recollection of a return visit, I thought that either he tapped a memory of the earlier session or that this offered some evidence that we leave our bodies without being aware of it. Robert Monroe, for example, thought we have OBEs during periods of deep sleep. Dreams, he thought, are byproducts or discharges of energy as we try to make sense of our extravehicular experiences on the way back to waking consciousness.

Three days later, Tom and I scheduled another session. The experience was much like the first session. However, a couple hours later, Tom woke, thinking I had returned. He relaxed and tried to sense my instructions. He later said that this time I did something different. Instead of working on his head, feet, and back, I shifted his energy to the left and then to the right. As I manipulated his energy, his dreaming body slowly separated from his physical body. He said our dreaming bodies congratulated each other on his success. He then floated out of his bedroom into the living room. Excited, he returned to his physical body.

Comparing notes, I told him that I was sound asleep during his OBE, not having slept that deeply for almost a year. We conjectured that I had to remove my conscious mind to bypass my normal technique and use another method. The experience taught me to relax more and try to deal with the moment at hand without preconceptions. Since I was not consciously manipulating his energy at that time, the experience offered Tom support that he could go out-of-body on his own. It also offered convincing evidence that we do travel out-of-body during sleep without conscious awareness of doing so.

About six weeks later, we scheduled a session for when he would be on a jet airplane flying from Florida to Arizona. At the selected time, I located his emotional identity. We all have a certain feeling which separates us from others. By focusing on this aspect of a person's identity, you can send your nonphysical energy directly to them regardless of their physical location.

Within several minutes, I became aware of myself as an oblong energy floating in the coach section of an airliner. I immediately saw Tom. He sat on the right side of the fuselage and had three seats to himself. He looked in my direction as though he were aware of my presence. A dark-haired flight attendant passed me, and I turned to follow her into the first-class section. I returned to the coach section and looked around. Tom appeared busy, and I didn't approach him. Just before leaving, I felt the airplane start to jostle about. I had the thought that it must have entered a storm. I returned directly to my physical body and jotted down the experience.

A few days later, Tom said that even though the airplane was almost full, he had three seats to himself on the right side. He mentioned that he had perceived a mental image of me sometime during his flight but didn't pursue this further as he was busy having dinner. When I asked him about the bumpy ride, he said that at the time I mentioned, the plane was descending into Houston and had entered a storm. He said he didn't remember the color of the flight attendant's hair.

It is also possible for a group of people to simultaneously visit the same location. Years ago, I gave dreaming workshops. One of the exercises was having all participants go to their individual rooms and aim to become aware of the same location. Individual reports confirmed the exact locations of others in the group, characteristics of the target location, and the participants' purposeful control of their awareness.

Seeing in Dreaming

In addition to the uses of dreaming mentioned above, don Juan placed keen emphasis on learning to *see* while dreaming.[11] While dreaming, you're in a type of heightened consciousness: images might be clearer and more intense, sensations more revealing, intent more responsive, and consciousness more expansive. This reduces stress on your physical body and permits you to *see* more powerful emanations. Remember, *seeing* is aligning with energy, becoming aware of deeper recesses of the wavefield. Without the advantage of heightened awareness, merging with the farther reaches of the unknown may allow too much energy to come into the energy body, which might be unsettling rather than affirming.

You also don't have the ordinary forces of daily life constricting awareness into consensus interpretations. *Seeing* is outside of description. Interpretation stems from your cohesion, which forms from self-reflection. Dreaming helps you step away from these pressures, making it easier to *see*. The better you stabilize dreaming, the better your *seeing*. In turn, this helps make new inroads for dreaming.

It therefore helps to have a firm, though not concrete, sense of direction. You need flexibility and resilience. From a stable dream, you can use the same procedures used in daily life to see. At an elementary level, for instance, you can problem solve by *seeing* a resolution.

Projecting consciousness for *seeing* other locations or dimensions, for another example, doesn't rest on having any type of body but rather a point of reference. Developing dreaming provides this precision. In daily life, we're taught to rely on muscles for physical intents of moving about. In dreaming, the skill is employing intents within the world of energy. The focus is on wavefield dynamics and internal systems of the energy body. *Seeing* in dreaming is therefore a valuable investigational tool.

Don Juan says that it was from this inquiry that old cycle shamans realized that only the flow of energy that intersects with the assemblage point becomes coherent perception; that moving the assemblage point permitted new streams of energy to intersect (and so new perception); that during dreaming the assemblage point moves; that the assemblage point can be extended outside of the energy body; and that it is possible to intentionally control these shifts.[12]

Another purpose of dreaming is to incrementally awaken a natural field, which is aligned with new cycle teachings. At each level of dreaming, you have greater ability to manage cohesion by making more intricate alignments with the wavefield. This permits more enhanced *seeing*. In leapfrog manner, these cornerstones stretch the known order of cohesion through the energy body. Over time, you're aware of a natural order beyond social consensus. For the few who can place their sights beyond this, the stage is set for the Fire from Within when a person's complete energy body is placed in the third energy field.

Phasing

As a term, OBE is often immediately recognizable. The topic routinely appears in comics and in off-hand remarks, for example. However, a more accurate term to understand OBE and the energy body is *phase*. While I was working at The Monroe Institute, Robert Monroe told me he had changed his interpretation of OBE. Rather than viewing OBE as actually leaving the body, he thought it was a shift in the phase of consciousness. Awareness isn't projected. It is displaced, phased, or aligned with another area of the energy body.

Likewise, I've come to regard OBE as a change in cohesion, a shift of the assemblage point. And just like changing the phase of matter from solid to gas, this can be accounted for by a change of cohesional phase. In physics, density and phase of composition relate to coherence, to how well pieces work together, which has direct application to cohesional dynamics. In terms of the energy body, OBE is a shift of energy, a change of energetic phase, a change in the interactions between the first and second energy fields. You may perceive yourself as being away from your body, but it is still within the energy body. You don't go out; you go different.

The findings of science provide perspectives for phase. A classical physicist, as previously mentioned, takes the approach that energy results from the composition of physical matter. New wavefield investigators, on the other hand, hold a shamanic-type view that there are no material particles, that matter originates from energy—the wavefield—and only appears to be material. In other words, there isn't material form at all, and states or phases of matter are actually types of energetic coherence or composition (cohesion).

In addition, biological coherence is determined by an electrodynamic field.[13] Optimally, the phases among different rhythms of the body strive toward a unified relationship, or coherence. Proper resonance among the body's systems indicates homeodynamics, a coherent state to which the entire body returns after disruption.[14] Stepping back, this sounds like a scientist describing how the cohesion of a natural energy field behaves.

Along these lines, it is also interesting to note the research of Hans Jenny, a scientist and medical doctor. Jenny coined the term *cymatics* in describing the effects of sound. Using different sound patterns, he showed how various material substances would form intricate patterns based on the vibrations of sound.

Jenny considered vibration to be an essential characteristic of nature, where "pulsation, circulation, pattern formation, [and] changes in phase" were all bound by a single process of manifestation. Remove one element and the phenomenon of something coming into existence would cease.[15] The absence of one element disrupts coherence, intentionality of what is being manifest dissipates, and the overall effects disappear. Of interest is that don Juan considered sound to be the new cycle's gauge of the alignment of energies.[16]

Therefore, dreaming, going from one state of consciousness to another, involves a change of cohesional phase. The content of cohesion changes, as does perception. Control of dreaming, including OBE, is deliberately altering the phase of coherence—rearranging the elements of cohesion—to bring about different perceptions. The same principles apply to perception in general. Perhaps, then, the dynamics of dreaming and any form of perception or state of consciousness can be thought of as "energy body phasing" to gain awareness of what already exists.

7 | Out-of-Body Aerobics

As though you're on an expedition to foreign territory, you need to prepare for your out-of-body travels. Aside from getting your life together and having a general lay of the land, there are no firm steps for dreaming. It's a matter of enactment and learning. Much of the drama about dreaming in Castaneda's book was due to Castaneda's personality. That said, don Juan considered dreaming to be a serious affair. Shamans go beyond natural and relatively simple states of OBE as they enter the deepest jungles of awareness. For most of us, the initial levels of OBE are like having dessert, with the later stages requiring more rigorous training and implementation.

For preparation, imagine you're moving into a new house and need to set up everything so that it feels like home. You select furniture, rugs, kitchenware, etc. and arrange it all. Likewise, for dreaming you select a few targets, places you want to go, and goals you want to achieve. You visualize what it might be like from stories you've read or heard and form the feeling of the endeavor. Don Juan thought that it's best to streamline experiences to remove bizarreness, that vividness is a barrier to fully enter a dream, and that a simplified focus leads to success.[1]

Maintaining unbending intent toward dreamtime objectives is a very effective way to enter and maintain OBE on a sustained basis. It is a skill best used for expanding consciousness and developing a natural energy field where you have all your resources at your disposal.

Basic exercises will get you started and will carry you through the levels of dreaming. Then dreaming automatically provides lessons of life and liberty.

AIMING FOR OBE

You can talk and read about OBE, and that's all well and good, maybe necessary. But by stepping into this world, you begin to fully realize the difference between descriptions of reality and reality beyond those views. Facing a world that you've always been told doesn't exist is ripe with challenges.

Preparation

Preparation automatically eliminates some hurdles and eases you over others. Keep in mind that much of what you learn in dreaming occurs on the spot. So don't lock yourself into a standard set of procedures. This is why it's best to acquaint yourself with a variety of perspectives. In addition, knowing why you want to dream focuses energies on specific results, minimizes stray influences, and grooms intent. Part of preparation is knowing what you're getting into.

At some point, you need to convince yourself that OBE is real. At the same time, you can nonpattern this by not buying into anything about it and just enjoying the process. Since dreaming produces natural shifts of cohesion, you need sobriety, and this comes from the balanced management of daily life (next chapters). This automatically leads to stronger dreaming and is, therefore, a principal means of preparation.

Dreaming itself teaches you how to adjust your life. For instance, people often tell me that a big difficulty is their hesitancy to enter dreaming in the first place. It seems they've always been told that the bogeyman lives there, so they'd just as soon not make the trip. When dealing with reluctance myself, I dreamed of a group of black panthers. Surprisingly, as soon as I saw them, I felt a strong affinity. I recognized their stealth as quality tracking, and associated their spirit with dreaming energy in general. I had the thought that although a panther may not be considered king of the jungle, it certainly was a sleek and powerful prince. Then, in a vision within the dream, I *saw* a panther saunter up to me. I scratched its ears. Then it curled up like a kitten into my heart. I felt rejuvenated, and my reluctance to try for a new dreaming level dissipated.

While this helped me out of an OBE slump, part of the problem remained. I still had a lingering malaise. But while resting in the blackness of level one, I intuitively realized I had to back off any preconceived notions of how I wanted dreaming to develop. I also knew I had to dive into it with an attitude combining experimentation and entertainment. These realizations placed me squarely back on the dreaming path.

You also need to prepare yourself for possible adventures in other dimensions. For this, you need to strike a balance. On one hand, entering other dimensions is highly instructional. You learn that other worlds are not imagination and that they exist independently of this world. On the other hand, it's easy to become wonderstruck and wander off the path. It may be best to not seek worlds outside of this one, but rather find your source of power in learning more of this world.

A general approach to preparation is to gain several perspectives about OBE and have a solid purpose for why you want to enter dreaming. Feel relaxed and capable. Find your own natural sense of self and timing, your pace as you go through the day. Don't lock yourself into one way of being, one identity. Deliberately select items of an inventory that develop dreaming cohesion.

Transitions

Dreams are often difficult to regulate and stabilize. Transitions into and within dreaming are even more problematic as they're highly dynamic where anything can occur. Yet they have definable characteristics that can help you recognize them, just like seasonal transitions of weather. Getting a handle on transitions helps learn the nuances of dreaming.

Transitions often reveal what you need to work on and what you're doing well. They speak to the entire workings of the energy body, how well the parts of your life cohere, and, therefore, the formation and use of cohesion. Dreaming provides direct experience of these mechanics.

For me, a troublesome aspect of learning dreaming was the transition from one state of consciousness to another. Years ago, the difficulty expressed itself as shark attacks. Practically every time I entered dreaming, I was attacked by a shark. By giving my emotions more free rein, the attacks diminished and eventually disappeared. The difficulty then became getting past an immense surge of energy when going into dreaming or when going from one dreaming level to the next.

This surge of energy also indicates a period when almost anything can happen. During a transition, you're in a high-energy, high-potential zone. It's as though the assemblage point is in a free-fall state. You're still in the influence of level two—lucid dreaming where the landscape randomly shifts. Until the dream stabilizes, you're susceptible to almost any influence. The slightest fluctuation of your mind, as well as any long-standing concern, can define the content of the dream. Managing a dream is like catching a wave when surfing. With practice, you learn to control your movement in and about the wave. Until you learn dreaming at this level, the wave is most likely to get the best of you and tumble you about.

With my shark attacks, for instance, I would find myself swimming in the ocean which is something I enjoy tremendously. I would notice a dorsal fin off in the distance. Rather than interpret it as a dolphin, I defined it as a shark. The experience unfolded as adrenaline kicked in, and ostensibly the shark would sense it and head toward me. This produced more adrenaline to which the shark vigorously responded. An attack ended the dream. I later realized the shark represented my emotions. And they were coming to get me, ready or not. The attacks abated as I learned how to surf transitions.

Dreaming contains a rich complexity of cohesion in which many influences are at play. When a shift begins you feel movement, anything from floating sensations to high-speed travel. Cultivate those feelings. Breathe easy and stay relaxed. You want the transition. Otherwise, you won't enter dreaming. Have a clear purpose so you can hook onto a dream. If you slip off track, try again. Then let yourself go. A common tendency is to check yourself and pull back. Often this is due to the unusualness of dreaming. If you pull back, you're likely to pull out of dreaming.

I've also noticed that prior to an OBE, I feel as though I have condensed energy inside my body. It's as though there is a warm block of ice inside my chest. Invariably, when I feel this type of energy, dreaming ensues. A friend of mine says she knows she will dream when she feels a line of pulsating energy extending from the front of her pubic area to one inch above her navel. She says that while this brings about associations with sexual energy, the pulsating energy is not sexual.

Don Juan advises that transitions are brought about by holding an image of where you want to go and turning off your internal dialogue.[2] You might then float away from your physical body in any direction. It doesn't matter providing you make the complete transition because that's the goal, not because there's necessarily any meaning associated with how you move out. You may not even notice a transition. You simply find yourself dreaming. If so, you did nothing wrong. However, being able to handle all the stages of dreaming, including transitions, might assist your overall practice. But again, you don't need to conform to procedure. The steps for everyone may be much the same, but the experiences are individual.

To regulate your speed, you need practice. One person told me he enjoyed OBE just because he liked the rush of energy during the transition and didn't give much thought to where he'd end up. Although I admired his rebelliousness, his approach is a little too disorienting for me, as I prefer to have a handle on why I'm entering dreaming and what I want to accomplish, even if the purpose is just to see what will happen. The main idea is to use OBE productively, to learn and grow as a person.

After a dry spell where I had no OBEs, everything simplified when I remembered that dreaming is an energy-producing endeavor. And maximum energy is needed to release completely into dreaming. Immediately upon making this connection while I was meditating, I felt suspended about one foot above my physical body, although looking down from my dreaming body it seemed my physical body was 20 feet away. I floated around the room and gently ended the event. The idea is that just having a few pieces of dreaming intent fall into place produced the shift.

In addition, before a dream stabilizes, you might perceive the dream waver as though it were undulating. It may also seem as though you are spinning. To counter this, don't focus on anything within the dream. But do focus on the dream itself, a wide-angle approach. As your cohesion shifts, your perception may not be stable until you master the transition. Commitment to dreaming not only produces it but also smooths out the transition.

Vibrations are also common during a transition. And they, too, might prove unsettling. For instance, one woman told me she thought her vibrations meant she was critically ill. After her physician told her she was fine, and after reading about vibrations associated with dreaming, she relaxed and turned her attention to the positive aspects of dreaming. In my dreaming, I recognized vibrations as something that often signals the onset of an OBE. For instance, during a dream, I saw a tornado. As it came toward me, I started shaking from its force. This transferred to vibrations associated with exiting the physical body. I then realized I was heading from a dream to an OBE. About a half-foot out, I started thinking about the tornado since I'd dreamed of them before. I thought that this was the real Wizard of Oz, and because I started laughing, I re-entered my body.

In another instance, while lounging around my house one afternoon, I heard a sound resembling a freight train. The noise increased, and it seemed like an invisible train hurtled through the living room. A vibration along my spine began and I gained control of it by moving it up and down then evenly distributing it through my body. I began to lift out. About six inches out, I stumbled upon discovering this new aspect of OBE. My self-reflection had interrupted the event. I returned to my body elated at not getting spooked and partially capitalizing on the sound and vibrations but deflated at losing my nonattachment and succumbing to the experience.

The content of a dream might also throw you off the mark. For example, during a dream, I found myself in a room that had a snake in a terrarium. It looked about three feet long. It was brown with dark brown markings. I checked to see if it had a triangular-shaped head which might indicate it was a poisonous pit viper, but it kept moving, so I couldn't confirm anything.

All at once, it was out of its container. I tried to remain calm. I then felt vibrations in my physical body. I realized I was dreaming, but the intensity of being with the snake prevented the complete transition. In a flash, the snake's body connected itself to the base of my spine and to the ground. I felt a powerful infusion of energy winding its way up through my body. I began to vibrate again but woke up wondering where the snake was.

You may also discover that the general novelty of dreaming is an obstacle. Dealing with sharks, snakes, vibrations, romantic interests, and whatever else comes up may surprise you back into your physical body. Plus, like the woman associating vibrations with illness, other occurrences may conjure equally distasteful illusions. For instance, while dreaming, your body may feel catatonic, or rigid. Several people have told me of their horror at finding they could not move their physical bodies shortly before or immediately upon returning from dreaming. It seems that this is common within the scope of OBE and is temporary. For another example, you might wake up feeling groggy or out of sorts. In most cases, this indicates you're processing experiences, perhaps your relation to life or dreaming, but the malaise soon passes.

Learning how to handle intent gets you over this hurdle as well. For example, one morning I woke up and realized my physical body was catatonic. I also had a split awareness of being in my dreaming body. From research, I knew it was okay for my body to be immobile. So I relaxed and enjoyed sensing the acute separation between the two bodies. Taking my time, I gently and slowly intended my awareness to refocus from within my physical body. In short order, I wiggled my toes and stretched my limbs.

As you work with dreaming, remember you're dealing with perception, not with hard-and-fast rules. Most borders and barriers are of your own making. Castaneda kept failing with *seeing*, for instance, because he couldn't get past his own thoughts. I had difficulty with dreaming because I wouldn't own up to my emotions. In getting over these types of hurdles, people tend to be amazed at how deeply imprinted are thoughts and emotions which they have long since failed to recognize.

Transitions in daily life mirror dreaming transitions. When substantially changing your perspective, especially a worldview, you might feel buffeted, a little disoriented, and out of control. Employing attributes of consciousness—focusing your attention on what's in front of you, being aware you are in a transition, and intending to stabilize new perspectives—helps with this just as it does in dreaming.

Emotional Intelligence

For OBE, EQ relates to applying the cornerstone of feeling. Robert Monroe began his OBE adventures after daydreaming about flying his glider. He loved the skies and the sense of flying. That connection precipitated his first OBE.[3] You could also easily imagine yourself on a sailboat with full sails and feel yourself gliding through the water. The sense of joyful movement can serve as a trigger to bring about OBE.

In daily life, attention is primarily given to social considerations: relationships of all kinds, corporate culture, how cities are built, and means of transportation are a few. In dreaming, your relationship with the environment is more potent and personal. EQ lets you sense your body, flow with transitions, and connect more deeply with a dream. One of the best ways to develop EQ is through what you do in your daily life. Deliberateness in your actions throughout the day promotes EQ, and EQ helps form deliberateness. From this comes a sense of security and capability. EQ then carries over into dreaming, allowing you to better control the pace and content.

Separation

After you enter an OBE, it will seem as though you took your physical senses with you, and they will most likely operate from a heightened perspective. Colors will appear deeper. Shapes will look clearer, sharper. Feelings will intensify. Sounds might seem magnified. It is possible to duplicate any of the five physical senses, although developing taste and smell may, in general, require more effort, while vision is usually the first to develop.

There will be times when your vision embraces a 360-degree panorama rather than straight-ahead, stereoscopic vision. Traveling as a sphere of energy readily lends itself to maintaining this perspective. In the beginning, however, your vision might appear foggy, and you may not have any of your other physical senses. With time and practice, difficulties clear.

Even though you perceive while out-of-body as though using physical senses, other physical requirements such as breathing don't matter. You may stay under water or in deep space for as long as you wish. Eating while in the dreaming body is irrelevant as well. You may also travel through physical objects such as walls and mountains. The rules of the road, the intents, are not the same as what you've grown accustomed to.

Partial Projections

It's common to experience a partial projection where you see or feel a non-physical arm or leg rise out of your physical body. This might seem dramatic, perhaps alarming. You may sense most of your awareness resides outside of your physical body, but you still feel partially connected with it.

Partial projections are more common during the early days of trying to have your first OBE. Later, they may occur because you need to resolve something in your daily life, so you can't completely let go. They may also occur because you are learning something new. They can be managed by paying attention and focusing on distinctly perceiving the physical or dream world.

Control

During an OBE, you now have at your disposal different states of awareness. You might hover about your room, fly around Earth, or go to other planets or dimensions. If you don't like a particular situation, it is up to you to travel away from the environment, not try to change your external landscape. You need to avoid using your personal power for manipulating your world.

Changing the landscape by movement is a key distinction between lucid dreaming and OBE and is accomplished by aligning thinking with feeling or, more precisely, with your intent. Merging your thoughts and feelings, something you have already learned by this time, creates a foundation for maneuvering intent. This provides the energy to travel. You may travel to any destination within the blink of an eye, or poke around. Often, as soon as you think about a place, you may instantly find yourself there.

You may also run into forces which are more powerful than you. Knowing that they exist and dealing with them in a manner like you would in physical experience makes them non-threatening. For example, people periodically drown in the southwest deserts as they attempt to cross a wash (a dry riverbed) in four-wheel vehicles. During flood seasons, washes may suddenly come to life as water thunders through them. Underestimating the force of the short-lived river may result in death as the vehicle meets a stronger force and is swept away. If you're aware of the season, of washes, and of difficulties associated with both, you can easily avoid this danger.

This analogy of OBE with physical experience stops short, however. If you encounter a situation where you feel overwhelmed, you always have the option to quickly leave or return to your physical body. Allow your experience to unfold without fear or concern. In such a circumstance, it might prove beneficial to adopt the attitude that you are participating in an educational or entertaining movie, or perhaps something in as ordinary as stepping into your backyard.

Landscapes

By now, I'm sure you've got the notion of the variety of dreaming states. Experience follows from the seeds you sow. If you organize your life in a certain direction for specific outcomes, related experiences follow. This applies to OBE as well. Keep in mind that off-hand or unexpected events may still occur. Any new event might happen only once, or it could signal the beginning of a new area you'd like to explore.

Preparation should include consideration of after-transition experiences in which you end up in an alternate reality. It might be normal but from different perspective, similar with differences, or totally different. Just as there are different countries, states, cities, and neighborhoods, there exist different dreaming landscapes. You might find yourself on another planet and learn about extraterrestrials. A visit to a neighboring state of consciousness might take you to a dreamtime Silicon Valley, where you discover how to design an electronic device. Or you might find yourself in a nonphysical equivalent of a church where you meet guides and helpers who offer insights on life or dreaming.

Returning

The return transition consists of refocusing on your physical body. Usually, just by thinking about returning or wanting to return, you will. Chances are you will return from an OBE before you want to.

I've heard people express fear of having a "false awakening," where they can't get back into their body because they've entered another dream but think they've returned to their body. I think viewing this as a false awakening is a matter of projection, and the intensity behind it produces a negative experience. From a shamanic schematic, learning to dream within a dream is an exercise to take dreaming to another level. If a person is not aware of this, unexpected experiences might be frightening. In addition, sometimes bad dreams are necessary to shake you from your slumber, to make you take a hard look at yourself.

Protection

Another concern of those interested in OBE is that an entity will try to inhabit the physical body after the dreaming body leaves it, or that a malevolent entity will attack the dreaming body. Perhaps the most common method of protection for both the physical and nonphysical bodies is to surround them in white light prior to entering the out-of-body state. Assigning a given meaning to white light establishes an intent that shapes cohesion to filter or block specific types of information or influence. Along with immersion in this light, many people use an affirmation such as, "I am in no danger, and I will not encounter any harmful experiences." At the least, these procedures help a person relax and feel more confident. As additional reference, white light is also associated with a chakra at the top of the energy body from which the rainbow colors matching the lower chakras flow.

This type of affirmation also serves as a means to condition or prime cohesion for positive experiences. It produces an intent that alters cohesion and changes experience. You're not going out of your body, you're phasing cohesion. Therefore, if your cohesion is coherent—well organized and flexible—it is automatically disposed to a beneficial OBE.

I've had to use this method of encasing myself in an energy field of white light only two or three times over years of OBEs, and even then only as a preventative measure when I became unsure of my whereabouts. I have found, however, that an excellent means of protection results from how I live my life. The more balance in my daily life, the less I worry about harmful experiences. The more you walk in light, the less darkness you have. You're in light and so don't have to create it.

If your intent is aimed at wholesome, productive OBEs, experience tends to follow. This is another reason for knowing why you want OBEs. The more you refine and purposefully direct your energies, the more you align yourself with constructive experiences. However, don't ignore less desirable feelings. Refusing to acknowledge exactly how you feel, even though it may be considered as negative, almost ensures that you will encounter those issues during an OBE at some time. Once you shake off the cobwebs of cohesion, your dreaming experiences align more accurately with your nature. You experience more of yourself.

OBE TECHNIQUES

Exercises can be effective but are limited. They are simulations. They help give a sense of what's involved, so you recognize them as part of OBE. They also help establish expectation and condition cohesion for the purpose of OBE. There comes a time, though, when you need to grow beyond technique into the intent represented by the technique. You need to get beyond a description and into the heart of the matter. Hold firmly to the goal of leaving exercises behind, and let that shape your awareness. Time, practice, and paying attention to what happens along the way is an avenue to success. You need to go beyond a driver's manual to actually driving.

There are two main approaches or styles. A forced method occurs when a teacher leans hard on a student, applies pressure to shift awareness, and excessively dominates. This brings results, but it does so at the cost of balance and harmony with purpose. Another forced way is by using psychedelics. By applying pressure to cohesion, drugs can give a bona fide experience but distort cohesion and take a toll on the body. I had an extended OBE after ingesting peyote, but I also felt an intense dread that I should never do so again. Another method relies more on a full-system approach based on understanding, gradual learning, and moderate implementation of dreaming procedures. It involves a light touch. Don Juan emphasized this approach, as the lessons better integrate throughout cohesion and take root. Although, due to the abruptness and power behind his efforts, his light touch didn't always seem very light.

With the following exercises, you'll approach OBE from several perspectives: while awake, during the state between wakefulness and sleep, after having a dream, and while pulling yourself into a dream. They also acquaint you with how to respond to unexpected situations. First, though, is a process related to transitioning to and from dreaming. Try repeating it after you've done the other exercises. Also keep in mind that by paying attention as you progress, you'll develop your own exercises to engage dreaming.

Transition
1. Determine a destination and two intermediate stops along the way. The two pit-stops and the destination should be places you enjoy visiting.
2. Center your energy within your physical body.
3. Send that energy directly to the destination, bypassing the intermediate stops.
4. Return to your physical body.
5. Go to the destination again, this time stopping briefly at each intermediate stop.

6. Return.
7. Head toward your destination, stopping at each intermediate place. This time, however, do not travel to the destination from the second pit-stop. Change direction and go to the first place that pops into your mind.
8. While in a meditative state, ask yourself why you traveled to the new destination.
9. Return to your physical body.

This next series of exercises is based on Robert Monroe techniques. He popularized them in his book, *Journeys Out of the Body*, and they are incorporated in TMI's programs.

Log Roll

1. Find a comfortable place to lie on your back.
2. Inside and down the length of your body, perceive a log of energy slowly rotating as though it were spinning along the axis of your spine. If you require assistance feeling this rolling energy, imagine the swirling hurricane symbol that television weather forecasters use. Place the eye of the hurricane in the middle of your physical body. Let the clouds extend through your skin and a few feet away from your body. Imagine the formation rotating, following the direction of the swirling clouds. Use that imagery to apply friction to the log of energy to get it rolling. This exercise assists in heightening your sense of nonphysical energy.
3. When you feel the log rolling, gently stop it.
4. Lift or project the log straight out of your body as though you were levitating from a lower to an upper bunk bed. Allow it to float about 4 to 5 feet above your physical body.
5. Reverse your intent and allow it to lower and return within you. This is a good time to learn how to regulate the return of your nonphysical energy into your physical body. As you return, tell yourself you want a smooth, gentle transition where all your energies are aligned and in harmony.

6. To add a little zest to this exercise, intend the nonphysical energy to pivot so that instead of hovering parallel to your body, it floats perpendicular to your body. Moving it about the room or playing in other ways exercises concentration and control.

That Sinking Feeling
1. Repeat steps 1 through 3 in Log Roll.
2. Just as you levitated up, slowly sink down through your resting area then through the floor.
3. Return.
4. A variation of the sinking method involves partially sinking and then meeting that energy with an equal and opposite force. As you begin to sink, imagine another force that comes from below you, and send it upward toward the sinking energy. Use the upward force to exert pressure on the sinking force so that both energies rest motionless in a state of equilibrium. When the pressure in between the two forces feels even, reverse the intent of the sinking force, and lift out, using the momentum of the lower, upward force to assist you.

The following exercises take a different approach to OBE. I learned them while scouting OBE. They provide additional practice in perceiving distinctions (sensations) between physical and nonphysical energies.

Straight Shooter
1. Repeat steps 1 through 3 in Log Roll.
2. Now, rather than lift, imagine that the energy log is hinged at your ankles. Then lift out so the energy log stands straight up at a 90-degree angle to your physical body. This is like stepping on the teeth of a rake, and the rake handle jumps up at you.
3. Reverse your intent and return within your body. Exit your body, again standing upright.
4. While your nonphysical body is standing up, just for the fun of it, do a back flip.

Bundle of Love
1. Collect or bundle energy inside your physical body akin to creating the energy log. You might even think of it as stuffing a sack full of potatoes.
2. Allow this energy to exit the top of your head as though it were vapor, gas, or fog.
3. Collect or bundle it again outside of your body.
4. Travel away from your physical body.
5. Pull it back into your physical body.

Vibing
During these exercises, or a real OBE, you may feel vibrations. It may seem as though you have waves of energy coursing through your body or your entire body is shaking, while to an observer, there is no movement whatsoever. Sounds may accompany these vibrations. It may even sound as though a freight train is rumbling through your room or ocean surf is crashing about you. Maintain your concentration. Learning to control these vibrations facilitates OBE. The vibrations and sounds will ease and abate when you have fully entered an OBE.

Merge Right
1. Find a comfortable place to lie down or sit.
2. Stimulate your physical senses. Feel your chair or bed, notice the texture of your clothes. Listen to the air conditioner or heater, the traffic, the clock ticking. Smell dinner in the oven, the remnant of hair spray, the flowers nearby. Feel comfortable in your physical body.
3. Close your eyes and gently look toward the middle of your forehead. You are now shifting from physical to nonphysical energy.
4. Relax attention to your physical senses, and pay attention to nonphysical sensations of color, images, intuition. Travel with any sounds.
5. If pressure in your head or elsewhere in your body suggests looking in another direction, do so. Dialogue with the pressure and find out why it is there. Release the pressure and return your vision to the middle of your forehead.

6. If any image appears, stay with it through relaxed concentration. If you try too hard, the image will disappear. If you don't try hard enough, the image will disappear. Don't immediately project toward it. You might interfere with an actual projection or a preferred destination. Relaxed concentration is the key.
7. Look for a sequence of images where you perceive a field of color, then a static image like a photograph, and then a fluid, streaming image like a motion picture. You may not experience this progression, however. You may start off perceiving a fluid image or not get past the field of color. The goal is to get to the fluid image (level two dreaming), so if you start there, you're that much better off. If you can only perceive color, practice longer and more often. Don't censor or edit the images. Perceive them however they appear to you.
8. You may feel pushing or pulling within your physical body as though something inside you wants to merge with the streaming image. You will probably notice that these moving images have a deeper feel to them or are more vivid than most mental images. Now the trick is to exercise patience. Wait until you sense sufficient energy enabling you to completely merge with the image.
9. Merging with the fluid image so that you perceive the environment from the perspective of being in the image, rather than from your physical body, indicates you're en route to an OBE.

The Force Is with You
1. Repeat steps 1 through 5 in Merge Right.
2. Rather than a sequence of colors and images, you may perceive a speck of white light or an eyeball.
3. Allow the light or eye to enlarge.
4. You may then feel as though a force from within the light or eye is pulling you to it. Gently hold back until you feel the tension becoming stronger.
5. Allow yourself to be pulled into and through them.

Let's Get Lucid

A classic maneuver of entering dreaming made popular by Castaneda involves finding your hands in a dream. Anything in a dream will do, says don Juan, but hands are always available.[4,5] Hooking onto an external element within the dream is difficult since they easily change. Your hands are a personal, inside-the-dream connection. As lucid dreams randomly shift, your hands establish a stable reference to maintain continuity, which then allows you to step completely into a dream.

It is also a natural approach to OBE because it works from within dreaming. It is a technique to bring about a lucid dream and from there cultivate OBE. The basis of it is learning to remain awake while you fall asleep.

1. Throughout the day periodically look at your hands, front and back. Stop your internal dialogue to produce a clear image of them. Stopping your dialogue while imagining something acts as a command, an intent to produce a goal; in this case, finding your hands.
2. Before sleep, command yourself through thoughts and imagery to find your hands during a dream. Tell yourself you want to find your hands, and why. Imagine lifting your hands to eye level. If you have the alertness to find your hands during a dream, you know you're dreaming.
3. As you fall asleep, be sensitive to changing levels. You might bypass the exercise and go directly through lucid dreaming to an OBE.
4. When you find your hands, remember why you did so. A few times, I found my hands and, since I didn't remember why, nothing happened.
5. If you wake up, tell yourself that you will return to dreaming; better yet, feel that you will.
6. Break patterns of falling asleep. Rolling over on your side might signal that you're ready for sleep. Remaining on your back can send another message.
7. Stabilize the dream. Remember, the difference between a lucid dream and OBE is that the environment is stable. Lucid dreams shift from dream to dream, from scene to scene. Scenes in an OBE

don't shift unless your dreaming body moves to another location. Stabilize the dream by picking three or four objects in the dream and holding them in your awareness without them shifting or dissolving. If the objects begin to change, return your attention to your hands until you feel the energy has stabilized or evened out. Look back at the objects. When the objects no longer shift, you have entered an out-of-body state.
8. To refine your control, practice traveling to other locations. Fly around your neighborhood. Zoom off to England or Asia. Discover the magic of the moon. Allow your internal guidance to direct you.
9. To refine your control even more, learn to correspond the time of day or night where your physical body is with the time where your dreaming body is. Locate both bodies in the same time zone. This step is an exercise for enhanced control, not something you must do to have OBEs.

Finding your hands places a charge of energy within the dream and provides a link to transfer into it, so the novelty can be disconcerting. It is easy to fixate on something in a dream and lose track of the wider picture. The fixation can be simply distracting or more complex. For instance, I once noticed my hand with a ring. I started to focus on the hand but was thrown off the mark when the ring turned into a grotesque tumor and began to grow. When I recognized this as a machination of mind, the tumor disappeared. Yet it was too late to enter the dream because I'd lost that thread.

Castaneda said he found success after he gained control of his life.[6] My sense of this is that a person develops the capacity to manage their life based on having a path forward and a positive relation to life. The person has a sense of him or herself which is delivered by their link to EQ. The person knows where he or she fits in and what and where to avoid. This stance in life permits better dreaming. Being inaccessible to whims and distractions of others is the art of the mix.

The 3 E's

As a result of my experiences with don Juan, TMI, talking with people who have had OBEs, and my own explorations, I developed a three-step process for inducing, or bringing about, OBEs. This "3E" method focuses on expectation (opening perception), excitation (balancing perception), and exploration (focusing perception). Most of the exercises in this approach involve preparation. Expectation, for example, concerns opening and clearing awareness so that OBE can be considered an attainable goal. During this stage, you begin sensing the movement of energy.

Excitation involves taking raw energy, shaping it, and balancing with it. Whereas expectation generates new awareness, excitation starts refining that energy. You mold your energy with the objective of harmonizing your activities in daily life with those of dreaming. You blend your actions with your goals, which balances mental, emotional, and physical energies, which, in turn, provides greater energy and direction for your goals.

The exploration stage involves simulating actual OBEs, or deliberately focusing energy toward having OBEs. As you work with various techniques to develop out-of-body awareness, you gradually develop the intent of OBE. This is the focus of energy that produces OBE.

You will find that the 3E method also provides an approach to increase out-of-body abilities. The expectation stage now reflects your openness to enhancing OBE. The excitation stage requires further balancing of mental, emotional, and physical energies. You begin building and harmonizing this energy as your experiences allow you to familiarize yourself with different landscapes of awareness, which then allows you to formulate how you want to use OBE. During the exploration stage, you develop control of OBE as you realize your goals. You travel to precise locations or perceive written material (books, lyrics, business proposals) that you can put to paper after you return to your physical body.

Blending Techniques

You might not bring about an OBE from the methods presented here. Use techniques as guidelines, not as hard and fast rules. Keep yourself open to new ways and shortcuts. If you bypass the color and static image portions of an exercise and get right to the fluid image part, good for you. Don't hold yourself back just because you read or heard it was supposed to happen a certain way. Once, for example, while practicing the exercise of levitating straight up, just for the heck of it I pivoted 90 degrees while hovering in mid-air. Suddenly, without my intending it to, the energy came back down and went inside my abdomen, where it formed into a sphere of energy and then floated out of my body.

You may also find yourself in the middle of a dream, abruptly wake up, and then enter a transition. In addition, you may purposefully blend different techniques. For instance, the deep meditative experience of the in-between exercises offers a superb situation to condition yourself to find your hands during a dream. As a rule, find or create techniques that work for you. Tailor your entire life to fit you well.

OBE Intent

Through empowering yourself, what you're trying to achieve is the ability to transcend technique to arrive at the actual experience. To do this, you will develop OBE intent, a compact feeling which acts as a vehicle or tunnel that begins or causes OBE.

OBE intent, when awake, feels centered inside my physical body. This energy is then projected outward. When in between waking and sleeping, the intent feels like I'm connecting with something outside of my body. It feels like I am pulled by it, or else I am reaching out and grasping it to pull myself out.

As you align your energy through clearly thinking about your goals, refining your desires and emotions about them, and behaving in ways that support their realization, you consolidate energy. Feelings coagulate into compact energy. Shaping and then focusing this energy delivers you to the experience. The more exacting and purposeful your quest, the more power or intensity you place behind your intent. Once you consolidate your intent, dispense with the exercises. OBE then becomes another technique of expanding consciousness, a more refined and powerful technique than those used to develop it.

TOP 40 OBE TIPS

The following rapid-fire suggestions may prove beneficial for OBE. They are in no order of importance.

1. Cultivate EQ for a steady cohesion to allow easier, more controllable transitions.
2. Participate in daily life as though it were a dream.
3. Staying centered within the physical body offers one of the most powerful exercises for OBE. Don't wander off. Pay attention to physical movement. Feel what it is telling you.
4. Be open to new experiences.
5. Be nonchalant to keep loose and open, but not arrogant.
6. Don't tie yourself to the results of your actions. Use nonattachment to do what you want without worrying whether you'll succeed.
7. Build thoughts toward OBE from inner relaxation, not from an outer hardness of thinking "I must do this."
8. Take care of your worries prior to sleep. At least come to some kind of agreement with yourself that enables you to relax.
9. Don't force OBE, or anything else for that matter.
10. Let yourself go without letting go of yourself.
11. Stay active, keep fit.
12. Draw, sketch, or otherwise loosen your imagination.
13. Aim for the meaningful, the purposeful.
14. Try to stay light-hearted.
15. Listen to the sounds of the world. Doing so opens doors of new awareness.
16. Speak freely, but wisely. This gives a sense of regulating the flow of information while being in your body and thoughtful.
17. Remember the clash of symbols. Not getting caught up in views of reality helps to remain inaccessible to worldly concerns. This doesn't mean to block yourself off from the world. It suggests that you don't become ensnared in worldly matters.
18. Try to stay calm.
19. Confront your fears and put them to rest.

20. Know what you want; do it.
21. Don't hurry, have patience.
22. Strive to concentrate on the here and now, and on the flow of your life.
23. Humility and efficiency will provide strength in developing OBE, as well as in the explorations this ability enables.
24. Meditate often.
25. Think that OBE is possible.
26. Without becoming obsessed, stay focused on the goal of having OBEs.
27. Try not to be a petty tyrant.
28. Be kind to and tolerant of all life, including yourself. And learn to do so while standing your ground.
29. Visualize yourself from the point of view of your dreaming body.
30. Relax and cultivate feelings of floating.
31. Mentally project yourself to a target destination. See if you can perceive what is going on there.
32. Feel like you're a rocket taking off or a plane flying to simulate a sense of lift-off or skimming over the water. The feeling of movement is the important element.
33. Upon waking, you're sensitive to cohesional dynamics, so take a few minutes to reflect on your dreams or any situation in daily life that comes into awareness.
34. Allow your feelings to roam wherever they want while trying to keep them centered in your physical body.
35. Keep your travels and experiences simple and practical. Avoid extravagance as that takes energy away from learning the next level.
36. While OBE is a serious endeavor, look to have fun. Approach it as a sport or form of entertainment.
37. Have a purpose for dreaming that is aligned with daily life.
38. Try not to feel so committed to the goal that you become uptight or inflexible.
39. From time to time, suspend what you know and believe.
40. Be patient. Just as a child learns, you need sensation prior to recognition, and recognition prior to control.

* * *

As mentioned, your relation to your daily life and physical body are key determinants in OBE. Toward that end, the following chapters focus on these topics with an eye toward OBE. As part of this, they include ingredients for the understanding and expansion of consciousness.

8 } In-the-Body Experience

Travels through daily life are, for good and ill, where it all comes together. You're looking to make things happen, to manifest circumstances from the portions to the whole of your life. The processes are no different than learning OBE. If cohesion defines all aspects of your behavior, then energy body exercises apply to how you go about your day and how you create what you bring into the world. It's a matter of attention, awareness, and intent—the ingredients of consciousness.

Life is traveling the omni-present currents of the wavefield, including the currents of job, family, friends, etc. With the swirling streams of many influences throughout the day, we tend to squeeze out dreaming energies. Yet daily life can be preparation for OBE. As it did for Castaneda, gaining a felt-sense steadiness of your life leads to dreaming proficiency.

Our daily world is much like a dream only on a slower schedule, time seems thicker. Dreaming can have the same practical effects and value as daily life, and daily life affects dreaming. The stepwise merging of daily and dream experiences results in an expansion of cohesion that accelerates development of the energy body.

Consensus reality dominates daily life. It is a dream on a large scale of agreement. Groups have power, especially if the energy among participants harmonizes. The more a group is in alignment with each person and a common goal, the greater the amount and focus of energy toward the goal. EQ as a type of alignment pertains to how the individual relates to other individuals and to the group. A cohesive group has its own sense, its own EQ.

The foundation of consciousness, though, is the individual. For the most part, OBE is not part of contemporary social consensus. It therefore doesn't exist, and yet it does. To build the energy for OBE, you need to claim your own life while making determinations of where you do and do not fit in. When cohesion is thrown out of balance, which will happen sooner than later, you can apply everything you've learned to restore harmony. In the process, you learn how to intentionally regulate cohesion and also develop multiple skills associated with energy body dynamics. You'll be paying attention to new influences and processes. Your daily life will be enhanced, as will your dreaming.

ELEMENTS OF MANIFESTING

Life abounds with potential, a natural state of the wavefield. As microcosms of the wavefield, humans cohere their own creations by utilizing similar dynamics of resonance, transfer of information, intentionality, alignment, and all aspects of consciousness. In other words, the wavefield produces wave packets, and humans have within them some of these same wavefield processes. This allows humans to develop or cohere their own objects such as tools and technologies.

Manifesting is harnessing information from the environment and translating it into observable form, into a coherent organization of energy. In other words, manifesting brings something into view, crystallizing something out of the wavefield. In addition, from the wavefield creating your energy body to your job requirements to the influence of your significant other, the environment shapes who you are. One way or another, you become your environment. And the environment you're aware of is preordained by your cohesion.

Your state of mind, your cohesion, is the primary lens determining how much possibility you entertain, what you can bring into this world, and what can be perceived as having become manifest.

Dreaming experiences result from how you tune your cohesion: preparation, purpose, attention, and intent. This is also evident in daily life, with your environment being the equivalent of your dream world. How and what you place into motion has effects and consequences, making personal responsibility essential.

The initial condition from which manifesting occurs is the moment at hand, the immediate state of consciousness. For shamans, there is no fixed reference of reality. This allows the unexpected, if not the impossible, to occur, like the physical world turning into a sea of luminous energy or instantly finding yourself on the moon. Interestingly, quantum researchers hold that wavefield calculations assign probabilities of what might—not will—happen.[1]

Wavefield dynamics place events into motion, animating creation. If you have a strong desire to accomplish something, the wavefield already holds that potential. The quality of the result hinges on how well you balance your goals with the natural intention existing in the wavefield. The basic mechanics of the energy body are the same for waking and dreaming. The first and second energy fields balance the energy body's alignment with the environment. Intent places energy in motion for all actions and reactions.

Part of this harmony includes processing information and participating with the flow of energy toward the goal. An individual's work is to cultivate the intention associated with the goal, to do everything required for success, and to let that process happen. This is conscious behavior regulating the content and effects of cohesion. Excessive self-reflection can get in the way of success because it interferes with a solid environmental connection. It is self-defeating because it blocks the flow of information to, from, and within the wavefield. It dampens cohesion.

By paying attention to your body knowledge, you can sense the state of your cohesion. Is it jittery, relaxed, or attentive to a goal? You can also sense how your cohesion is intertwined with the environment and produces environmental results corresponding with your energy. This can be as simple as noticing that if you're nervous, a job interview may not go very well.

Dynamics

In relation to a shamanic inventory, manifesting results from the interplay of the first and second fields, and these in relation to the environment. The first field is what has been realized, and the second field is potential, or order that is waiting to be revealed. Both are within and without the energy body. With this essential dynamic forming cohesion, wavefield, social, or individual intent produces a focus or directive for energy to cohere, a process that produces something from potential.

Manifesting in the human sphere involves consolidating elements of an inventory to produce something that is bound by that inventory. As microcosms of wavefield coherence, humans carry the essence of bringing something to life. Their information is released into the environment, which changes the environment. This then affects not only what has been created but what will be manifest. If the world is made of energy, it's malleable and not fixed forever in place. From this principle, you can alter the conditions of your life by purposefully engaging mechanism and method of manifesting.

Furthermore, you can alter your cohesion and the environment by changing the items of your inventory. The inventory you feed to your energy body forms your reality. If the elements of an inventory don't cohere, if they're not harmonious, you're not going to get very far. If wood was used for brake pads in an automobile, the auto would burst into flames. Wood doesn't cohere, doesn't fit, within a viable inventory of brakes. Yet it fits as a stylish complement to the interior of an automobile.

By cohering energy of what might be produced, an automobile engineer brings that awareness into existence. The engineer may fully envision the new model but still needs to enact the step-by-step process of bringing that new inventory into acceptance. This necessitates working with consensus views, since manufacturing parts, assembling parts, and distributing products all require social interaction and common language. Intention is a way to latch onto the potential of building something such as an automobile, and it also affects the manner of bringing automobiles to life. During this undertaking, the alignment between internal and external conditions becomes increasingly enhanced. Aligning is facilitated by tuning with EQ, using feeling to measure and build.

The same applies for other endeavors. Someone who wants to earn a college degree or become a mechanic adjusts their cohesion to those external requirements. And so the person studies, takes tests, and perhaps changes geographic locations, all to bring about success. In effect, you tune your energy body—dreaming, feeling, *seeing*, inventory—to your goal.

It may be that tuning cohesion is what coheres something out of potential. Then again, it may be a matter of tuning into something that already exists. The interpretation of time originates from and solidifies your take on reality. (This relates to the Betwixt and Between exercise in chapter five.)

To review, energy is the ability to do work, to effect change. Power is how much energy is available. Personal power equates with possibilities. It provides a means to accelerate manifesting. For example, dreaming is an avenue for cultivating personal power. You can use it to boost your awareness. Dreaming is also a procedure to bring awareness of a dream into existence. I've mentioned the professor who finished his textbook in a dream, that Castaneda learned to dream his books, and that other apprentices of don Juan built their livelihoods through dreaming.

In addition, you can apply lucid dreaming lessons to daily life. In dreaming, the lesson is not to use, let alone abuse, power. In waking life, the lesson is the same. In both instances, the subsequent lesson is that you're not powerless.

Decisions

Don Juans says decisions are in the realm of the nagual.[2] A decision, he says, is acquiescing to this domain that permeates the wavefield. It is aware of everything.[3] Since the nagual is also within the energy body, to sense it is a matter of learning to skillfully employ body awareness.

From this perspective, decisions relate to the wavefield processing information in order to produce new conditions, new variations in all environments, and whatever else the wavefield creates. These creations also inform the wavefield which alters its intent and its decisions. This is the power of the wavefield. Your cohesion operates in similar fashion.

Your decisions are therefore governed by your cohesion, which is determined by your connection with the wavefield and the extent to which you've made that connection. You have conditioned yourself to respond to life in certain ways, to make decisions based on your cohesion. At the same time, your decisions create cohesion. If you make decisions based on new awareness and new inventories, you expand cohesion and the possibilities for action. The deeper you enter dreaming, the more daily decisions align with the wavefield since you're more in tune with it.

Looking at this from another angle, when you have sufficient energy, you automatically create a new cohesion, a new set of commitments, and new decisions. As a result, your life is refreshed, and you grow. Grooming body knowledge is becoming more aware of cohesional dynamics. Don Juan says that your body knows if you made the right decision, and other bodies also know.[4]

Decisions also result from ordinary environmental pressures which are an effect of the nagual. A decision forms from how much of the environment you're conscious of. If a friend is in need, a decision follows. If your interpretation of life is based on material objects, compatible decisions follow. You can't sidestep the power behind the environmental pressure produced by the interlocking structure of a worldview. You can, however, be aware of it in order to make better decisions, to acquiesce to more information and awareness. On a larger scale, however, the wavefield evidently has it all under control and this notion takes us into the heart of the nature of free will.

On a practical basis, decisions result from goals. Once you decide on a goal, for success in realizing it, you must act in alignment with the goal. If you don't, the energy hovers in potential. As a result, it's not set fully into motion and dissipates, and your decision becomes more difficult to realize. On the other hand, when cohesion is relaxed and receptive, it automatically provides awareness based on your questions or goals, which are forms of intent. Intent aligns you with your goals, and cohesion responds accordingly.

Furthermore, consistency is a hallmark of decisive behavior. A well-formed cohesion results in steps from sticking with decisions that are made deliberately, consciously, and enacted without reservation. This produces unbending intent. A way to be deliberate is to use your death as an advisor and assume responsibility for your behavior. In addition, you can be accessible to parts of the environment and inaccessible to other parts. Each of your actions then adds to or subtracts from your personal power.

Intent

Odorless, colorless, and tasteless, intent rules our lives. There are extremely powerful forms of intent, such as wavefield emanations, and there are intents of lesser intensity, such as wishing your dog wouldn't shed as much. But make no mistake, each form of intent is focused energy and is therefore a form of power. Even idle remarks can produce unintended events. The popular saying, "Be careful what you say, it might come true," carries weight.

When you apply your intent, you place energy into motion, you direct your *will*. Beliefs can place considerable energy behind your intent. If you feel wronged, for example, your emotional energy augments your focus. You become more determined to produce a desired outcome. On the other hand, beliefs may bind you. Regarding Earth as a material object for exploitation is a belief. Hear it enough and you might abide by it. Repeated by your teachers, parents, bosses, and friends, a belief becomes an unquestioned fact within a worldview.

Intent is the essential dynamic of the wavefield. For both the wavefield and the energy body, intentionality dictates intrinsic operations whereby flows of information establish coherence, resulting in manifestations. The formation, lifespan, and dissolution of observables, including sentient beings, give evidence of wavefield intentionality. Don Juan thinks that intent is a universal force whereby wavefield emanations act as commands, and from which everything is created.[5-7]

As part of the wavefield, any observable has within it its own intent based on its inventory, organization, and overall nature. In this regard, everything has purpose, character, and essence. As a wave packet, an energy body's behavior is another indication of its composition in that each movement, thought, or action stems from any number of intents built into it. The rhythmic beating of the heart, standing up and walking, and designing automobiles are all different forms of human intentionality.

Across the board, intent is central to manifestation for perception, experience, and products. All your intentions form cohesion, and this produces your alignment with the wavefield. And your alignments create cohesion. Experience flows from this relation between self and environment. From an energy body perspective, alignment between internal and external emanations generates perception. The better the resonance, the better the result.

Thoughts, feelings, and behaviors need to harmoniously line up. If cohesion is unbalanced, if it isn't coherent, you'll get discordant results, as your internal and external worlds don't mirror each other. If you're argumentative within yourself, you'll produce reactive contentiousness with others. But you can also use external conditions to change your cohesion. You can take classes, seek wisdom from a mentor, or notice how your behavior affects others.

The same process of alignment pertains to individuals and groups. Both are constantly sending and receiving information. Over time, individuals build social consensus, and this creates an intentionality that produces effects such as agreeing on how to build a house, automobile, or reality. Old cycle shamans established a variety of intents embodied in the dreaming levels. New cycle shamans refined this with an eye toward forming a natural field.

All these actions are clearly visible without accounting for the wavefield, although wavefield dynamics offer a clearer, deeper picture of intentionality. However, because we don't have this expanded reference, we step away from a fundamental, balanced relationship with life. We become lost in unregulated self-reflection to the extent where acting out of self-interest dictates what will be manifest for groups.

Climate change reveals that humans isolate themselves from the environment due to the stultifying effects of self-reflection. Humans primarily focus on the human part of the world, acting for their own benefit.

Intent to develop technologies that delicately balance with and help sustain the environment is often not part of human behavior. The lack of awareness that humans are part of an environment extending beyond themselves impedes a more natural flow of information and behavior. The results are clear, and nature is now restoring balance on its own terms—because the natural environment is conscious and more powerful.

A practical application of understanding manifesting is that you have a way to build each part of your life and make it consistent with every other part. This transformation is dramatic and makes unerring sense when you understand it. Exploring intent hinges on educating yourself about the mechanics of your energy body and the types of energy in the world about you. You then recognize different energies, how to awaken them, and how to skillfully use them. You learn the effects of placing them into motion. You can then build a life consistent with a natural energy field. Shamans, says don Juan, aren't really learning shamanism but rather the nature of intent and the skill of using it.[8]

On an individual level, intent consists of harnessing *will*, or unbridled energy. In this way, intent can purposefully shift cohesion. The result hinges on coherence, how well elements of the intent were gathered into a composite whole. Several intents combine for employment, for instance, such as the type and purpose of a job, required education or training, benefits, corporate culture, travel distance, etc.

Decisions create and reflect an intent. They focus energy and modify how you're connected with life. Holding fast to your decisions produces unbending intent, a well-organized, precise focus. To act consistently after having established a new cohesion is to act from knowledge. This is what produces the changes in your outer world. As don Juan says in simpler terms, emanations obey intent.[9] The only thing that will change this force is making another decision.

Unbending intent provides a clear, steady stream of information into the wavefield, thereby affecting its dynamics which, in turn, affects individuals. Intent is also the ability, direction, and singular force of alignment, and is therefore the wherewithal to change cohesion, to move the assemblage point upon personal command, to manifest different perceptions and experiences. Out of all possible outcomes, success necessitates bringing your entire mind, your entire cohesion, to bear on your goal. This type of intent supersedes those generated by science, mysticism, or consensus reality. It's a statement of your personal power.

When you have different energies focused, and there is nothing dampening or contrary to this composite energy (like worry, doubt, or fear), you also have unbending intent. Unbending intent shifts and stabilizes cohesion and thereby supports manifesting your goal. Without it, you can never muster the energy to plow through conditional energy fields. They have too much power, and we're too bound by them. The shift from being in a materialistic world to participating in a world of energy, for instance, is where fundamental effort resides because in making the shift you're dealing directly with energy, and that is what intent uses to change awareness.

The challenge is not letting unbending intent become brittle. Excessive focus and implementation prevent obtaining new information. The self-imposed barriers of perception form a hardened boundary, throwing the overall balance of living off the mark.

Visualization

Shamans hold that there is no world at large, no definitive reality, only what has been visualized and described.[10] Visualization is also important for new wavefield theorists to develop their views of wavefield dynamics.[11] It allows the exploration of ideas and concepts. It activates imagination to begin grasping abstractions and making sense of them. It helps to picture circumstances and scenarios in order to crystallize concepts into something recognizable, relatable, and usable.

It also primes intent. In psychological experiments, athletes who used visualization improved their abilities at rates higher than those who just practiced. They used their imagination to refine their "athlete" cohesion, which translated into better performance in the physical world. Some studies included the use of hypnosis and overall found the subjects learned how to relax and concentrate better.[12]

For our purposes, visualization may be considered a form of dreaming. You can alter the content and the effect of a dream on the spot, and you can test and measure your steps more easily. It's like running a software program to explore the goal and processes for success. In daily life outside of dreaming, visualization is a means to keep focused and to build your life. The basic mechanics are constant in both applications.

It is not difficult. You visualize different scenarios, feel if they make sense, and let your body adjust to that energy. Start by visualizing a goal, the possibility of it. This sets the stage for determining, organizing, and focusing more on what's needed. Then the required pieces to achieve the goal come to mind. The effects of placing this into motion become apparent, producing feedback regarding quality resonance with the goal. Adjustments are then made to continue toward success. Your body awareness helps you reconstruct the program in your outer world and thereby manifest it.

Furthermore, you reinforce your image of yourself throughout the day by what kinds of images you create. Notice how you think, feel, and view yourself at various times of the day. These imaging sessions occur in a split second. But over time they build a self-profile. This, in turn, aligns you with that image of yourself, which then manifests that result. And this applies to health, monetary prosperity, how you drive, and how you talk; in short, it applies to all facets of your life.

You can use imagination to open yourself to any potential. Pick a far-fetched goal. Tap that energy, play with it, imagine it. Track it. Let it stretch your thoughts and feelings into new worlds. Allow your visualizations to freely develop. The general idea is not to force visualization but rather to allow it to happen. Based on your goal, let awareness beyond your self-reflection inform you. This is an interactive process of establishing an intent and letting it work out within your imagination. This allows for new approaches to manifesting.

Waiting

Waiting is a posture of focus and allowing events to unfold. Related to this, patience is learning to regulate the flow and timing of energy. You learn when to hold off and when to move forward. It is a maneuver of balance requiring EQ. You need intent to establish focus, patience to not force something into existence, and power to claim your goal when it manifests.

Waiting involves developing an alignment with goals and doing so free from fear or ambition. You need to get out of your own way, your own desires, and allow what it is you're manifesting to come into existence. You step outside of self-reflection to participate more fully with life. You let the processes of waiting unfold as things come to you. As don Juan says, when someone is impeccable, the rest comes of itself and by itself.[13]

You therefore need to pay attention in a different way than what you're accustomed to. Multi-channel listening is a must. You become aware of thoughts and feelings that either support or interfere with your goals. In the world of energy, this is known as constructive and destructive interference. Your sense of continuity rests with the whole environment, and you trust this connection to guide your steps. You'll feel the pushes and pulls of social influences and must decide when to act and when to wait. As a result, you're exercising the three attributes of consciousness.

Waiting may seem passive, but it's not. It is being active in an unusual manner. You communicate with life. Serene, centered, and determined, your EQ establishes resonance, and things come to you as a matter of course. This is how the interactive exchange of information works. It's like fishing: you use the right bait, cast your line, wait for signs of a bite, then use your skill of bringing in the fish. If you fret, you're accessible and will throw yourself off the mark.

With patience comes the rhythm and meaning of life. This involves pace, timing, and clarity of manifesting. Shamans balance a sense of having no time (death as an advisor) with the responsibility of knowing what they are waiting for. In other words, you're not rudely bending the environment out of shape just to fulfill your desires. You have wavefield manners.

NAVIGATING LIFE

As part of the infinite wavefield, each manifestation is at once at the center of everything and at the furthest reaches of eternity. It is in part known, unknown, and unknowable. Forms of guidance, of navigation, to make headway through life are therefore indispensable. No matter the type of guidance, focused consciousness delivers answers, and body knowledge is the centerpiece to listen, act, and learn.

A worldview is a primary form of guidance. Within this are all types of group consensus. Corporate directives inform behavior. Parents teach their children. Philosophies, be they science or mysticism, provide guidance. Furthermore, a near-death experience can give direction, your feelings offer ways to proceed, and *seeing* is revelatory.

All of these direct behavior by establishing boundaries of what is considered meaningful and true. We surrender to them because we don't have other options. The more you can suspend thought and allow new information to enter consciousness, the less susceptible you are to a bureaucratized reality. Personal communication with, and guidance from, the wavefield—the top-end category of reality-breaking navigation—comes into play by consciously participating with life.

For practical application, we'll look at types of guidance relating to internal and external circumstances. Both involve interactive communication with the environment. Each requires personal responsibility and the gumption to act. Let's begin with a type of guidance that incorporates both internal and external conditions.

Path with Heart

As a form of guidance, a path with heart is central to shamanism. As an avenue to your uniqueness, it is an ongoing procedure to invigorate your life at any age. It stretches across personal, social, and professional situations. It produces the intersections of internal and external environments. It is a method to deliberately forge cohesion and re-envision your connection with the environment. It creates the circumstances for the time of your life. It pertains to values, judgements, and goals in making your decisions.

A path with heart develops self-regulation and responsibility. It brings to the fore dynamics of the energy body. Orchestrating all the elements of your life develops intentionality, awareness, and attention.

It is purposeful self-conditioning that generates the rhythm of living. Because such a path nourishes coherence, it offsets the effects of decoherence.

Your path is what delivers a meaningful life. Circumstances can quickly change, and a path with heart offers consistency. It is a way to reorient yourself and get your feet back on the ground after an experience that splinters your sense of reality. It is also part of making a living, having a "right livelihood" as some mystical disciplines refer to it.[14] For most people, earning a living is a necessity. How you go about it is where you align with a path with heart.

While elements of the environment formed your cohesion during childhood, your behavior since then most likely became robotic due to this conditioning. A path with heart restores your original nature. And yet, you wouldn't gain this appreciation of life without having had it removed.

Each person is a conglomerate of energy. The bundles of energy that once floated in the wavefield and that formed coherence require harmony to produce a stable life. We often shift moods and change our minds in a manner that indicates a lack of direction. Some people seem to shift with the wind. Yet we also lean toward certain behavior; we have predilections. We might get a charge out of studying art, business, or diesel mechanics. Or we might tend toward contemplation, while others are always on the go. All too often, however, we find ourselves estranged from our predilections, from our natural selves, and from the world.

A path with heart offers a way to structure your life to pull forth and live your deepest predilections. By finding the dreams you want to dream, by extending your reach into consciousness, you simultaneously develop your first and second energy fields. Dreaming is a way to enter the second field and expand awareness. To make practical sense of these explorations, the effort needs to be grounded in the first field, an orientation which a path with heart provides. As a result, you strengthen first-field integrity which propels you deeper into the second field. This sense of yourself and your path also augments awakening *will*.

In addition, purposeful predilections serve as shields. As we are constantly bombarded with immense energy, shields buffer these effects and filter energy into meaning. Redefining your shields purposefully redefines what you perceive. If you lose your shields, you're open to stray influences. You might become more accessible to discordant influences of dreaming, for instance. Shields also provide a focus to restore your awareness when the seas of daily life throw you off the mark.

To help create a natural energy field, don Juan had his apprentices revamp their shields, their activities in daily life.[15] For anyone engaging warriorship, ordinary shields, such as the pursuit of money, sex, and popularity, are thrown out. Then, forging a path with heart relies on basing your decisions for your job, relationships, hobbies, and anything else on peace, joy, and strength. Over time, you will have forged a path aligned with personal growth. Part of the process is hooking thoughts, feelings, and behaviors together, a step toward becoming whole—a measure of elevating your EQ. The effect is that you create a life that is strong, joyful, and peaceful. This doesn't mean there will be an absence of strife. You will, though, have the means to regain balance when you lose it.

Workable shields contribute to your well-being. Your predilections override the harshness of the slings and arrows of life. Each predilection gives you something that you love doing and provides ample challenges. Each carries its own intent. Like individual branches that combine with a trunk to form a tree, predilections combine to form another intent: the path with heart.

Navigating life by heart rather than by intellect or societal norms gives you firm direction and purpose. It brings your uniqueness to the foreground. It also offers a sense of power to effectively manage any concern. People often feel powerless and find themselves readily upset at any social injustice. Sexism, bigotry, and other forms of discrimination plies awareness into a sense of inadequacy or outrage. Having a path with heart delivers you beyond normal responses. This doesn't mean you automatically become indifferent to social problems. The idea is that regardless of how you fit into the social order, you fit into the natural order. You have your own life, and only your death can remove you from it. Without becoming embroiled in self-importance, you'll be able to clarify your life and say, "This is who I am, this is what I do, and here's where I'm headed."

Finding your path is a matter of expanding your awareness. Disrupt routines to avoid complacency. Nonpattern to dislodge the assemblage point. Use your death as an advisor to trim your life and enhance your focus. Gaze to stretch your awareness. And decide without reservation that you want to find your path.

This is a gradual, systematic process. As with anything else, you must put in the time and energy to realize results. Rest assured, though, that doing so changes your life for the better—and in ways you can't currently imagine. A path with heart is a way to fully engage the world and derive nourishment from the path itself. Once you've cultivated your path with heart, you've found patience and learned how to wait.

Following are two procedures that may prove helpful:

Developing a Path with Heart
1. Develop an acute sense of your death as a physical being. Or, turned around, how do you truly want to live your life?
2. To prevent this awareness from becoming debilitating, apply nonattachment to everything.
3. Deliberately select several things for personal and professional relationships that you want to learn and involve yourself with. The measurement for selection is simple: Does the activity provide peace, joy, and strength?
4. Test and retest these selections to ensure their strength in your life.
5. These items should assist you in obtaining and maintaining both balance in and control of your life.
6. Select items for the physical, emotional, mental, and spiritual sides of yourself.
7. Go ahead and dream, selecting items which give the deepest meaning to your life, so you may live a life worth living.

Robert Monroe's ABC Method to Find and Complete Your Life's Work
Recognizing the importance of balance in everyday life, Monroe had his version of a path with heart.

1. Make an 'A' list with all your worries, anxieties, and concerns about which you can do nothing.
2. Make a 'B' list with all your worries, anxieties, and concerns about which you can do something, large or small, today.
3. Make a 'C' list with all your needs, hopes, goals, and desires yet to be fulfilled.
4. Destroy the 'A' list knowing that you're also dismissing it from your consciousness.
5. Take some kind of action, large or small, for each item on the 'B' list. If you're addressing your problems, you're gaining control of them and not letting them control you.
6. Take some kind of action, large or small, for at least one item on the 'C' list, and know you're building momentum and direction.
7. Do this each day until you have no 'A' list, no 'B' list, and are completely devoted to your 'C' list.
8. You then will serenely complete your human life purpose.

Petty Tyrants

A result of invading armies, old cycle shamans had fun making categories of tyrannical behavior. These stretched from the primal power of the wavefield to human behavior based on the degree of pettiness. This practice continues. So critical are petty tyrants that shamans deliberately find them, should one not cross their paths. They magnify and promote understanding of social interactions, bring EQ to the fore, and intensely stimulate self-importance, with the latter causing a tremendous expenditure of energy. Due to this effect, petty tyrants help make it clear what you need to work on. They stimulate you to crystallize your values so you can decide what to focus on: self-importance or a more meaningful goal.

Ideal petty tyrants have authority over you; the more manipulative they are, the better. You get to deal with office politics, outright back-stabbing, subtle and not-so-subtle bigotry, blind hate, and explosions of rage. But you deal with this as a form of exercise, balance, and losing self-importance. The process quickens EQ, a primary means of navigation, and pertains to the management of all adverse challenges in life. Don Juan says that if you can deal with petty tyrants, you can easily deal with the unknown.[16] Put another way, gaining control of your daily world stabilizes cohesion, which also translates to achieving constancy in dreaming.

To find success, learn how to let go of your expectations, and then let go of everything else. Reduce your personal agenda by throwing out your conditioned responses, and strive to remain unaffected at each turn of your path. Avoid confrontations, unless you want to generate more heat from your oppressor. Then be willing to take it on the chin for a greater strategy. Otherwise, let confrontations diffuse.

This doesn't mean to become wimpy. There are times when you need to make a stand and deal directly with authority. How you do this is part of the petty tyrant lessons since a primary goal is to not become one yourself. During your skirmishes, you'll find that your path with heart keeps you focused. It soothes you when your nerves are frayed and lets you laugh when all seems lost. All the while, though, continually assess your strong and weak points, and plug the holes where energy leaks.

Skirmishes with petty tyrants give you ample practice to regulate your resources. Always keep in mind that you're in a petty tyrant relationship. Over time, you feel yourself getting less caught up in the ordinary affairs of the world and more dedicated to freedom. Remember you're placing yourself through a mind-numbing obstacle course. You'll suffer lost battles. There will be times when you're overwhelmed and highly reactive. But the overall effect of engaging petty tyrants is that you continually lessen irritations, and so the petty tyrant course eventually becomes mind-liberating.

The skills learned from petty tyrant interactions may be applied to all irritants and environmental challenges in your life. They become a matter of understanding and adapting. The more you push yourself into a greater awareness, the less effect they have. Due to the external pressure on your energy body, you learn to be inaccessible. With time, you also learn that your control prevents you from blindly reacting and your discipline enables you to assess what's taking place even though you're feeling pummeled. And you learn to persevere while patience allows for deliberate resolution.

Basic management skills applied to petty tyrants include erasing personal history to throw the tyrant off his or her mark. The person then can't fully assess your energy, find your weak spots, and try to manipulate you. Nonattachment gives you a little space to remember your strategy, what you're involved in and how to get out of it. And you'll find that being inaccessible helps buffer the tyrant's onslaughts. Overall, it is your path with heart that lets you not only persevere but transcend petty tyrant influences.

Inner Guidance

In some way, shape, or form, all guidance hinges on body knowledge. As such, all guidance requires paying attention to what the body senses and to how you relate to any given event. Proficiency relies on having a cohesion that responds to these types of information. The essence of body knowledge is knowing that you're connected with the environment and that you have the cornerstones at your disposal. Then it's a matter of listening, paying attention, waiting, and acting. For inner guidance, listen to your innate modes of perception: dreaming, feeling, and *seeing*.

Dreaming

Some people say that you must have the same dream several times for it to be considered revelatory or meaningful. From personal experience, dreams that repeat themselves usually mean something is at work, and the message within the dream is begging for attention. At the same time, while a one-time-only, very vivid dream might be the result of too much pizza, such a dream might carry enough weight by itself to be considered as portent, as signaling bona fide guidance.

The way to figure out which is which is to educate your intuition. Sense what a dream tells you. Does your body tell you that your interpretation feels right? Examine the dream to discover its meaning. Did you eat too much, or does it carry a prophetic note? Dream dictionaries can help, but you'll eventually have to make your own. This helps you better discern your feelings.

You may also set up dreaming to find specific guidance. Carry a question into dreaming, for example, and let your dream play itself out. Pay attention to the images and to how you feel. Don't censor your dream. Let it work itself out, and discover where it takes you.

In general, dreaming levels offer guidance for developing OBE, just as the entire structure of shamanism provides direction for the overall expansion of consciousness. These are valuable roadmaps, just don't get lost in the map by thinking that these frames of reference are reality.

Feeling
Realizations stemming from emotional outbursts are fleeting and useless, says don Juan.[17] This means that when you have insights that are packed with emotion, they tend to be of very limited value and don't withstand the test of time. Hence the need for educating emotions, feelings, intuition, and thereby increasing EQ.

In this way, you cultivate the feeling cornerstone as a viable method of guidance. Feeling acts like a collection house. It gathers and connects with information from many influences and then delivers appropriate insights. Feeling may even be thought of as having tentacles extending throughout regions of consciousness. This means you can be intuitively aware of something without a rational foundation to explain why. As you can imagine, managing such complex behavior requires experience and the recognition that it is possible.

Letting go of how you think the world is in order to abide by intuitive guidance can be difficult. It is fraught with challenges. I'm not advocating how to go about this, should it be something you want to pursue. From personal experience, guidance provides the insight to make new alignments with life, and abiding by this guidance is necessary to consolidate a cohesion that reflects a new direction.

Seeing

Seeing is like peering through something, through outer manifestations into deeper root energies. This makes it a marvelous technique for guidance. Like any skill, it requires training. With practice, it becomes a direct link with intent, a direct way of knowing. You may also notice a silent voice that informs you of exactly what is what.

Keep in mind that the visual nature of *seeing* may be misleading. While there may be a visual component, it hinges on merging the entire body with what is being *seen*. It's not something that's done just with the eyes. It's full body awareness. From revealing immediate circumstances to understanding why a situation is developing to forming a worldview, the different forms of *seeing* provide daily guidance.

Outer Guidance

It's common for someone to say he or she noticed a sign, something that gave meaningful direction for their life. A good example of this, and one that can be learned and used in everyday life, is using omens as directional signs from the wavefield.

The use of omens has been around for a long, long time. Julian Jaynes, for example, explores many varieties of omens in his book, *The Origins of Consciousness in the Breakdown of the Bicameral Mind*.[18] From comet trails to cloud formations to eclipses, from facial characteristics to dreams to the flight of birds, deciphering omens has always been part and parcel of human behavior. And there is no doubt it is a key element in a shaman's lifestyle.

Until you get a good handle on intuition and *seeing*, omens serve as an excellent bridge to understand the interactive communications of life. Plus, until you establish a firm direction in your life, they also help guide you through the random influences that push and pull at you. Omens are like the signposts found along the highway. By serving as external reference, they help take you out of your normal habits. They help transform your ordinary feel of the world into the perception that daily life is a type of dream where mystery abounds. What might be interpreted as an inconvenience to the flow of your daily life could be a note from the wavefield. You let your body make the calculations.

Intuition is key to deciphering omens. When you initially witness an omen, don't tell yourself what just occurred. Nonpattern it and let it be. Then ask yourself what it means and wait for an intuitive reply. Make sure you don't bend an interpretation to suit your personal desires. As you build your omen vocabulary, you'll recognize some omens immediately. Others will be filed for future reference. You'll have to wait and watch how your life unfolds then match the omen on file with whatever occurs. You can begin building this language by determining your positive and negative colors, your "yes" and "no" omens.

For example, during a recent trip to London, my companion and I were walking about town as I explained omens to her. Since she wanted to try, I set up an omen by telling the world I wanted it to show us what her positive color would be for the day. I told her she could change it later, but for practical purposes we needed references for that afternoon. As I asked, a red automobile pulled up to the curb and stopped in front of us. Okay, red it was. I then asked for her negative color. A white taxi turned from another street in front of us. Now, part of the omen was that these events were out of the ordinary, or at least obvious. We had not previously seen any red cars stop in front of us, nor had I seen too many white cabs that day. They stood out, which is often but not always part of what omens are all about.

We then had fun walking about town while reading these signs. She asked about heading in a certain direction, then based on what color car drove by us, a yes or no response was evident. We then decided to eat. She was not familiar with the area, so she wanted to turn left and head back to where she knew the area. I said, let's use omens. As soon as she agreed, a red car passed us heading in the opposite direction. We turned around and followed. After walking three blocks, a woman dressed in black stopped, bent over, and adjusted her shoe. To me, black means death, which means the event gets an exclamation point. Black is not necessarily good nor bad; it means paying greater attention. (There are times when it does mean death.) We then noticed a white car parked just beyond the woman, and immediately to our right was a pub. I asked if this is where we should eat, and a man wearing a red shirt walked inside.

I had been hungry for a traditional English meal of roast beef and vegetables. It turned out that this was the pub's evening special. My friend had fish and chips, which she raved about, saying the pub was a true find and she had to return. This example illustrates the preliminaries. Over time, you'll create your own list of symbols, not unlike creating a dream dictionary.

False Echoes

Due to projection, you also need to consider false echoes. Your desires, for instance, can alter your interpretations of any type of guidance because you want your guidance to shape up based on your reflections. You might expect a response and imagine it occurring out of the corner of your eye. It may also be that you think you have sufficient information to consider and close yourself off to more information, which makes other forms of research valuable avenues of guidance.

When it comes down to it, the responsibility of abiding by your own counsel sets the stage for navigating your life. Energy body skills stand ready to assist. Stopping your internal dialogue gives space between desire and action. Nonattachment and being inaccessible also help. Due to stubbornness, ignorance, lack of experience, or any other manifestation of self-importance, there will also be times you simply want to overrule guidance and act in a head-strong manner. The remedy is to pay attention, prioritize personal growth, and then apply yourself to learning the ins and outs of guidance. It's a way to enjoy your time in this and other worlds, connect with the wavefield, and perhaps make it through life more gracefully.

9 } Life with an Energy Body

How conscious you are of your energy body includes how much you are aware of it and its dynamics; how well you groom, condition, and educate cohesion; the state of your health; how you apply your resources; and how you grow as a person. All of this relates to your understanding the tonal, the state of your energy body. Your tonal is your primary connection to life, and to everything about you, including health.

Health makes having a quality life possible. You don't have to divert energy and other resources to correct illness. We begin this chapter, then, by examining aspects of health, including the tonal, and then follow up with elements of personal growth.

DYNAMICS OF HEALTH

Health and illness tell stories about people, and depending on the worldview there are many ways to interpret them. How to treat illness follows from the interpretation. You can approach this physically as with drugs and diet, energetically as with Reiki and chakra therapy, and cognitively with a mind-over-matter approach.

Healing is standard practice for old and new cycle shamans. Some of their ways of going about it have remained consistent. Using plants for healing was a common practice for ancient shamans and remains a staple for modern shamans, for example. One of don Juan's colleagues, Vicente, used plant extracts for healing.[1]

Good health is characterized by *homeodynamics*, a term that is catching on as it is more descriptive than *homeostasis*. This refers to having an internal stability that can resist change and that provides balance while interacting with an ever-changing environment.[2] This requires maintaining equilibrium of the entire body during constantly fluctuating conditions. Cell division, embryonic development, genomic transcription, and the required death of cells are each a study in themselves, yet each is influenced by other parts and the whole. Conditions within the body are dynamic. Energetic cohesion is no different. A natural energy field contains the blueprint for health, although thoughts, feelings, and environmental circumstances can overrule this and produce ill health.

According to at least one wavefield scientist, brain science and biology don't yet offer a complete framework for understanding the whole organism.[3] A modern, yet increasingly outdated, model of how the body works relies on viewing the body as a material object. Modern medical practices are also technologically oriented, often overlooking the vital, energetic force of the patient. The cause of a disorder may be an imbalance among internal and external environments. This may not be in current textbooks because the whole body, acting in concert with the environment, hasn't been described at a scientific level.

Molecular interactions throughout the body occur as part of an array of interconnected events. This view of how the body works is consistent with how energy behaves. A defining element of homeodynamics, the skillful processing of information, is the orchestration of systems, the timing and rhythm of when biological events occur and when they don't. Like the highly integrated parts and systems of a jet airplane, the body is an intricate array of cells, tissues, organs, and systems relying on precise, well-timed exchanges of information. Synchronization among all parts and systems is the difference between health and disease. Stating this in another way, how well the parts and systems cohere and work in unison determines health or disease.

Stress occurs throughout the day. Some stress is beneficial, as it is required for mental, emotional, and physical processes. Others forms of stress interfere with health. The appropriate response to stress of all forms is therefore a crucial element of maintaining homeodynamics. Proper timing of the body's processes counters unnecessary stress, allowing the body and mind to function better. Some of the mystics' contributions to health are meditation, yoga, and other techniques that are proven to reduce stress and facilitate homeodynamics.

From an energy body perspective, health is a well-functioning cohesion. An excessive conditional field may place undue stress on the physical body. A natural energy field relates to optimal health and reflects energetic homeodynamics. Part of a natural field is the balancing of tensions within the energy body and between the energy body and environment. In this way of viewing health, physical conditions reflect those of the energy body. A full accounting of homeodynamics therefore takes the energy body into account.

In cohesional homeodynamics, health is the proper phasing or regulation of cohesion. Health is regarded as the natural state. Disease occurs from disrupting this balance and manifests as a distorted cohesion, which can be measured by the position of the assemblage point. Regaining health is moving the assemblage point back to the position indicating health.

Part of this effort is merging daily and dream worlds, balancing the first and second fields internally and in relation to the outer world. Don Juan says that cures are easy in dreaming.[4] This means that when awareness is in dreaming, cohesion is not bound by the rules and order of the daily world. It is freer, and when aligned with a natural field, cohesion adjusts toward its optimal state. Establishing an intent to discover what is needed to restore health is a skill learned in lucid dreaming. You don't lose your sense of your known world when dreaming. You minimize it to allow more options.

There may be other processes equally at work. I remember don Juan saying that he was severely scarred after falling into a fire. The scars disappeared after he entered the nagual several times. I had a similar experience. When I was a toddler, I tripped and fell into a wood burning stove, which caused severe burns. Doctors, my parents told me, were amazed when I had no scars after healing. Afterward, though, I didn't have the sense of a meaningful life. To feel was to feel pain. It was easier to be absent, not absentminded but vacant from life.

A powerful psychological effect may have resulted from being thrust into another dimension by the pain. The immersion in another state of consciousness for which there were no references in daily life, no means to orient myself, caused me to be oddly inattentive. It was only after becoming somewhat skilled with energy body dynamics—especially sensing the tonal-nagual relationship—that I was able to get my feet on the ground and have a more solid relation with my daily world.

I sometimes speculate that the shock of being burned catapulted me into the second field, perhaps the nagual, where the natural effects of being more focused within another dimension produced physical healing. In other words, accenting the second field brought to bear cohesional homeodynamics, which resulted in what might have been remarkable healing. It may also be that miracles and other unexplained healings can be accounted for by a similar sudden shift in cohesion brought about by faith, belief, or intent. This is partially addressed in the placebo section later in this chapter.

Since scientists categorize OBE, NDE, ME, and survival after death as "extreme" phenomena, it would be wise to include rapid, spontaneous healing as an extreme event that warrants further scrutiny. This would eventually lead to regarding these experiences as ordinary and thereby change the social base of reality.

Since the energy body offers a broad-based accounting for behavior and health, an understanding of cohesional therapy would revolutionize medical care. It would also indicate the acceptance of the existence of the energy body. The body contains its own intelligence for healing. When cohesion can't support this, intervention is needed, and therapies arise. Oriented to cohesional homeodynamics, a natural field allows healing to occur. This doesn't mean the end of illness. It is, though, another approach to health.

Personal Tonal

Don Juan says that the tonal consists of everything we are and everything we know.[5] It is anything imaginable. It begins at life and ends at death, he says.[6] The first and second energy fields are within the tonal. In contrast, as mentioned in chapter three, the nagual is the part of the wavefield and the energy body for which there is no description, no words, and no knowledge other than knowing it exists.[7] There is also an individual component to the tonal—the personal tonal—that organizes awareness and produces meaning on an individual basis. It relates to the development of your entire energy body, the first and second fields combined, and all cornerstones of awareness.

The tonal is life, and to slide completely off it ends in death. You also need your tonal to perceive and make use of the nagual. The nagual has a distinct feel to it and dreaming also grants access. Conversely, awareness of the nagual promotes dreaming. But it is the tonal that bestows meaning to excursions into the nagual, including how it feels and its relation to dreaming. To one degree or another, this means you're always subject to projection, to making sense of experience based on your cohesion. The relationship between the tonal and nagual affects how much power you have and therefore what you can achieve. You begin by knowing about them, that they exist. Then you need to shine up your tonal, followed by appropriate actions to follow through on the intent. The cleaner your tonal, the more accurate your perceptions. Reflective of warrior discipline, this is a vital step for exploring consciousness as it provides clarity, objectivity, and personal integrity.

Your tonal organizes itself based on its inventory, how it formed due to upbringing, education, and enculturation. Broadly speaking, a technology is organizing and manipulating the tonal for a specific result. At a personal level, the tonal embodies all aspects of your consciousness. It is your means to travel through life. A stronger, more flexible, and more resilient tonal offers a means to navigate worlds based on consensus as well as those beyond. While internal and external environments influence health, it is your tonal that gives an immediate indication of your state of health.

Don Juan says that a personal tonal has two sides: a rugged, surface side that relates to action, and a softer, more yielding side prone to decisions and deliberation.[8] Having a "proper tonal" is when these sides are balanced, harmonious. There is no internal conflict, no dissonance between thought and action. This reflects homeodynamics. And for this, you need a tonal that includes a balanced relation between first and second fields and between the entire energy body in relation to the environment. This results from applying the basic procedures of energy body management found in previous chapters. In the process of assuming responsibility and disrupting routines, for example, you reorder the tonal and recondition your energy body. Doing so, says don Juan, removes the need for drugs.[9]

With awareness of the tonal and nagual, you begin to apply the attributes of consciousness in a different way. Before, you isolated different characteristics of the first and second fields, your daily and dream worlds, the known and unknown, and how they influenced each other. The nonordinary world became ordinary. Now, your focus is more expansive as you relate more to your entire energy body. The emphasis on the second field has served its purpose of expanding awareness to this level. You've integrated first and second field mechanics, although these lessons continue as you progress through dreaming levels. It's just that your relation to what you're learning has shifted.

OBE helps illuminate the dynamics of both the interplay of the first and second fields and then that of the tonal and nagual. Cleaning the tonal keeps dreaming free of clutter and distractions. In other words, your cohesion determines the content of OBEs. A well-organized and clean personal tonal results in more constructive and enjoyable dreaming.

Don Juan also says that the greater understanding and implementation of the tonal and nagual pairing falls squarely with advanced applications of dreaming in combination with a notable development of overall consciousness. He characterized this as a stage of growth beyond shamanism, to having become a person of knowledge.[10] This corresponds with having stabilized a natural energy field. Arriving here is a premier goal of shamanism, a necessary step to avoid becoming lost in the bureaucracy of shamanism, which is no different than getting lost in the bureaucracy of any other reality.

This overarching stability granted by having a natural field includes adaptability. Environments, both internal and external, change. Being sensitive to this helps prevent forming a bureaucratic mindset. With sufficient awareness of an environment, you can recognize, measure, and predict changes. Providing you don't try to use your personal power to control the environment, this knowledge allows for the continued development of the energy body. A proper tonal permits this personal evolution.

You can sense your tonal by gazing at other people. Gaze at their energy bodies, not their physical bodies. Your assessment will result from apprehending the state of their energy, not from their social status. This also provides a measurement for *seeing*. You can then apply this awareness to yourself.

Aging

Aging provides an example of the tonal in relation to health. Since we've built our world on a sliver of the energy body, without cleaning the tonal, we remain on the fringes of life. In daily practice, our health stands to suffer, as we've set aside a significant portion of available energy. Youth is not a barrier to a deteriorating tonal, says don Juan. A person drinks heavily due to having a poor tonal, not vice versa.[11] Due to a lifetime of bad habits, we may condition ourselves to have a weak tonal, resulting in poor health.

Decoherence, the deterioration of the energy body, occurs with aging. There's no getting around it. But the process can be mitigated or accelerated by the level of care given to oneself. A proper tonal addresses some of these effects. We're constantly told that with old age comes ill health and declining abilities. When people condition themselves to that education, they almost ensure that result. Social conditioning can increase the rate of decoherence, the dissipation of energy. Extended self-reflection, likely enhanced from having gained a lifetime of experience, makes cohesion stiff and unbending. Physical movement follows suit, and cognitive ability may decline as well. Citing the benefits of a clean tonal, which reflects a flexible cohesion, don Juan says that a shaman's energy is noticed as youthfulness and vigor.[12] Based on numerous stories found from a simple web search, with proper attention youthfulness during old age isn't something exclusive to shamans.

Age-related health problems are part of life. But the education of what's involved with aging isn't always up to par. The conditioning and expectation of deteriorating health and falling, for instance, may produce that effect as a person gradually succumbs to a poor tonal based on the aforementioned social conditioning. As decoherence takes hold, it therefore becomes important to know about having a proper tonal, energy body dynamics, and how to deal with aging on another level. Even if someone (young or old) has an infirmity, a disability, it doesn't have to define his or her life.

Simply due to the amount of experience gained, there is a relationship between age and knowledge. However, this doesn't automatically mean anything other than that someone has increased potential for using life's lessons. More likely, the person wants to impart his or her wisdom but often at the cost of not learning too much more. The potential to expand cohesion applies to gaining new levels of proficiency with energy body skills, something that requires unlearning a lifetime of habits. Not many people know of this option, and much less want to take on the challenge. The advantage for an elderly person comes with the possibility of using extensive experience to actively build a broader base of knowledge than previously encountered. Energy body mechanics provide a means for learning at any age. For both young and old, continued growth is a matter of managing self-reflection while targeting a natural field.

A natural energy field can offset what is considered normal aging. It offers additional perspectives of homeodynamics, reformatting the diagnosis and treatment of illness, and of aging in general. And a path with heart promotes having a natural field. There's nothing like knowing your place in the world, finding sure footing no matter your age, and discovering the peace that comes with having purposeful pursuits. The effect is realizing that your life becomes revitalized each and every day.

APPROACHES TO HEALTH

For the most part, western medical science is based on a material world. It has been built using classical science descriptions and interpretations. The physical body is material, technologies to diagnose and treat are material, and homeodynamics pertains only to the physical body. This is all well and good. I owe my life to it. But scientific research also considers the effects of thoughts, feelings, and energy. Bioenergetics, for example, is frontier inquiry. It is "the study of the flow and transformation of energy in and between living organisms and between living organisms and their environment."[13] Cohesional dynamics fits this definition and provides context that can further research by providing a rich pathway for exploration. The burgeoning field of energy medicine gives us a foothold.

In energy medicine, homeodynamics involves the choreography of energetic rhythms within the physical and energy bodies. Even from a classical perspective, biological coherence is determined by an electrodynamic field.[14] The various phases among different rhythms strive toward a unified relationship. Proper resonance among the body's systems indicates homeodynamics, a coherent state to which the entire body returns after disruption.[15]

From an energy body perspective, homeodynamics indicates the well-functioning coherence of a wave packet. The moment-to-moment processing of and response to information is how the wavefield works and therefore how the energy body works. In both classical and quantum perspectives, then, health and disease are tied to energy. Some researchers think that a disease has its own type of energy field that needs to be released.[16] But not all diseases fit neatly into this schematic. A broken bone is a broken bone, for instance. While pulsed magnetic therapy, a form of energy medicine, has demonstrated effectiveness for healing bone fractures,[17] overall treatment still requires an old-fashioned approach.

Even so, from an energy body perspective, all healing modalities seek to establish an intent that influences cohesion, restores coherence, and moves the assemblage point back to a position of "health."

With cohesional homeodynamics, there is a constant flow of information into and through the energy body, which is then emitted back into the environment. If the flow isn't properly managed, it can distort cohesion and produce illness. For shamans, a proper tonal is viewed as a baseline for health, with therapies supporting or restoring that condition. Optimally, a well-functioning tonal removes the need for therapy.

Like material technologies, therapies related to energy medicine can give you time to make changes and address underlying conditions that lead to a disorder. Treatment in relation to a natural field is holistic, as you're addressing the entire person based on homeodynamics. To illustrate, let's look at a few therapies in this category.

Drugs

There is a class of drugs that affect states of consciousness. It has various names depending on the use and context, such as entheogens, psychedelics, and hallucinogens. A common feature is that due to their energy, their coherence and intent, they significantly alter consciousness. People often regard these chemically induced experiences as aberrations. Yet this attitude is changing due to the success of using marijuana, psilocybin, and LSD in therapeutic situations, including for the treatment for PTSD, epilepsy, and a range of emotional disorders including depression and end-of-life anxiety.[18]

Along with other healing practices, shamans have a reputation for the use of altered states of consciousness. Psychedelics are one way to bring these about. By acting as a catalyst or trigger, they can provide glimpses of transcendent states and help acquire knowledge but may also cause fixations and addictions. The immediate environment and the intention for using them are known to influence the drug-induced experience.[19]

Psychedelic drug episodes are often considered hallucinations, events that are somehow not real or valid. Some investigators connect hallucinations with shamanic procedures.[20] Shamans regard them to be as real as any other experience.[21] Such events occur due to a shift in the assemblage point,[22] and the shifts can be mild or dramatic, producing revelations or complete changes in one's relation to the environment.

The altered states are then incorporated into the daily world, expanding the known aspect of cohesion.

In the early stages of Castaneda's apprenticeship, psychedelics were integral to his learning shamanism. He initially thought they were the basis of don Juan's teachings. However, he later realized that this thinking was erroneous. Castaneda came to understand that don Juan gave him several types of plants to shift his assemblage point, to alter his cohesion and gain nonordinary experiences. Don Juan thought that Castaneda would be slow to catch onto the teachings without them. But once Castaneda grasped the meaning behind their use, he stopped using them.[23]

Acupuncture

Acupuncture consists of inserting needles into the skin at precise locations along meridian pathways in order to alter the flow of energy. This works directly with energy and can be considered a technology consistent with cohesional dynamics. Meridians form an energetic system of the energy body and therefore influence cohesion. Acupuncture treatments can dissipate patterns of energy that produced a disorder and instruct the body to restore or maintain cohesional and physical homeodynamics.

Having a Taoist influence, acupuncture also offers the benefit of looking at disorder from a different angle. For instance, you can relate what a meridian is associated with to better understanding your discomfort. If a meridian relates to the gall bladder and this pertains to decisions or dissonance producing tension, you can examine yourself and make behavioral changes to remove the dissonance. In addition to direct therapeutic value, acupuncture is a valuable support to provide relief while you're figuring out the underlying problem.

Some researchers are quick to point out that meridians have not been shown to exist, and therefore acupuncture is quackery. Yet studies using infrared technology have mapped their existence.[24] Also of interest is that medical insurance companies now reimburse the cost of acupuncture treatments for some ailments, an indication of effectiveness.

Massage and Touch Therapy

Both acupuncturists and massage therapists use the term "the issues are in the tissues," which points out the value of body awareness. Massage therapy removes tightness and blockages in the muscles, tissues, and other body parts. It promotes relaxation, a key part of maintaining homeodynamics. Muscles store information and are a key to cohesion. Don Juan emphasized their use beyond just looking fit.[25] According to the biophysicist James Oschman, muscles are integral to a matrix of energy that affects health.[26] Massage can also bring to awareness issues that need to be addressed, situations that may be causing muscle tension in the first place. There are many styles of massage, just as therapists have different approaches.

Related to this are therapies such as Therapeutic Touch and Reiki. Here, the energy of the therapist is part of the treatment. Optimally, therapists try to be channels for a purer flow of energy to occur, thereby assisting cohesion back to health. But, as with massage, completely removing their energy from the picture doesn't occur, as they are the channel. Chakras are often used as a reference for the flow of energy. And touching a client or patient isn't always needed, as it is the resonance of the energy of the therapist in relation to the patient that is the mechanism.

While don Juan called attention to the importance of the physical body, he regarded it as one of two necessary parts of the total human. He maintained that without awareness of the energy body, the physical body was a "lump of organic matter" and that for most people, the energy body is dormant and unaware of many things.[27] The notion here is that with the right therapist, coupled with purpose, sensing both sides of your nature can be facilitated with body work.

Mind over Matter

Areas of science that mesh neatly with shamanism are found with *placebo* studies. A placebo is something that produces a positive healing response but is not itself a therapy. The classical way of looking at it is someone taking a sugar pill and then getting better without the aid of an actual therapy. The expectation of healing produces that outcome. However, if we harness what is known about placebo responses and clinically apply that knowledge, then that procedure becomes a bona fide therapy and revamps what is known about placebo. This fits cohesional dynamics relating to how cohesion forms and to the effects of intent. Expectation is an intent that influences cohesion, for instance.

As with energy medicine, environmental influences themselves affect health. In terms of placebo responses, how doctors' offices are decorated and how patients are emotionally treated can affect a person's health. So much so that if a physician thinks and says only the right things, but the tone and tenor strike the patient poorly, it can produce a *nocebo* response whereby the patient becomes ill. The emotional environment is therefore a significant factor in shaping health, just as the wavefield environment shapes the coherence of what it manifests. Mental and emotional behaviors, therefore, contribute to forming cohesion, which then affects physical health. This corresponds with beliefs generated by a worldview affecting behavior since worldviews regulate cohesion.

Bruce Lipton, a former medical school professor and author of *The Biology of Belief*, holds that beliefs markedly influence biology. He says that thoughts can control cellular behavior as strongly as a prescribed drug. And he regards the placebo response to result from one's beliefs.[28]

Lipton also thinks that based on negative expectations, nocebo responses hold the same power as placebo responses.[29] He makes the point that doctors are usually not trained to consider the impact of placebo responses even though some historians have made a compelling case that the history of medicine relates to the history of placebo, to the ability of mind to affect health.[30]

Placebo investigations provide a compelling avenue to examine the human mind and its effects on health. Because we're talking about mind, we're talking about cohesion—if not the entire energy body, if not the entire person. And because cohesion pertains to the physical body, we're also talking about the effects of cohesion on health. As mentioned, scientific investigations are contributing in some way to the understanding of this relationship. In so doing, researchers provide details that zero in on mind-body healing. By comparing this with energy body concepts, these scientific findings might also provide evidence for how the energy body works.

However, even when someone learns new information, recognizing new possibilities doesn't indicate that the person can or will apply it. A patient or physician may intellectually understand and accept placebo research but still not have the desire or ability to apply it in any meaningful, deliberate way. Doing so requires additional context and skill.

I've mentioned my ulcer story in the first chapter as well as in my other books. Doing so has become tedious. But the topic continues to assert a primary lesson: the value of body knowledge and the capacity for healing with the mind, the totality of oneself. The situation offers a reference for most, if not all, mind-body interactions, which is pretty much the condition of all human life. I was in the hospital for a long time but eventually healed myself by working with my energy body. For me, this established the value of using the energy body for personal development and health.

I had unintentionally conditioned myself for illness and I later reconditioned myself for health by paying attention to what my body was telling me—and it was telling me exactly what to do. Whether addressing the ulcer or some other problem, changing cohesion provided relief. As with anyone's health, this is an ongoing pursuit. It is a learned skill where it's best not to take things for granted.

Some medical thinking holds that ulcers are caused by bacteria. But even by scientific standards, correlation doesn't equal causation. While the presence of bacteria as first cause fits within a medical science worldview, it shouldn't be the final assessment. Therefore, the question needs to be asked, "What conditions exist that allow bacteria to grow and cause an ulcer?" If we relate this to cohesion, medical thinking enters new territory. A wider view results from, and produces, new interpretations. Without continually peeling back the layers of influence relating to health and disease, we come up short in our understanding. And, like nocebo responses, not doing so potentially results in harm.

Yet even armed with shamanism or science, humans are not invincible. Disease is an ever-present risk of life. The degree of illness can override the person's capacity to change. The patient continues to have poor health, or drastic intervention like surgery is needed. Generally speaking, body awareness provides a means of navigating health and reducing risk. Shamanism offers a map of what this means and the means to use the map.

Cohesional dynamics offers valuable perspectives to examine and treat disease and to promote health. In these examples, cohesion can be diagramed as the first cause of health or disease. Cohesional dynamics takes into consideration energetic anatomy, states of mind, the resonance between patient and therapist, other aspects of the environment, and the intent of a therapy and of the practitioner.

If medical science were to examine health based on the energy body, the results would be startling. Such research would yield an entirely different way of understanding the human body, changing the practices of diagnosis, prognosis, and treatment. It would bring the practice of science even more into line with ancient knowledge. Part of this knowledge is recapitulating your cohesion, which is a method to revitalize the energy body.

Refreshing the Energy Body

For a properly functioning energy body, you need to refresh it just as you shower to cleanse your physical body. Another way of looking at this is you need to update cohesion just as software programs need updating. Some of the influences shaping cohesion are embedded so deeply, causes of your behavior are unknown and robotic. You can't think straight about why you react in certain ways because you're not aware of the situations producing those behaviors. So you first need to recognize that these influences exist, then you relive them in order to let them go and regain balance.

In shamanism, a principal means to spiff up your tonal is through the *recapitulation*.[31, 32] This consists of methodically reviewing, releasing, and recharging your energies. It is a process of moving forward. By providing a means to review everything that has formed your cohesion, the overriding maneuver of this technique is allowing a natural energy field to surface.

The recapitulation applies to specific events as well as the entirety of your life. It is a means of moving energy, working through matters of concern, and cleaning the tonal. It is another means of dealing with "issues in the tissues." It results in cohesion becoming more supple and fluid. This grants greater ability to change perception and make substantial changes in your life. Past difficulties, if not traumas, are released, and the path forward becomes more apparent. Over time, you will easily sense the pressures within your physical body and recognize whether you're tightening or releasing cohesion. This will help you better trust yourself and what your body is informing you of.

The technique allows you to let go of blockages in cohesion naturally so you may then let go of worry, discomfort, or that argument you just had. It is a type of healing. It is also a form of forgiveness, considering that you can't change cohesion, and therefore your behavior, unless you let go of the old cohesion to make room for the new. You don't let the past command who you are now or want to become.

Paying attention to the breath is often an initial reference no matter the method. In Zen Buddhism, for instance, breath is the doorway that connects inner and outer and acts as a centering mechanism for meditation. Adherents of Tantric Yoga use their breath as a fulcrum to consciously move energy through the body, as well as to release and remove blockages of energy in a similar manner as outlined here. Body massage may perform a similar function as memories and toxins stored in the connective tissues are released.[33] And writing this book served as a personal recapitulation. The following exercise may help you better relate to the applications that follow it.

There are two primary methods: formal and informal. The formal approach requires making an inventory of your life, a list of events beginning with what is pertinent. The informal way is fluid with no schedule. You work with whatever comes to mind. For both styles, self-observation during and after the exercise provides ongoing assessment of any effects. You observe your behaviors and how they relate to your cohesion. You'll discover your behavior has been predetermined by upbringing and professional conditioning. In addition, emotional upheavals happen anytime, anywhere. By familiarizing yourself with the following exercise, you can release emotional events as they occur.

The recapitulation lets you sort through all of this to gain your own sensibilities. The breath is used as a hinge to connect with the topic under examination and then to discharge that energy. But it isn't vital after you gain proficiency. It's a way to get started.

This is a variation of a shamanic recapitulation.[34]

1. Place your chin near your right shoulder. Now move it in a smooth, sweeping motion to your left shoulder. Then back to your right shoulder.
2. As you repeat step 1, inhale through your nose as you sweep from right to left, and exhale through your mouth as you sweep from left to right. That's the mechanics of it. Repeat with your chin near your right shoulder.
3. As you inhale, intend your breath to pull in the energy of the event, person, or feeling under examination. Feel yourself connected with your subject of study, and then use your breath as a bridge to bring that energy into your body. To get a sense of this, pick a minor event that is still somewhat troubling to you.
4. As you tap memories, work from the items surrounding the event, to the people involved, to your feelings. All the while, keep inhaling and exhaling as you sweep your head back and forth.
5. Let your body do the work. It knows what to do. Your part is to engage the exercise and, above all, intend the recapitulation: review, release, and recharge. If you feel your head wants to move in a different rhythm or direction, that's fine. Let your body be in charge, not these directions.
6. Immerse yourself in your memories without indulging. Allow yourself to fully relive the event. If your images or thoughts move to a different subject, allow this to occur. You may need to process something else first and then return to sort out the prior occurrence.
7. Allow the energy to dissipate of its own accord. This facilitates realigning your energy.

8. With experience, you'll find that your intent sets the recapitulation process in motion with or without performing the breathing sweeps. What matters most is intending the recapitulation, not the specific manner of doing so. You may then feel energy moving and releasing anytime, anywhere. When proficiency in recapitulation has been developed, it is possible to gather the full sense of the process, eliminate the steps, and then just apply intent for the same results.
9. Get in the habit of reviewing and releasing anywhere, anytime. Even in the middle of a business conference, you can unobtrusively make one or two breathing sweeps and release energy.

Recapitulation is an essential tool for energy body management. It is key to moving the assemblage point. It assists in redeploying energy. Dreaming and recapitulation work together, for instance. By setting energy free, the assemblage point can move.[35, 36]

In addition, you need to let problems and negative conditions surface in order to deal with them, otherwise they continue to influence your behavior without you knowing why. We carry all the insults and injustices we've experienced or have inflicted on others. These need to be recognized and processed for you to be free of them.

You also need to let go of positive experiences so your cohesion can shift. You don't lose the memories of anything; you lose the fixation. You gain the ability to recognize problems and have the means—the context and skills—to deal with them. Having heartfelt goals assists in moving beyond the past as you capitalize on the effects of your recapitulations. It's not only what you relinquish but also how you move forward. From the recapitulation, you learn to listen to what your body is telling you. Discovering the secrets your body holds will change your life.

Over time, the discharge and realignment of energy becomes conscious. You will also find yourself releasing tensions as they arise. Having a path with heart assists this process. Eventually, you will become aware of composites of energy, gestalts of experience that almost instantly evaporate. Letting go of energies is also a step toward letting go of realities. Letting go is not disregarding, ignoring, or pushing away.

It doesn't mean to lose something you hold dear. It does mean you are tempering your energy body.

Based on anecdotal reports from those who have used this technique, it appears to be a useful psychotherapeutic technique to stimulate memory, relaxation, and learning. It may also prove to have application for the treatment of mental, emotional, and physical disorders, as it provides insight into the cause of a problem and may even resolve the underlying condition by releasing energetic fixations. Unrecognized past trauma affects current behavior.

Another health-related application pertains to relaxation. For many, relaxation has become an altered state of consciousness. Daily tensions build, thereby distorting cohesion. Relaxation reduces inflammation, which is known to be a cause of many disorders.[37] EQ, a benefit of recapitulation, indicates a more balanced cohesion having learned from past mistakes and successes and being more capable of moving forward. Remember, relaxation has also been associated with unplanned OBE.

Furthermore, your past experiences are baked into your cohesion. Once cohesion stabilizes in your formative years, it is difficult to move beyond the conditioning influences. Behavior becomes robotic. Children absorb the energies from others, primarily from parents due to proximity and the need for survival, something children are instinctively in touch with.

Cohesional imprints occur extensively in early development. And you also inherit some of your parents' cohesions. By influencing cohesion to release these fixations, you can change your relationship to what has come before. For the person who has suffered abuse, recapitulation may lessen that hold and allow more self-empowered behaviors. All this is more fodder for research.

Another application relates to reincarnational topics. Don Juan says that while in the throes of death, the dissolving force of the universe normally squelches individual awareness, but it can instead accept a likeness of it and allow individual awareness to remain. He adds that the wavefield wants experiences, raw information, but not a person's life force.[38, 39]

Extensive recapitulation is a way to provide a duplicate of experience and retain one's life force. During a life review in the throes of death, the composites of information reflecting one's life no longer have tension to interact with the dissolving force, and so there is nothing to break apart and remove the awareness of individuality. By entering the third energy field, engaging the Fire from Within, the person might survive death. For a simpler application, recapitulation helps you remember where you came from and your purpose, a memory don Juan says we forget at birth (chapter four).

EXPANDING CONSCIOUSNESS

Decoherence, or the dissipation of the tonal at death, is one thing; shrinking the personal tonal is based on having a proper tonal and increasing awareness. This is another procedure to manage the energy body. It involves reducing or minimizing attention to the daily world and shifting attention deeper into the energy body. This allows more information to enter consciousness.

Ordinary embarrassment gives a reference for shrinking the personal tonal. It disrupts the focus and continuity of awareness. Usually, the reaction is to engage in self-importance as you defend yourself to regain your non-embarrassed self and fend off ridicule. To use embarrassment, you need to forgo this reaction in order to become aware of unusual things outside of usual responses. You simultaneously feel the effects of embarrassment yet remain open to new awareness. In other words, you let pieces of the unknown become conscious by allowing embarrassment to shrink the tonal and the ordinary references to your known world. You need to let go of your self-reflection to become aware of new territory. In addition, the more you sink into the feeling of embarrassment, the more the circumstances producing your reaction become apparent.

When you enter dreaming, you encounter the same dynamic. Your continuity of experience changes, and you reflect on whatever is happening. By reducing your tonal, you go beyond self-reflection, and then by focusing your intent, you can go deeper into dreaming. If you can maintain a minimized tonal, you'll find that your inventory doesn't hold as much sway over you as before. Perception is freer. You're now on fertile ground to grow in ways that were once beyond imagination.

While dreaming, you access more order of the wavefield. Making sense of this relies on using the tonal's order. This is like saying your conditional field filters awareness. Put yet another way, it is taking the tonal into dreaming that allows for meaningful or recognizable experience. This allows you to integrate your dream travels into cohesion and expand awareness, making the entire process a conscious endeavor. As a result, you become the knowledge gained while dreaming. This solidifies an expansion of consciousness as you increase your personal power.

The hallmark of the tonal is organization, and this cuts to the heart of reason. The make-up of the tonal provides meaning but also blinds us to environments outside of its known barriers. The trick is to make expanding consciousness, entertaining new levels of order, reasonable. This keeps the tonal alive and well while lessening its effects. You can then slide away from it to expand consciousness yet grab back onto it to prevent it from falling apart, an event which would make the experience meaningless.

Grooming a well-ordered life that is also flexible supports this ability. It grants the security to risk shrinking the tonal. Don Juan says you don't leave the tonal, you manage it, and do so in a way that maintains balance and health.[40] Dreaming is an exercise to do just this, and it also sets the stage for the general expansion of consciousness. Aimed in the right direction, this leads to a natural energy field.

Being Natural

Holding the tonal too firmly in place, holding fast to a conditional energy field, prevents new awareness. You just recirculate current information, and consciousness remains static. Stopping your internal dialogue is therefore central to stepping away from this whirlpool. A path with heart helps balance the tonal with all parts of the energy body, and the energy body with the environment. From efforts such as these, a natural field gradually takes root. When you bring this into concert with the tonal and nagual, you position the energy body for remarkable feats such as the Fire from Within.

To expand consciousness, the main goal is developing a natural energy field. Boosting the first field by having more awareness of the second field allows for greater innovation and generally increases the options for manifesting. This same process but with an added measure of cultivating the tonal and nagual leads to a natural field, the quintessential condition of humans. You may suddenly experience it, but sustaining it is a different matter. The dynamism of life constantly throws people off balance, although energy management exercises help restore it.

A natural field involves consciously blending the tonal and nagual. As decisions result from acquiescing to the nagual, to maintain this state you need to use different means of navigation than what you're accustomed to. If the nagual is aware of everything, then it is aware of circumstances relating to you that are beyond your current consciousness. Navigating this requires an artful dance of inaccessibility and accessibility. You don't abandon yourself to anything, yet you also abandon yourself to your life.[41] And for this, you need to accurately assess yourself, which brings in the recapitulation along with basic energy management skills. For instance, you'd generally be accessible to the wavefield and inaccessible to other environments.

As a rule, we tend to overly accent and deplete the tonal's resources while completely overlooking another vital aspect of consciousness. One effect of this is that once you get a sense of balance, you'll want to take charge of your life and make decisions based on self-reflection. However, doing so interferes with skillful energy management and removes you from the power of the wavefield and the ability to further expand consciousness. While you need to be responsible for your actions and remain in charge of your life in this way, you simultaneously need to abandon yourself to the flow of the wavefield. You therefore participate with the nagual while allowing your tonal to temper your awareness. This permits the wavefield to reshape your cohesion, rather than it being formed by social circumstances. The secret of this balance is found with body knowledge.

A natural field indicates an optimal alignment within and without, producing clear coherence that permits an interactive flow of information. It is the intersection of the energy body and wavefield. It demonstrates cohesional homeodynamics. This is the energy body's nature, and the nature of *being*. Even when placing the Fire from Within aside, cultivating the nagual is essential for *being*. In a way, it is like a river that guides one's steps. From another angle, it is an emptiness that allows the tonal to awaken. Steps toward a natural field include giving way to this silent power.

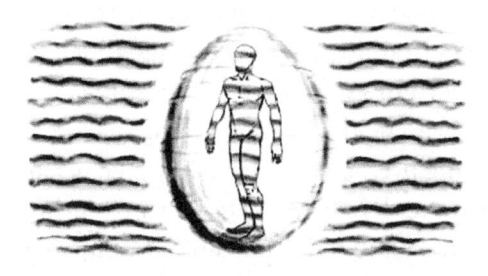

Figure 9.1
A Natural Energy Field
The energy body blending and harmonizing with the wavefield characterizes a natural field.

When internal energies are at rest, says don Juan, they match external emanations. If we let that happen, he says we become fluid, eternal, and we discover what we really are.[42] He adds that intent is a universal force, and it is possible to merge with it.[43] He maintains that, upon doing so, you don't think so that you can think clearly.[44] By not letting self-reflection get in the way of a felt, and more accurate, appraisal, you then act in an appropriate manner without having plans.[45] This marks the state of *being*, and energy management exercises of meditation, nonpatterning, and stopping the internal dialogue act to bring internal energies to rest. Thought then occurs from your complete mind rather than just as a mental process. You become thoughtful and more in touch with self and surroundings.

At some point along this journey, all interpretations and descriptions evaporate, and you are left with the fullness of experience. You're living in the moment, you are the moment, which is when the energy body functions best. It's an effect of a proper tonal and natural energy field. Awareness is less filtered by consensus, self-reflection is minimized, and EQ is enhanced—all leading to a sense of spontaneity appropriate to the environment and without expectation of reward. For this, you need a flexible, resilient, and stable cohesion.

Guidance then occurs in many forms, all depending on the situation at hand, and you don't try to make the world conform to your thoughts. It's bigger and stronger than you, and you'll automatically be out of balance. This state of *being* is difficult to manifest, even more so to sustain. It is a common goal of shamans and other mystics, with procedures to attain it. For example, the person becomes accessible to the wavefield while remaining inaccessible to disruptive influences. Erasing personal history allows the person to let go of the past to become more than before. Disrupting routines allows the flexibility to adjust to changes. Responsibility tempers the energy body, while using death as an advisor results in boldness. A path with heart develops inner peace, and petty tyrants provide the skills to manage the trials of daily life. Combined, these practices form a curriculum for learning about the energy body.

From this, you have both map and meaning for your travels, and a natural field yields new experiences without effort. Not to overstate my experience, I've briefly entered this state on occasion. Once, it lasted for several days. I didn't think much and made my decisions based on feeling. The timing of meeting people was incredulous and the flow of events smooth. I also had several OBEs that occurred seemingly on their own. They just happened throughout the day and night. This led me to understand the importance of cultivating EQ for ordinary travels throughout the day and for OBE. It is the feeling of centeredness within while aiming for your next steps. This sense of *being* stimulates the activation of *will* en route to a natural field.

The travails of following a path toward a natural field are many. Aside from the daily difficulties of shifting to your energy body, you'll feel beaten up by petty tyrants and discouraged you can't get it right, no matter the situation. People you know will criticize you, maybe due to their lack of understanding or maybe not. But when you realize progress, when you connect more deeply with the wavefield, it'll all be worth it. You'll have turned your defeats and triumphs into stage plays of learning. As don Juan says, you will have realized the fortune of having found a challenge.[46]

ELEMENTS OF LEARNING

Everything in this book, all of it, relates to learning. Getting comfortable with new concepts, techniques, and worldviews involves learning. How I came to write it, how you came to read it, and what you or I are doing about it all relate to learning. Therefore, let's look at a few basic forces, pressures, and conditions related to learning (another name for expanding consciousness), and how each fit with what we've been reviewing.

The way to know more is to prioritize learning over knowing. Many of the problems humans face result from not wanting to learn and change behavior. On top of this, knowledge is a form of power, yet we're usually not taught how to learn, but only what to learn, by those already having power. The natural and human worlds are quickly changing, as are the needs for innovation and survival. Learning is the crucial element of manifesting needed change. Mistakes yield valuable information, as does getting it right.

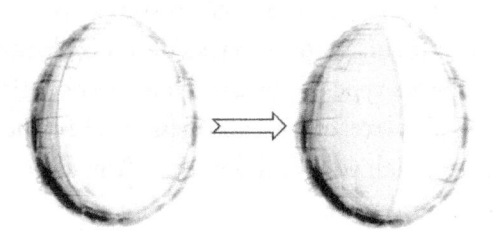

Figure 9.2
Learning
Learning expands the first energy field, the known world, through the energy body. Skills related to all forms of nonpatterning apply, with minimizing self-reflection being the imperative. These give the energy body space to grow. OBE opens you to traveling far and wide, giving you fresh perspectives and pushing the first field further across the energy body.

As for the energy body, basic management exercises combined (chapter five) render the dynamic element of learning. This involves expanding the known order of the first energy field by accessing more of the unknown potential within the second energy field. From another angle, cultivating the second field pulls the first field into it. Different styles of learning yield similar proficiency. Both require destabilizing cohesion for it to expand and restabilize. In other words, you need to be thrown off center to progress, to learn a new balance at a more comprehensive level.

Creating imbalance so that a more comprehensive balance can be achieved is why shamans induce altered states of consciousness. Psychedelic drugs perform this function; energy management skills do it better. Petty tyrants greatly facilitate the process within daily life while dreaming does a superb job within the second field, keeping in mind that true balance comes from uniting the first and second fields.

Control

In general, learning results from stretching awareness further into the environment. As you become more aware, you gain the ability to control events. You then have more influence. While this represents having become more conscious, it also is a substantial impediment to continued learning. Because you have an ability to shape people's awareness and events, you can easily lose yourself to your sense of power, to having this control. But this ability smacks of old cycle machinations. If you don't sidestep this type of power, if you don't continue expanding awareness beyond this level of consciousness, you become locked within yourself and never reach your full potential. You close yourself to life, and perhaps become abusive.

Closure

It is difficult to learn if you keep telling yourself how much you know. This leaves no room to obtain new information. Consciousness becomes locked in place, closed to more awareness. Yet closure is necessary to gather meaning, to chart a course, and to survive. It relates to having a type of knowledge and skills. It is an effect of stabilizing learning, yet it also closes off additional learning by making the known into something too concrete.

Problems arise when closure commands perception to the extent where you can't open the windows for fresh air. We remain in a particular inventory, lost within a worldview. When you hear or read something new, that information is forced into what is already known. OBE can't be legitimate because it results from a broken brain. Other worlds don't exist because those who have power say it is impossible. Perhaps the best way to counter this force is to use your consciousness: pay attention to matters outside of yourself, be aware that closure exists, and intend learning.

Entrainment

This is a type of alignment. Whether an environment is educational, medical, religious, social, or whatever, we become the environment because our cohesion incorporates it. We absorb environmental energies into cohesion. We align internal and external environments. We take on those characteristics and mannerisms. We fall into line with and accept these influences. We fit in.

Our social world develops through an enormous number of entrainment influences that combine to form reality. Confining perception to the physical world of objects results from entraining to that reality. When other abilities surface, such as OBE, we have been taught to disregard those observations since they do not fit the world we have been taught to perceive.

A child is inundated with environmental energies, taking them on as a matter of necessity and without conscious intention. As you grow, you become your parents, as the saying goes. Plus, the culture of your upbringing holds dramatic sway over your perception. If you consort with criminals, you stand an increased chance of entraining to their energy. If you associate with people who are principled, you are influenced to be this way. If you fully entrain to a worldview, you become fundamentalist. If you entrain to source energy, you might step into a mystical experience.

Entrainment can be managed by being accessible or inaccessible at any turn in the road. The more accessible you are, the more environmental energies shape your cohesion. But openness to the wavefield is one thing, participating in dysfunctional behavior another. It helps to find environments that let you breathe easier, grow quicker, and have more fun.

Contrary Evidence

Regarding entrainment, in our efforts to maintain a stable cohesion we tend to ignore perceptions that don't fit with the way we think things ought to be. Regarding nonordinary realities, we are often taught to ignore the substance of dreams as they are just something we do during sleep. OBEs can be chalked up to flights of imagination.

However, any manifestation of the cornerstones of awareness is contrary evidence pertaining to a rigid, material world. *Seeing* energy contradicts what has been taught, as does having an OBE. Like traversing any path, assessing contradictions always rests in your hands. Whether you find fallacy, or flush out the details, you've benefited. If you don't take the time to fully examine the situation, you're certain to remain within a hardened conditional field.

By failing to recognize contrary evidence, at best we remain off balance with ourselves. We can't develop awareness by refusing awareness. At worst, failure to pay attention produces a false sense of invincibility, the same feeling that led to the downfall of the old cycle shamanic world and to human-made climate change.

Simply put, this means not arbitrarily dismissing evidence. At the same time, being onto something doesn't mean you've found it. You can't manage knowledge by taking a scrap of information, associating it with your interests, and then generalizing the scrap into a broad-base conclusion.

The Bureaucratic Mind

Another area that sheds light on the effects of belief and the formation of conditional fields is the bureaucratic mind, a situation where perception, thought, and behavior are organized in line with the status quo.

This results from an over-accentuation of self-reflection that forms a mental bureaucracy where thinking is compartmentalized, departmentalized, and passed on to others with minimal examination of value.

A form of fundamentalism, reason becomes bureaucratized by conditioning, authority, and a desire for belonging in a group. Expectations shape what you perceive and develop from what you think. The firmer your expectations, the more you're bureaucratized, and the more you filter out what is in front of you.

In addition, groups tend to become bureaucratic. This often results in dogmatic, inflexible rules that are unyielding to new requirements. Groups with harmonious interactions can significantly increase productivity for individuals and the group. But while you may participate in a group for the betterment of everyone, there may come a time when the group becomes a hindrance. You then need to decide how to proceed. You can try changing group dynamics or leave the group. Effectiveness with either is a sign of personal power. If you leave, it doesn't mean you completely step away from groups. You're just more deliberate in your choices.

What occurs with having a bureaucratic mind is that throughout the course of the day, a person adheres to a particular mindset. Any deviation from what is considered normal, especially if it suggests new pathways, is ignored. Or, worse yet, pressure from others is applied to bring the person's thinking around to accepting the bureaucracy. Reality becomes stereotyped, and behavior falls in line. Options for living have become significantly reduced. In modern times, we have no idea the dreaming part of human life exists. We're rarely taught about it. Worse yet, the teachings that do exist are often labeled errant because perception must conform to the current view of reality.

Plus, authorities seek to maintain the power of their knowledge and position, which not only addresses the topic at hand but the use and abuse of power. Societies tend to be structured in terms of power, with those at the top of the chart having the most, or at least designated as having the most. Wise power brokers understand the effects of their actions and employ their authority in harmonious ways.

In all cases, the bureaucratic mind creates a perceptual prison. Cohesion is constricted, with stress possibly leading to ill health. A way out is recognizing this as a form of the petty tyrant. Adhere to energy body fundamentals without becoming fundamentalist. Remember that everything is an interpretation in an ultimately unknowable world.

Experience

The only way to handle information is to taste it with experience, says don Juan.[47] Tension is needed to shift cohesion, and action is a quickening agent. Experience provides both. Part of learning is setting up conditions of pressure, and knowing why you're doing this is another part. Experience results from alignments of energy. It sets the stage to change interpretations, to open the doors to new worlds, and to verify what you're already thinking. Experience broadens the scope and flexibility of cohesion. By acting just for the sake of it without anticipation of reward, you might find you have interesting experiences that fill in gaps of learning.

Experience is based on action and, as don Juan says, new actions produce new reflections.[48] This forms new realities. Pertaining to the energy body, new experience comes from developing each cornerstone. This accelerates learning, expands consciousness, and adds to personal and professional growth. Categorizing dreaming levels, which pertains to individuals and also reflects a sub-technology of shamanism, resulted from the experiences of dreaming combined with *seeing* the overall dynamic of utilizing dreaming for the expansion of consciousness.

Method

Teaching shamanism relies on two primary methods: those of reason and *will*. Reason gradually builds a foundation to move the assemblage point. Over time, experiencing nonordinary reality becomes reasonable. The other method, the use of *will*, places the student squarely and immediately, with no thought, in another cohesion, another world.

While the second remains in practice, new cycle shamans prefer the use of reason to develop understanding and a keener sense of the path, but only up to the time when *will* and the complete energy body take precedence. As the potential of the second field becomes realized and there is less of a sense of the division between the first and second, the relation to life dramatically shifts. It also becomes obvious that shamanism is a method to arrive at the full energy body and is not, itself, reality.

Scientists' principal references for learning are books, journal articles, and instruments while shamans rely on the cornerstones. The practice of science requires that an experiment be successfully repeated; replicated, in scientific terms. If enough scientists can do this, a consensus develops that what is studied is on the right track. Shamans build consensus but only require validation of experience based on two similar events to move forward. This is like journalism where one source must confirm the information of another. This doesn't by any means preclude additional sources, but the basic requirement to move forward has been met. In both cases, consensus allows a wider grasp of knowledge but may also impede innovation, as it can dampen the progress of research that has great potential.

Both shaman and scientist must remain as clear-eyed and objective as possible, given that both are seeking to participate in their respective descriptions of reality. In practice, a change of consensus for a new worldview requires acceptance of radical experience. This takes time but doesn't necessarily hold back intrepid people willing to forge new paths. They'll just be marooned for a while. In the meantime, having a goal that requires substantial learning pushes you off your current mark, makes you look at life anew, and, in this way, renews your life.

A TRAJECTORY OF CONSCIOUSNESS

This book covers a fraction of human capability which, overall, concerns our ontological makeup. As used here, ontology focuses on the general state of consciousness and its relation to the world, if not the cosmos. It relates to the nature of *being*, which corresponds with a natural field. Its wide-angle consciousness incorporates multiple forms of awareness and dimensions of existence. It includes the full breadth of human capacities. Your current ontological state determines how you live your life and what you experience. This is where you put it all together and every element of your life forms one neat package.

Ontological intelligence means consciously connecting with and learning the natural order of life. From an energy body perspective, you align more fully with the world at large without losing sense of yourself. This requires attention to be placed within the body. Material technology displaces body knowledge. It requires attention to an external, material world. A similar effect occurs when relying too much on book knowledge when intellectual learning becomes overly authoritative. While both can help orient you to your body and activate *will*, at that time entirely different skills are needed to navigate life. Your experience of reality has markedly changed.

Addressing this is a matter of stretching further into the first field, which expands your known world. This process can be boosted by use of the second field, by being open to that energy and learning to intend effects, a positive use of personal power. Dreaming is therefore a path for ontological development, and when oriented to a natural field, each dreaming level further expands consciousness. The effect is that you become more plugged into life, have more options at your disposal, and have a way of being. You can access your totality.

A trajectory of awakening the totality, says don Juan, involves learning to free existing energy, using the energy of dreaming to develop the energy body, and then using this awareness to place the physical body in other worlds. He maintained that under the leadership of top-tier shamans, entire civilizations have disappeared into another dimension, never to return.[49]

Put another way, the first stage pertains to grooming a proper tonal. The second stage consists of developing dreaming to a level that includes awareness of, and increased sensitivity to, the tonal and nagual. This allows for managing cohesion fluently, which leads to the ability of modifying uniformity. This grants proficiency to align with and scout dimensions beyond the ordinary human bandwidth of the wavefield. Doing so sets up conditions for the third stage, where the energy body fully awakens in a flash of consciousness then jumps outside the human domain as it enacts the Fire from Within.[50]

The trajectory stages correlate with focusing awareness on the first, second, and third energy fields. The underlying process involves shining the personal tonal, gaining proficiency with dreaming, and merging the first and second fields with increasing degrees of efficiency to tap other dimensions. Each of the three stages influences the others. It is a matter of using your complete range of consciousness that determines your focus and ability to manage perception.

Along this route, you become less influenced by social consensus. You find yourself to be self-contained, balanced with the environment, and with your wits about you. Throughout this journey, strive to maintain harmony with life, a highly animated undertaking requiring flexibility, wherewithal of skill, and ongoing learning. Finding your path with heart, for instance, helps enact OBE. In turn, OBE can help you find your path. Combined, they provide meaningful experience, afford practice for adaptability, generate a fuller sense of life and living, and accelerate the expansion of consciousness. The more skills you have and the more confident you become in your abilities, the faster you learn. You increasingly become more aware in large chunks of knowledge, the gestalts of awareness as previously mentioned.

Energy management skills provide the foundation for this path, and the dreaming levels offer a roadmap for achieving competency in the stepwise progression of blending the first and second energy fields. All of this is guided by an EQ profile of patience, perseverance, and boldness. The end goal doesn't need to be the Fire from Within, although for some that might be an option. Arriving at a natural energy field is itself a lifetime accomplishment. It is a path of constant change, of releasing yourself to life, participating with the wavefield, and witnessing your personal journey of realizing your totality. This is the quest, says don Juan, "...to know, to discover, to be bewildered."[51]

Our totality is the complete energy body: uniformity, cohesion, chakras, meridians, first and second energy fields—everything. It offers the essential human experience. Don Juan says we become aware of it at death when the energy body expands, disintegrates, and earthly cohesions evaporate. He adds that this is also when we learn the mystery of life. He then poses the question that if we die with our totality, why not live with it?[52]

LIVING THE UNKNOWABLE

While life may be inherently unknowable, this doesn't mean you throw up your hands and stop learning. Human understanding pertains to the structure of life, and the ultimate story will always remain out of reach. When we're not learning, life is mechanical, robotic, and devoid of meaning. Learning is discovering better ways to understand and use the immensity about us, and how to better navigate it with less distortions.

New cycle shamans and modern scientists are together forming a new consensus reality where the wavefield is front and center. While this may be light years ahead of traditional shamanism and classical science, it is still a description from which interpretations follow. It is notable that both shamans and scientists acknowledge this.

It is against the backdrop of the unknowable that don Juan says the shamanic description of the world is an "explanation that doesn't explain anything."[53] In other words, while it enhances the options for consciousness, the extensiveness of this worldview needs to be checked by the understanding that it is still a description. Physicist Fritjof Capra similarly says that modern physics has confirmed the mystical view that "the concepts we use to describe nature are limited, that they are not features of reality, as we tend to believe, but creations of the mind...."[54]

Our energy bodies reside in a sea of infinity that cannot be completely collapsed into a worldview. The best we can do is have navigational maps that help us get somewhere, all the while knowing the map only provides options of where we can travel. Life itself is beyond our comprehension, and this yields the sense of awe don Juan prescribes.

The shaman is not bound by reason but by natural order. While shamans have kept this knowledge alive, the ability to use and derive benefit from the energy body rests firmly within all of us. Basic elements of shamanism as presented herein provide perspectives and practices designed to develop your energy body and arrive at a natural energy field and do so regardless of your interest in shamanism. By using your energy body, you stand to claim the fullness of yourself. You become aware of what already exists but is buried from sight due to the pressures of daily life.

At the same time, the practices are props, guideposts to facilitate this type of journey. Along the trajectory of increasing awareness, it becomes more important to live a meaningful life rather than to live a description. Ultimately, life is about performance. It is going through the day using all your resources. The outcome, how far you travel, rests with how well you power up your energy body.

References

CHAPTER 1: ENTERING THE LUMINOUS WORLD
1. Castaneda, Carlos. *Journey to Ixtlan: The Lessons of Don Juan*. New York: Washington Square Press, 1972.
2. -----. *The Teachings of Don Juan: A Yaqui Way of Knowledge*. New York: Washington Square Press, 1968.
3. -----. *A Separate Reality: Conversations with Don Juan*. New York: Washington Square Press, 1971.
4. Following Castaneda's lead and don Juan's request, I'm not using the name he gave me. I use don Juan to indicate the continuity of his teachings with those of Castaneda.
5. Monroe, Robert A. *Journeys Out of the Body*. New York: Doubleday, 1971.
6. Eagle Feather, Ken. *Traveling with Power: The Exploration and Development of Perception*. Charlottesville, VA: Hampton Roads Publishing, 1992, 1996.
7. Smith, Kenneth. *The Complete Energy Body: A Space Age Exploration of Consciousness, Life, and Reality*. Wilmington, NC: EB Dynamics, LLC, 2022.
8. Eagle Feather, Ken. *On the Toltec Path*. Rochester, VT: Bear & Company, 2006.
9. Castaneda, Carlos. *Tales of Power*. New York: Washington Square Press, 1974, 122.
10. -----. *Separate Reality*, 5.
11. -----. *The Power of Silence: Further Lessons of Don Juan*. New York: Simon & Schuster, 1987, ix.
12. -----. *The Fire from Within*. New York: Washington Square, 1991, 3.
13. -----. *The Active Side of Infinity*. New York: HarperCollins, 1998, 178.
14. -----. *Fire from Within*, 48-49.
15. -----. *The Art of Dreaming*. New York: HarperCollins, 1993, 3-4.

CHAPTER 2: CREATING THE ENERGY BODY
1. Castaneda. *Art of Dreaming*, 3-4.
2. -----. *Fire from Within*, 14-18.
3. Projection. Encyclopedia Britannica. https://www.britannica.com/science/projection-psychology, accessed March 14, 2023.
4. Healthy Relationships. https://www.monikahoyt.com/projection-in-relationships, accessed March 14, 2023.
5. Tart, Charles T, ed. *Altered States of Consciousness*, rev ed. New York: HarperSanFrancisco, 1990, 581-599.
6. Kornfield, Jack. *A Path with Heart: A Guide through the Perils and Promises of Spiritual Life*. New York: Bantam Books, 1993, 120-122.
7. Castaneda. *Fire from Within*, 4.
8. Ibid, 2-6.
9. Ibid, 33.
10. Castaneda. *Ixtlan*, 91.
11. Deikman, Arthur. *The Wrong Way Home: Uncovering the Patterns of Cult Behavior in America*. Boston: Beacon Press, 1990.

12. Castaneda. *Infinity*, 115.
13. Smith, Kenneth. *Shamanism for the Age of Science: Awakening the Energy Body*. Rochester, VT: Bear & Co., 2011, 4-12.
14. Oschman, James. E-mail correspondence, May 19, 2005, June 11, 2005.
15. Wolff, Milo. E-mail correspondence, October 14 and 15, 2005.
16 Zurek WH. "Decoherence and the transition from quantum to classical – Revisited." *Los Alamos Science*, 27, 2002, 2-25.
17. Ho, Mae-Wan. *The Rainbow and the Worm: The Physics of Organisms, Third Edition*. Singapore: World Scientific Publishing, 2008, 298.
18. Folger T. "Crossing the Quantum Divide." *Scientific American*, July 2018, 28-35.
19. Schlosshauer, M. "The quantum-to-classical transition and decoherence." Cornell University Library. https://arxiv.org/abs/1404.2635, accessed July 25, 2018.
20. Castaneda. *Infinity*, 178.
21. -----. *Fire from Within*, 38-39.
22. Schlosshauer. "quantum-to-classical transition."
23. Zurek WH. "Decoherence and the transition from quantum to classical." *Physics Today*, October 1991, 36-44.
24. Zurek. "Decoherence – Revisited."
25. The Information Philosopher. "The Quantum to Classical Transition." http://www.informationphilosopher.com/introduction/physics/quantum_to_classical.html, accessed July 23, 2018.
26. Ho, Mae Wan. "Quantum Coherence and Conscious Experience." *Kybernetes*, 26(3), 1997, 265-276.
27. Information Philosopher, "Quantum to Classical."
28. Castaneda. *Fire from Within*, 37.
29. Stanford University on-line library. https://plato.stanford.edu/entries/information/#HisDevMeaTerInf, accessed November 15, 2017.
30. Ananthaswamy A. "Essence of Reality: Hunting the universe's most basic ingredient." *New Scientist*. https://www.newscientist.com/article/mg23331112-900-essence-of-reality-hunting-the-universes-most-basic-ingredient/, accessed February 1, 2017.
31. Kelly K. "Why the Basis of the Universe Isn't Matter or Energy—It's Data." *Wired*, 02.28.11.
32. Vedral, Vlatko. Oxford University Physicist. https://www.youtube.com/watch?v=QfQ2r0zvyoA, accessed November 2, 2017.
33. Castaneda. *Fire from Within*, 38.

CHAPTER 3: ENERGY BODY DYNAMICS
1. Castaneda. *Art of Dreaming*, 9-11.
2. Ibid, 228-229.
3. Light bulb image. http://clipart-library.com/clipart/yikrq9XbT.htm, accessed August 18, 2022.
4. Castaneda. *Fire from Within*, 65, 66.
5. -----. *Art of Dreaming*, 12.

6. -----. *Tales of Power*, 116-209.
7. Ibid, 272.
8. Ibid, 124-131.
9. Ibid, 120-126.
10. Ibid, 125, 140.
11. Ibid, 4, 98.
12. Castaneda. *Ixtlan*, 193.
13. -----. *Fire from Within*, 3.
14. -----. *Art of Dreaming*, 3.
15. -----. *Tales of Power*, 277.
16. Ibid, 93.
17. Hobson, J Allan. *Consciousness*. New York: Scientific American Books, 1999, 2.
18. Stillings, Neil A, et al. *Cognitive Science: An Introduction. Second Edition.* Cambridge, MA: The MIT Press, 1995, 15.
19. Oschman JL and Pressman MD. "An Anatomical, Biochemical, Biophysical and Quantum Basis for the Unconscious Mind." *International Journal of Transpersonal Studies,* 33(1), 2014, 77-96.
20. Castaneda. *Tales of Power*, 239.
21. Cognition. https://www.britannica.com/topic/cognition-thought-process, accessed June 25, 2023.
22. Blackmore, Susan. *Consciousness: An Introduction*. Oxford: Oxford University Press, 2004, 13.
23. Stillings. *Cognitive Science*, 15.
24. Castaneda. *Power of Silence,* 166.
25. -----. *Art of Dreaming*, 3-4.
26. Ho. "Quantum Coherence."
27. -----. *Tales of Power*, 130.
28. -----. *Fire from Within*, 46.
29. Information Philosopher. "Quantum to Classical."

CHAPTER 4: OUR MULTI-DIMENSIONAL WORLD
1. Wall, Mike. "Perseverance rover spies signs of ancient raging rivers on Mars," Space.com, May 11, 2023, https://www.space.com/perseverance-rover-ancient-raging-river, accessed July 3, 2023.
2. Lovelock, James. *Gaia: A New Look at Life on Earth*. Oxford: Oxford University Press, 2016.
3. Castaneda. *Fire from Within*, 204.
4. Mohawk JA, et al. "Central and Peripheral Circadian Clocks in Mammals." *Annual Review of Neuroscience,* 35, 2012, 445-462.
5. Holzman DC. "What's in a Color? The Unique Human Health Effects of Blue Light." *Environmental Health Perspectives,* 118(1), January 2010, A22-27.
6. Cosic I, et al. "Human Electrophysiological Signal Responses to ELF Schumann Resonance and Artificial Electromagnetic Fields." *FME Transactions,* 34(2), 2006.

7. Balser M and Wagner CA. "Observations of Earth-Ionosphere Cavity Resonances." *Nature*, 188, November 19, 1960, 638-641.
8. Kandel ER, et al, eds. *Principles of Neural Science, Fourth Edition*. New York: McGraw-Hill, 2000, 916-917.
9. Cosic. "Human Electrophysiological Signal Responses."
10. Babayev ES and Allahverdiyeva AA. "Effects of geomagnetic activity variations on the physiological and psychological state of functionally healthy humans: Some results of Azerbaijani studies." *Advances in Space Research*, 40, 2007, 1941-1951.
11. Palmer SJ, et al. "Solar and geomagnetic activity, extremely low frequency magnetic and electric fields and human health at the Earth's surface." *Surveys in Geophysics*, 27(5), September 2006, 557-595.
12. Cherry N. "Schumann Resonances, a plausible biophysical mechanism for the human health effects of Solar, Geomagnetic Activity." *Natural Hazards*, 26(3), July 2002, 279-331.
13. Merrill RT. *Our Magnetic Earth: The Science of Geomagnetism*. Chicago: University of Chicago Press, 2010, 177-178.
14. Rusov VD, et al. "Can Resonant Oscillations of the Earth Ionosphere Influence the Human Brain Biorhythm?" Cornell University Library. http://arxiv.org/pdf/1208.4970.pdf, accessed 28 March 2016.
15. Medvedev MV and Melott AL. "Do extragalactic cosmic rays induce cycles in fossil diversity?" http://arxiv.org/pdf/astro-ph/0602092v3.pdf, accessed March 28, 2016.
16. Zirker JB. *The Magnetic Universe: The Elusive Traces of an Invisible Force*. Baltimore, MD: The Johns Hopkins University Press, 2009, 128-129, 252-264.
17. Arthur, W Brian. *The Nature of Technology: What It Is and How It Evolves*. New York: Free Press, 2009, 28.
18. Castaneda. *Infinity*, 268-270.
19. -----. *Fire from Within*, 31-46.
20. Ibid, 43.
21. Ibid.
22. Ibid, 109, 122-124.
23. Ibid, 50.
24. Zurek. "Decoherence and the transition from quantum to classical."
25. Castaneda. *Infinity* 189-191.
26. Ibid, 199.
27. -----. *Fire from Within*, 175.
28. -----. *Art of Dreaming*, 115.
29. Rees, Martin. BBC Future. "If alien life is artificially intelligent, it may be stranger than we can imagine." https://www.bbc.com/future/article/20231025-if-alien-life-is-artificially-intelligent-it-may-be-stranger-than-we-can-imagine, accessed November 4, 2023.
30. *Los Angeles Times*. "Navy releases video of 'unidentified aerial phenomena." https://www.youtube.com/watch?v=PLbosBj9Dow, accessed April 28, 2020.

31. Conte M. "Pentagon officially releases UFO videos." CNN. https://www.cnn.com/2020/04/27/politics/pentagon-ufo-videos/index.html, accessed April 28, 2020.
32. Marshall P. "Mystical Experiences as Windows on Reality," in *Beyond Physicalism: Toward a Reconciliation of Science and Spirituality*. Kelly, Edward F, et al., eds. Lanham, MD: Rowman & Littlefield, 2015, 42.
33. Castaneda. *Tales of Power*, 272.
34. James, William. *The Varieties of Religious Experience*. New York: Macmillan, 1961, 292-294.
35. Dimitropoulos S. "Trying to Lose My Religion." *Discover*, September 2017, 26-27.
36. Kelly, Edward F and Kelly, Emily Williams. *Irreducible Mind: Toward a Psychology for the 21st Century*. Lanham, MD: Rowman & Littlefield Publishers, 2007, 531-535.
37. Schlosshauer M. "The quantum-to-classical transition and decoherence." Cornell University Library. https://arxiv.org/abs/1404.2635, 1-22, accessed July 25, 2018.
38. Ho MW. "Quantum Coherence and Conscious Experience." *Kybernetes* 26(3), 1997, 265-276.
39. Kelly. *Irreducible Mind*, 411-427.
40. Ibid, 394.
41. Weiss, Eric M. "Mind Beyond Body: Transphysical Process Metaphysics," in *Beyond Physicalism*, 457-459.
42. Kelly. *Irreducible Mind*, 372-373.
43. Ibid.
44. Ibid, 374-376.
45. Castaneda. *Fire from Within*, 290-291.
46. Ibid, 259.
47. -----. *Infinity*, 202.
48. -----. *Tales of Power*, 52.
49. -----. *Infinity*, 202.
50. -----. *Art of Dreaming*, 197.
51. Wallace, B Alan. *The Taboo of Subjectivity: Toward a New Science of Consciousness*. Oxford: Oxford University Press, 2000, 5.
52. Stevenson, Ian. *20 Cases Suggestive of Reincarnation, Second Edition*. Charlottesville, VA: University of Virginia Press, 1980.
53. Stevenson, Ian. *Where Reincarnation and Biology Intersect*. Westport, CT.: Praeger, 1997.
54. Tucker, Jim B. *Return to Life: Extraordinary Cases of Children Who Remember Past Lives*. New York: St. Martin's Griffin, 2013.
55. Leininger, Bruce and Leininger, Andrea. *Soul Survivor: The Reincarnation of a World War II Fighter Pilot*. New York: Grand Central Publishing, 2009.
56. Weiss, Brian. *Many Lives, Many Masters. The True Story of a Prominent Psychiatrist, His Young Patient, and the Past-Life Therapy That Changed Both Their Lives*. New York: Simon & Schuster, 1988, 10, 43.

57. Castaneda. *Tales of Power*, 132, 254, 272.
58. -----. *Infinity*, 2, 191, 267.
59. -----. *Fire from Within*, 42, 67, 114, 247.
60. Ibid.
61. -----. *Art of Dreaming*, 73.
62. -----. *Power of Silence*, 103, 122-123.

CHAPTER 5: MANAGING YOUR ENERGY BODY
1. Castaneda. *Infinity*, 224.
2. -----. *Art of Dreaming*, 204.
3. -----. *Ixtlan*, 26-25.
4. Deikman AJ. "Deautomatization and the Mystic Experience," in *Altered States of Consciousness, Revised*, Tart, Charles T., ed. San Francisco: HarperSanFrancisco, 1990, 34-57.
5. Castaneda. *Ixtlan*, 181-199.
6. Ornstein, Robert. *The Psychology of Consciousness*. New York: Penguin Books, 1986, 37-38.
7. Castaneda. *Tales of Power*, 238-242.
8. -----. *Ixtlan*, 39.
9. -----. *Fire from Within*, 170-171.
10. Csikszentmihalyi, Mihaly. *Flow: The Psychology of Optimal Experience*. New York: HarperPerennial, 1990, 26-27.
11. Castaneda. *Art of Dreaming*, 124.
12. -----. *Fire from Within*, 40.

CHAPTER 6: A FOUNDATION FOR OUT-OF-BODY EXPERIENCE
1. Castaneda. *Tales of Power*, 11, 62.
2. -----. *Fire from Within*, 237.
3. -----. *The Eagle's Gift*. New York: Washington Square Press, 1981, 54.
4. -----. *Fire from Within*, 179-180.
5. -----. *Art of Dreaming*, 200-231.
6. Gabbard, Glenn O and Twemlow, Stuart. *With the Eyes of the Mind: An Empirical Analysis of Out-of-Body States*. New York: Praeger, 1984, 27-39.
7. Penfield W. "The Role of the Temporal Cortex in Certain Psychical Phenomena." *The Journal of Mental Science*, 101(424), July 1955, 451-465.
8. Penfield W and Perot P. "The Brain's Record of Auditory and Visual Experience." *Brain*, 86, 1963, 595-696.
9. Modi, Shakuntala. *Remarkable Healings*. Charlottesville, VA: Hampton Roads Publishing, 1997, 89.
10. Besant, Annie. *Study in Consciousness: A Contribution to the Science of Psychology, Second Edition*. London: Theosophical Publishing Society, 1915.
11. Castaneda. *Art of Dreaming*, 50.
12. Ibid, 19.
13. Burr HS and Northrop FSC. "The Electro-dynamic Theory of Life." *The Quarterly Review of Biology*, 10(3), September 1935, 322-333.

14. Ho. "Quantum Coherence and Conscious Experience."
15. Jenny, Hans. *Cymatics: Wave Phenomena, Vibrational Effects, Harmonic Oscillations with their Structure, Kinetics, and Dynamics.* Basel, Switzerland: Basilius Presse, 1974, 7-8.
16. Castaneda. *Fire from Within*, 55.

CHAPTER 7: OUT-OF-BODY AEROBICS
1. Castaneda. *Ixtlan*, 99-112.
2. -----. *Tales of Power*, 12.
3. Monroe. *Journeys.*
4. Castaneda. *Ixtlan*, 110-112.
5. -----. *Art of Dreaming*, 21.
6. -----. *Tales of Power*, 10.

CHAPTER 8: IN-THE-BODY EXPERIENCE
1. Folger. "Crossing the Quantum Divide."
2. Castaneda. *Tales of Power*, 249.
3. -----. *Infinity*, 182.
4. -----. *Tales of Power*, 217-218.
5. -----. *Infinity*, 10.
6. -----. *Fire from Within*, 40, 42-43, 76.
7. -----. *Tales of Power*, 140.
8. -----. *Power of Silence*, xi-xii.
9. -----. *Art of Dreaming*, 11.
10. -----. *Tales of Power*, 122.
11. The Information Philosopher. "The Quantum to Classical Transition."
12. PSI Research, "Visualization Improves Athletic Success," *Venture Inward*, 11(4), July/August 1995.
13. Castaneda. *Tales of Power*, 23.
14. Smith, Huston. *The World's Religions: Our Great Wisdom Traditions.* San Francisco: HarperSanFrancisco, 1991, 108.
15. Castaneda. *Teachings*, 160-161.
16. -----. *Fire from Within*, 19.
17. Ibid, 282.
18. Jaynes, Julian. *The Origin of Consciousness in the Breakdown of the Bicameral Mind.* Boston: Houghton Mifflin, 1977.

CHAPTER 9: LIFE WITH AN ENERGY BODY
1. Castaneda. *Separate Reality*, 30.
2. Miller, Benjamin. *Miller-Keane Encyclopedia and Dictionary of Medicine, Nursing, and Allied Health, Seventh Edition.* London: Saunders, 2003.
3. Ho. "Quantum Coherence and Conscious Experience."
4. Castaneda. *Art of Dreaming*, 37.
5. -----. *Tales of Power*, 122.

6. Ibid, 123.
7. Ibid, 125, 140.
8. Ibid, 140, 143.
9. Ibid, 242.
10. Ibid, 120.
11. Ibid, 135.
12. Castaneda. *Art of Dreaming*, 130.
13. *American Heritage College Dictionary*, 3rd ed., Boston: Houghton Mifflin Company, 2000, 139.
14. Burr and Northrop. "The Electro-dynamic Theory of Life."
15. Ho. "Quantum Coherence and Conscious Experience."
16. Hunt, Valerie V. *Infinite Mind: Science of the Human Vibrations of Consciousness*. Malibu, CA: Malibu Publishing, 1996, 244-247.
17. Oschman, *Energy Medicine*, 74, 206, 209.
18. Brodwin E. "Evidence is mounting that psychedelic drugs can help treat diseases." *Business Insider*. https://www.businessinsider.sg/most-promising-uses-psychedelic-drugs-medicine-science-2018-10, June 14, 2019, accessed April 24, 2020.
19. Earleywine, Mitch, ed. *Mind-Altering Drugs: The Science of Subjective Experience*. Oxford: Oxford University Press, 2005, 27-28, 35-36.
20. Hobson. *Consciousness*, 306-307, 315-317.
21. Castaneda. *Separate Reality*, 6.
22. -----. *The Second Ring of Power*. New York: Washington Square Press, 1977, 324.
23. -----. *Ixtlan*, vii-ix.
24. Schlebusch KP, et al. "Biophotonics in the Infrared Spectral Range Reveal Acupuncture Meridian Structure of the Body." *The Journal of Alternative and Complementary Medicine*, 11(1), 2005, 171-173.
25. Castaneda. *Tales of Power*, 82.
26. Oschman, James. *Energy Medicine: The Scientific Basis*. Edinburgh, Scotland: Churchill Livingston, 2000, 227.
27. Castaneda. *Art of Dreaming*, 135.
28. Lipton, Bruce. *Biology of Belief: Unleashing the Power of Consciousness, Matter and Miracles*. Santa Rosa, CA: Elite Books, 2005, 135, 84, 137-141.
29. Ibid, 127, 142-144.
30. Ibid, 138.
31. Castaneda, *Eagle's Gift*, 285–289.
32. Victor Sanchez, *The Toltec Path of Recapitulation: Healing Your Past to Free Your Soul*. Rochester, VT: Bear & Company, 2001.
33. Oschman J and Oschman N. "Somatic Recall," *Massage Therapy Journal*, 34(3), Summer 1995, 36-45, 111-116.
34. Abelar, Taisha. *The Sorcerer's Crossing: A Woman's Journey*. New York: Penguin Arkana, 1992, 42–65.
35. Castaneda. *Power of Silence*, 124-125.
36. -----. *Art of Dreaming*, 148-149.

37. Yale Medicine. "How Inflammation Affects Your Health." April 8, 2022. https://www.yalemedicine.org/news/how-inflammation-affects-your-health, accessed July 31, 2023.
38. Castaneda. *Art of Dreaming*, 149.
39. -----. *Infinity*, 148.
40. -----. *Tales of Power*, 155, 245.
41. -----. *Separate Reality*, 151, 180.
42. -----. *Fire from Within*, 56-57.
43. -----. *Infinity*, 10, 72.
44. -----. *Power of Silence*, 123.
45. -----. *Ixtlan*, 159, 165.
46. -----. *Tales of Power*, 55.
47. -----. *Infinity*, 182.
48. -----. *Tales of Power*, 24.
49. -----. *Fire from Within*, 5.
50. -----. *Art of Dreaming*, 185-186.
51. Ibid, 75.
52. Castaneda. *Tales of Power*, 132, 245.
53. Ibid, 252, 272.
54. Capra, Fritjof. *The Tao of Physics: An Exploration of the Parallels Between Modern Physics and Eastern Mysticism*. Boston: Shambhala, 1999, 181.

Illustrations

Figure 1.1: The Energy Body, 20

Figure 2.1: Cup or Faces Paradox, 30
Figure 2.2: Environmental Emanations, 48
Figure 2.3: A Meeting of Minds, 51

Figure 3.1: The Assemblage Point, 55
Figure 3.2, a & b: Assemblage Point Shift, 56
Figure 3.3: Chakra Locations, 57
Figure 3.4, a & b: Ancient and Modern Meridian Charts, 58
Figure 3.5: Light Bulb Aura, 59
Figure 3.6: Energy Fields, 62
Figure 3.7, a & b: Conditional and Natural Fields, 64
Figure 3.8: The Expansion of Consciousness, 75

Figure 6.1: Centers of Dreaming Levels, 126

Figure 9.1: A Natural Energy Field, 213
Figure 9.2: Learning, 215

Index

Accessible and Inaccessible, 102–103, 165, 174, 179, 190, 212
Alignment, 43, 54, 60–61, 67, 71, 75, 79, 83, 86–87, 98, 108, 111, 122, 141, 155, 164, 168, 170, 173–176, 213, 217, 220–222
Assemblage point, 55–57, 61, 93, 101, 124, 193, 208
Astral projection, 26, 129
Attentions, levels of (see Energy fields)
Aura, 59–60

Being, 213–214, 221
Bioenergetics, 44–46
Body knowledge, 77, 100, 112–114, 170, 173, 180, 186, 212

Capra, Fritjof, 224
Castaneda, Carlos, 9–10, 24–25, 126, 144, 201
Chakras, 19–20, 57–59, 67, 72, 85, 93, 128, 155, 202
    kundalini, 128, 150
Coherence, 47–50, 54–60, 65, 81, 86, 142–143
    wave-packet, 47
Cohesion, 53–59, 61, 86, 107, 110–111, 127, 131, 141–143, 147, 169, 173, 181, 193, 204, 206, 209
    cohesional dynamics, 142, 166, 173, 199, 201, 203, 205
Conditioning, 29, 32, 63, 86, 198, 204, 219
Consciousness, 9, 21, 74–76, 79, 101, 126, 169, 211
    trajectory, 221–223
Consensus (see Social agreement)
Cornerstones of perception, 67–74, 100, 108, 113
    see talking, feeling, nagual, reason, *seeing*, tonal, *will*

Csikszentmihalyi, Mihaly, 113
Cymatics, 142–143
    sound, new cycle gauge, 143

Death, advisor, 10, 104–105, 111
Decoherence, 47–50, 65, 98, 197–198, 210
    wave function collapse, 49
Deikman, Arthur, 43
Division of Perceptual Studies (UVA), 95
Dreaming (also see OBE), 10, 17, 60, 70–71, 124–125, 145, 147, 170, 193, 210–211, 222–223
    entering dreaming, 127–128
    landscapes, 153–154
    levels of, 125–127
    lucid dreaming, 21, 128–130, 161–163, 193
    seeing in, 140–141
    with others, 137–140
Drugs, 8–9, 33, 156, 196, 200–201
    power plants, 9

Eagle Feather, Ken, 22
Earth
    circadian rhythms, 81
    cosmic rays, 82
    energies of, 81–82
    Gaia hypothesis, 80
    geographic, 79
    geomagnetic storms, 82
    Schumann resonances, 81–82
Edgar Cayce, 18
Emanations (see Wavefield)
Emotional intelligence, 68–70, 103, 112, 122, 151, 168–169, 172, 184–185, 214
Energy, 42, 172
Energy body, 15, 19, 39–40, 79, 101, 170, 172, 175, 181, 194, 198, 202

totality, 67, 93, 204, 222–223
uniformity, 53–54, 61
Energy fields, 60–66
    conditional, 63–64, 193, 211
    first, 25, 60–61, 171
    nagual, 65–66, 172, 193–196, 212–213
    natural, 64–65, 70, 73, 182, 193, 196–198, 211–213
    second, 17, 25, 60, 171
    third, 61–63, 96, 98
    tonal, 65–66, 194–197, 210–214
    tonal, personal, 66, 194–198, 206, 214
Environment, 64, 74, 79
    multi-dimensional, 39, 80, 85–86
Expectation, 29, 63, 198, 203, 219
Extraterrestrials, 89–90, 129, 154

Feeling (see Emotional Intelligence)
Fire from Within (also see Reincarnation), 97–99, 132, 141, 210, 212–213, 222–223

Gazing, 11, 59, 88, 117–121, 197
    fire, 120
    fog, 119–120
    people, 120–121
    shadow, 118
    water, 120
Genaro, don, 126
Guidance, 186–190, 214
    inner, 186–188
    false echoes, 190
    outer (omens), 188–190

Health and Healing, 8, 39, 191–194
    acupuncture, 201
    aging, 197–198
    cohesional dynamics, see Cohesion
    energy medicine, 199
    homeodynamics, 192–194, 198–200
    massage and touch, 45–46, 202
    meridians, 58
    nocebo, 203
    placebo, 202–203
    recapitulation, 205–210, 212
    relaxation, 209
    stress, 192–193
Ho, Mae-Wan, 47

Information, 24, 33, 47–50, 53–54, 56, 63, 78–80, 85, 192, 213
Inorganic world, 86–87
    elementals, 87
Intent, 14, 57, 61, 72, 75, 77–78, 83, 117–118, 125–126, 150, 152, 155, 164, 170, 174–177, 193
    unbending, 18, 174, 176–177
Internal dialogue, 47, 57, 67, 108
    stopping, 35, 68, 109, 114, 148, 211, 213
Interpretation, 24, 29–30, 36, 47, 49, 54, 63, 93, 109, 140, 213
Inventory, 30–31, 48, 53–54, 71, 76, 97, 171, 195, 211

James, William, 91
Jaynes, Julian, 188
Jenny, Hans, 142–143

Kornfield, Jack, 38

Learning, 60, 215–216
    bureaucratic mind, 218–220
    closure, 216–217
    contrary evidence, 218
    control, 216
    entrainment, 217–218
    experience, 220
    method, 220–221
Leininger, Bruce, 95
Lipton, Bruce, 203

Manifesting, 169–170
    decisions, 172–174
    dynamics, 171–172
    visualization, 177–178
    waiting, 178–179
Matus, don Juan, 9, 12–18, 97
Meditation, 106–107, 213
Meridians, 19, 57–59, 201, 223
Mind, 76–77, 169
Monroe Institute, The, 18, 83–84, 90, 93, 137, 157, 184
    Hemi-Sync, 18, 83–84
Monroe, Robert, 18, 25, 83–84, 129, 142, 157, 184
Mystic (see Mysticism)
Mystical experience, 90–92
Mysticism, 36–38, 42–43, 54, 64, 72, 120, 180

Nagual (see Energy fields)
Near-death experience, 44, 67, 84, 92–94
Nonattachment, 103–104, 130, 183, 186, 190
Nonpatterning, 105–106, 189, 213
    deautomatization, 105
    not-doing, 105, 109

Oschman, James, 45
Out-of-body experience (also see Dreaming), 9, 25, 61, 70, 124, 128–136, 144–147, 168, 196, 223
    control, 152–153
    emotional intelligence (see Emotional intelligence)
    entering, 129–130
    exercises, 156–166
    false awakening, 154
    flying, 130
    intent (see Intent)
    Mars, 80
    moon, 135–136
    partial projection, 152
    preparation, 144–146
    protection, 154–155
    returning, 154
    separation, 151–152
    silver cord, 136–137
    transitions, 146–151, 156–157
    travel, 128–132
    vibrations, 149–150, 159

Path with heart, 180–184, 211, 214, 223
Personal history, erasing, 10, 109–111, 214
Personal power (see Power)
Petty tyrants, 184–186, 214
Phasing, 141–143
Philosophy, 43–44, 116, 180
Physics
    classical, 37, 45–46, 48–49, 56, 76, 114, 124, 133, 142, 199, 224
    entanglement, 47, 49, 77, 87, 90, 105
    quantum (wavefield) physics, 19, 22, 24, 37, 44–48, 51–52, 86, 170, 199
Power, 8–10, 15–17, 21, 31, 40–43, 50, 54, 62, 65–68, 70, 88–89, 98, 101, 146, 171, 215–216
Projection (see Self-reflection)

Reality (see Worldview)
Reason, 41, 68, 220
Recapitulation (see Health and Healing)
Reincarnation (also see Fire from Within), 49–50, 94–99
Responsibility, 10, 110–111, 190, 196, 214
Routines, disrupting, 10, 107–108, 111, 130, 183, 196, 214

Scrying, 88, 117
Seeing, 10, 15, 22, 48, 71–72, 87, 117, 121–123, 140–141, 150

Selective cueing, 31–32
Self-importance (see Self-reflection)
Self-reflection, 13, 34–36, 38, 43, 54, 63–64, 97–98, 170
Shaman (see Shamanism)
Shamanism, 8–9, 20–21, 36–43, 46–47, 51–53, 61–62, 72, 98, 124, 175–176, 180, 191, 196, 200–201, 205, 224
    seer, 9, 24–25
    sorcerer, 24
    Toltec, 24, 39
    warrior, 9, 24, 42, 195
Social agreement, 32–34, 36, 44, 80, 97, 168–169, 219
    cognitive system, 44
    language, 33–34, 91
    social base, 33
    terminology, 23–26, 34, 42
Stevenson, Ian, 95

Talking, 67–68
Tart, Charles, 25, 129
Technology, 82–84
    cognitive, 83–84, 111, 124, 137
Tonal (see Energy fields)
Tucker, Jim, 95

Wavefield (also see quantum physics), 24, 46–50, 61, 77–78, 170, 172, 174, 211, 213
    dark sea, 49, 94–95
    Eagle, 49, 98
Weiss, Bruce, 96
Will, 72–74, 113–114, 116, 174, 176, 214, 220, 222
Wolff, Milo, 45
Worldview, 24, 28–36, 46, 51–52, 62, 217, 221, 224

About the Author

Kenneth Smith is the author of *The Complete Energy Body: A Space Age Exploration of Consciousness, Life, and Reality*. This landmark work provides far-reaching perspectives concerning science and shamanism, connecting these with the best-selling books of anthropologist Carlos Castaneda. By demonstrating that the central pillars of modern quantum wavefield theory and new cycle shamanism coincide, Smith provides a firm bridge between the worlds of science and mysticism, where scientific findings often follow those of shamans and other mystics. Writing as Ken Eagle Feather, he has published several books on shamanic philosophy, including the classic *On the Toltec Path*. His books have been translated into seven languages.

For his shamanic training, Smith apprenticed to Castaneda's teacher, don Juan Matus. Afterward, he was on the staff of Edgar Cayce's Association for Research and Enlightenment. He then went to the staff of The Monroe Institute, founded by sound and consciousness researcher Robert Monroe. Years later, Smith left his position as vice president of sales and marketing of an independent publishing company to become communications director of Beech Tree Labs, Inc., a discovery and early-stage development biopharmaceutical company. He also served as executive director of The Institute for Therapeutic Discovery, a non-profit research and education organization focused on bridging biochemistry and biophysics. In this capacity, he published a variety of articles relating to medical science. A formally trained and experienced journalist and educator, his current enterprise, EB Dynamics, focuses on the exploration and education of the human energy body. You may contact him at biz.ebdyn@gmail.com.

Made in the USA
Middletown, DE
06 November 2024